FROM ACQUAINTANCE TO FRIENDSHIP:

issues for people with learning disabilities

Hugh Firth

Mark Rapley

Illustrations: Anita Cameron

First published 1990

© **1990 BIMH Publications**

BIMH Publications is the publishing office of the
British Institute of Mental Handicap (Registered Charity No. 264786)

Published and distributed by: BIMH Publications,
　　　　　　　　　　　　　　Stourport House,
　　　　　　　　　　　　　　Stourport Road,
　　　　　　　　　　　　　　Kidderminster,
　　　　　　　　　　　　　　Worcs., DY11 7QG.

 *The work on which this book is based was supported by the Joseph
Rowntree Memorial Trust.*

ISBN 0 906054 71 0

Typeset by: Action Typesetting Limited, Imperial House, Russell Street,
Gloucester, GL1 1NE.

Printed by: Staples Printers Kettering Ltd., Trafalgar Road, Kettering,
NN16 8HA.

Contents

. . . acquaintances are made, relationships develop, and friendships are cemented through the things that we do with other people . . .

Acknowledgements

We did not set out with the intention of writing this book. It grew on us. Northumberland Health Authority District Psychology Service provided the initial finance for the appointment of one of us to conduct a literature survey. The Joseph Rowntree Memorial Trust then provided very welcome financial assistance, which allowed the continued appointment of one of us as well as much needed secretarial help. The grant from the Trust enabled us to review the resource materials which are described in the sizeable bibliography which forms Chapter 12 of this book. The Trust also initiated a particularly fruitful exchange of ideas by suggesting involvement with the steering group of another project which they were funding in this field. The resultant dialogue with Ann Richardson of the Policy Studies Institute and Jane Ritchie of Social and Community Planning Research influenced our ideas greatly, in many ways which cannot readily be acknowledged directly in the text. We have referred to their work where we have consciously used their concepts. The debt is much greater, however, as any dialogue both encourages clarification of personal ideas and results in assimilation of the ways in which others conceive of and approach an issue.

There are other individuals whom we especially wish to thank. The advice of Dr. David Towell of the King's Fund College on the initial literature survey gave us clarity of direction at the start: hopefully a little of that early clarity is still in evidence. We owe a particular debt to Dorothy Atkinson of the Open University. She commented on two previous drafts of this book in ways which drew us to deal with issues about close relationships which we otherwise would have neglected. We have not heeded everything she said – having held to our view of acquaintance as a process through which all friendships must pass, however quickly and easily – but we hope our view is clearer as a result of her comments.

We also thank those other individuals who contributed to the thinking behind this book. Dr. Melinda Firth, Dr. Roger Paxton, and Dr. Paul

Smith of Northumberland Health Authority helped us to formulate the aims of the original project. Dr. Linda Ward of the University of Bristol and Alan Tyne of Constructive Options commented on drafts of the text, although their comments have not always led to changes. Janet Mayor and Fiona Nelson very helpfully contributed some of their observations, ideas, and experience from training on these themes into the material in Chapter 10. We are grateful also to the many other colleagues who have shared ideas and observations with us, including staff of Skills for People, Newcastle, and BIMH Publications' anonymous reviewers who made very helpful and extensive comments on the last draft of the manuscript.

We acknowledge the generosity of the following publishers who have given us permission to reproduce material from their texts.

Pergamon Press: *Teaching Social Skills to Children : Innovating Approaches,* Eds. Cartledge, G., Milburn, J. (1986), for Box 17; *In Response to Aggression,* Goldstein, A.P. (1981), for Box 9.

Sage Publications: The Rules of Friendship, in *Journal of Social and Personal Relationships, Vol. 1,* Argyle, M., Henderson, M. (1984), for Box 1; *Human Relationships,* Duck, S.W. (1986), for Box 2.

Lifeskills Associates: *Lifeskills Teaching Programme No. 1,* Hopson, B., Scally, M. (1980), for Boxes 12, 13, 14 and 15.

Comedia Publishing Co. Ltd. *Organising Around Enthusiasm,* Hoggett, P., Bishop, J. (1986), for Box 6.

Policy Studies Institute: *Social Networks, Informal Care and Public Policy,* Willmott, P. (1986), for Box 5.

Jossey Bass Ltd.: *Problem Solving Techniques in Childrearing,* Shure, M.B., Spivack, G. (1978), for Box 10.

Ohio Society for Autistic Citizens: *Personal Relationships for Persons with Developmental Disabilities,* (1985), for material in Chapters 2 and 11.

We particularly wish to record our indebtedness to the secretarial staff who have spent many hours on our repeated drafts, Mrs. Anne Chapman, Mrs. Mary Eddy, and Mrs. Kathleen Kilgour. Without their hard work there would be no book.

Finally, we seek forgiveness from family and friends for tolerating so well the disruption to life which they endured while this book was being written.

Hugh Firth and Mark Rapley

How to use this book

This is a book of ideas for readers to draw on which are concerned with the issues surrounding relationships for people with learning disabilities. Thankfully, these are now beginning to be discussed more widely, with a view to increasing the range of opportunities people have to develop friends and relationships. It is not a book on "how to do it". Partly that would beg the question, "What needs doing?" What this book does attempt to do is to offer a series of options as to what may need doing, and to provide some ways forward on how to start.

The scope of any discussion of relationships is so wide that readers will need to choose their own approaches from the ones offered here. The style of presentation is intended to facilitate this. The early chapters offer information and a point of view. Later chapters offer ideas on developing and using opportunities and skills to develop relationships.

We have also included, however, three chapters which are particularly intended to be of practical help. Chapter 9 addresses the contribution educators, relatives, care staff, and managers, for example, may each be able to make. Chapter 10 briefly describes three different approaches to teaching and training in this area, including one which we have developed ourselves. Finally, Chapter 12 describes a lengthy list of useful resource materials. For each of the items in this bibliography there is an indication of which audiences may find them most useful, besides a description and commentary on their usefulness in this context.

Some readers may wish to skip all the text we have laboured over so carefully, to dip into the sections on resources and training options. Others may begin with Chapter 9, and (hopefully) work their way backwards to Chapter 1. Some may browse and skim their way amongst the illustrative boxed material and the highlights in the text, abstracting a few ideas of particular interest to them at present.

Early drafts of this book caused some consternation amongst those who saw it, because we use the word "acquaintance" in a particular way. Not only do we employ it to mean someone whom one knows only slightly, but also to describe the process or stage through which all relationships pass if they develop into friendship. Our reasons for using the word in this way are given early in Chapter 3. For readers who choose to browse and skim, we offer this warning here.

We hope many readers will treat the book in the (supposedly) conventional manner, beginning at the beginning, selecting the insights which are new to them, and then moving on to consider what our chapters have to offer for practical action. Our intention, after all, is for the book to stimulate such action. We hope it will encourage some people to do things differently (and hopefully better!) than they might have done otherwise.

Use it how you will: only do use it.

. . . personal relationships may bring company, security and intimacy, opportunities for experience, a sense of self-identity . . .

CHAPTER ONE

Introduction –
the value of personal relationships

SOCIAL RELATIONSHIPS AND FRIENDSHIP

Social relationships vary, from the brief conversation with a stranger who gives us directions, to complex and long-lasting relationships within the family, close personal relationships, and marriage. People are involved in social relationships with others in school or work, in day-to-day commercial transactions such as buying a newspaper, at home or in the family, and in their leisure time. Many of these relationships are with people who are known by name. In these situations people typically know something about each other and about one another's life beyond the immediate needs of the situation: these are more personal relationships. Thus, we often know quite well some of the people with whom we work. Sometimes we know almost nothing about the people who live next door. Others may know their neighbours very well.

Personal relationships are of many kinds. They include the many different relationships we have with different members of our families. Sometimes a particular brother, or sister, or cousin will also be a good friend to us. More often people tend to distinguish between their family and their friends: they perform different functions. Often, people have difficulty in saying exactly who their friends are.

WHY THIS BOOK?

Many people with learning disabilities*, whether living on their own, in their parents' home, in a hostel or hospital, or in other forms of community accommodation, have either never got to know many people,

*We have referred throughout the text to people with "learning disabilities", rather than to people with "mental handicaps", in the belief that this phrase distinguishes the disability from its social effect – the handicap (Heron and Myers, 1983).

or have not got to know people as well as they would like, or have found it difficult to get to know people. This book is intended to help examine how their wishes and needs may be tackled.

Increasingly it is recognised that the quality of life of people with learning disabilities is not only about the physical environment in which they live. Nor is it only about the choice and value derived from work, training, education, or other activities. Different kinds of social life suit different people. But for almost everyone, with or without a disability, the relationships with the people with whom they live, together with other social relationships, are a major contribution to the quality of their lives. Quality of life is very much limited by financial circumstances and the choices which money affords. Nevertheless, as Atkinson and Ward (1986, 1987) have pointed out, the quality of life of many people with learning disabilities living in the community is very largely determined by the range and type of their social relationships.

THE BACKGROUND

In recent years much attention has been paid to the physical locations in which people with learning disabilities live. Despite the fact that most of them have always lived as part of a local community, often in their parental home (Bayley, 1973), it is only lately that the current drive to run down and phase out large mental handicap hospitals has begun to focus attention upon the social, occupational, and recreational needs of people with learning disabilities who live, and relate to others, in their local community.

This attention has been slow in becoming evident.

In the 1970s, service agencies in Britain were concerned with trying to develop services to meet the needs apparent at the time. These were summarised in the government review *Better Services for the Mentally Handicapped* (DHSS, 1971). Attention was focused on services to help support families, and to provide occupation and training, especially in self-help skills, for people with learning disabilities. The education of all children, however severe their intellectual impairment, had only recently been integrated professionally and organisationally with that of other children. Health and social service agencies were attempting to move away from the damage done to people's lives through institutionalised practices. Depersonalisation and social distance were described and clarified, epitomising the impersonal nature of institutionalised living (King, Raynes, and Tizard, 1971). Institutionalisation, however, was by and large seen as occurring in large institutions: the realisation that life in small hostels or other living accommodation can involve social and emotional isolation to just as great a degree has been appreciated only gradually. The focus was on the physical, emotional, and social ill-effects of large institutions (Jones, 1975; King, Raynes, and Tizard, 1971;

Oswin, 1978), rather than upon the relationships of the people who lived in them.

It is the recent attempt to move away from large institutions, rather than towards clearly defined local community services, which has led to an acceleration of hospital rundown and closure, and the widespread "resettlement" of people with learning disabilities. This has occurred in response to a policy with a central vision that is far from clear (Malin, 1987). The impact of such resettlement has been justly criticised for its effects in breaking apart people's friendships and relationships (Social Services Committee, 1985).

In the 1970s service planners' and providers' attention was drawn to developments such as those in Nebraska (Thomas, Kendall, and Firth, 1978) where residential services were provided for people with severe or even profound learning disabilities in ordinary housing. Gradually such models for residential services have gained acceptance in this country. But as new residential provision is being made in small living units in local communities, so professionals and consumers are now confronting the fact that living in houses in ordinary streets does not in itself constitute a life *as part of* a community. People live as part of a community when they share their work, social, or leisure activities with other members of that community (Shearer, 1986). It is social relationships and the activities associated with them which are central to community life. This book is one contribution towards the recognition of that fact.

The King's Fund publication *An Ordinary Life* (1982) stated:

> "Our goal is to see mentally handicapped people in the mainstream of life living in ordinary houses in ordinary streets, with the same range of choices as any citizen, and mixing as equals with the other and mostly not handicapped members of their own community"

and it went on to add:

> "The community is also likely to be, for any individual, the place where he finds the people who are most important to him: his family, friends and acquaintances he meets regularly in everyday life".

That document assumed that local residential services would be planned as part of a wider range of comprehensive services to help support people with learning disabilities to live like others in their community.

But this has not happened. Too often ordinary housing has been provided and services have been left to end there (Social Services Committee, 1985). The apparent neglect of the area of personal relationships, however, does need some explanation. Perhaps the overriding interest in the nature of residential services, and the focus upon issues like access, locality, and proximity, has dominated perceptions and priorities. Perhaps planners and professionals have not thought about, written about, or considered relationships because it has not been clear that they were an issue. The needs of individuals for close personal relationships have become more apparent over time and through experience. Many people actively engaged in rehabilitation and resettlement schemes thought initially about services, training, and support. It is only with time, perhaps, that they have "discovered" a set of needs that have hitherto been neglected.

Yet the need for a choice of personal relationships was recognised in *An Ordinary Life* (King's Fund, 1982):

> "It is only when mentally handicapped people live in the community that they can *begin* to be guaranteed the opportunity to make a full range of relationships. These range from the casually supportive relationships with shop keepers and others who provide the 'cement' to community life, to closer relationships with friends who share the same interests, to mutually supportive relationships between two people . . ." (our emphasis).

That report said little about how such a range of relationships might come about. This book may help a little in this respect.

THE VALUE AND IMPORTANCE OF PERSONAL RELATIONSHIPS

Rewarding or supportive personal relationships are of great value as a contribution to the quality of life of all people, whether they have a learning disability or not.

Personal relationships also have both a direct and indirect influence on the mental and physical health of individuals. Brown and Harris (1978) showed, in a classic study, how support from one close friend or relationship was important in preventing depression amongst women who would otherwise have been at risk. There is now other extensive evidence of the impact which social support can have on people's mental and physical health. (Readers who are interested may read reviews by Cobb, 1976, 1979; Kaplan, Cassel, and Gore, 1977; Lynch, 1977; and Greenblatt, Becerra, and Serafetinides, 1982.)

But personal relationships are of value in many other ways beyond protecting people's mental and physical health. Our view, which draws on the work of Richardson and Ritchie (1989), is that they may bring:

company;

security and intimacy;

opportunities for experience;

a sense of self-identity;

self-esteem; and,

practical help.

Looking at these points in a little more detail, relationships, especially friendship, can provide company. They can bring a variety of important new opportunities to learn, and to experience new sensations, perceptions, events, and feelings. They may also bring intimacy, a sense of closeness and trust which most people find important as an essential and enriching part of their lives.

Relationships can bring practical help in little, day-to-day ways, as well as in times of major disruption or celebration, such as birth, marriage, or death. Richardson and Ritchie (1989) have distinguished the provision of company, intimacy, and practical help as three chief functions which friendship provides.

Close relationships are, for many of us, a vital way of gaining pleasure in success, support in difficulty, and a sense of our own worth and value, through other people. Indeed the ability to give to others may be one of the most important ways in which relationships may enhance self-esteem.

Relationships can provide a way of confirming and validating our experiences. People who value us provide us with positive feedback. This is important to the development of a valued self-identity, a positive self-image, and self-esteem. The feeling that we are valued, and a sense that we are making a contribution to the lives of others around us, can only be gained through personal relationships.

Thus, relationships of all kinds help to define who we are. By helping to build and reinforce our self-esteem, they can allow us in turn to choose to be either the same as, or different from, other people. But without relationships with others we cannot know what we are like, or what kind of people we would like to be.

Acquaintances and friends bring with them opportunities to learn in several different but interlinked ways. They allow us to:

learn *about* others;

learn *from* others;

learn *through* others; and

learn about *ourselves*.

They provide us with the opportunity to learn *about* others – their lives, thoughts, feelings, and beliefs. They give us the opportunity to learn *from* others – from their experience and from their feedback to us. They offer us the opportunity to learn *through* others – through the experiences they report to us which we ourselves may never have. We may learn, through them, about the thoughts and feelings of others, which might otherwise never have occurred to us.

Friendships also give us opportunities for experiencing and developing choice in many ways: for instance, in day-to-day decisions about what to eat or drink, or in choosing new leisure or work activities. They provide us with experience of people, which may allow us to make choices as to those with whom we will spend time. Moreover, many relationships bring opportunities for meeting other people, so widening our circle of experience.

Most of all, however, acquaintances and friends provide us with repeated opportunities for learning from others *about ourselves.* We cope successfully with many difficulties because of what we have learnt directly or indirectly from others, rather than through personal experience. The influence of friends on smoking and drinking habits is but one example. It is clear that personal relationships have as much to contribute to the lives of people with learning disabilities as to the lives of people without disabilities.

Yet many people with learning disabilities lead what may be seen as impoverished social lives. The evidence for this is laid out in Chapter 2. At this point, however, it is sufficient to quote from the report of a recent conference:

> "Most people with developmental disabilities have few opportunities to interact with persons outside their residence or outside a network of other persons with disabilities. For individuals living at home, family members are most often the only source of interaction. Persons with disabilities (often) have little opportunity to interact with non-handicapped people except for paid staff either in residential or day programmes. Seldom have they been given the opportunity to establish a personal relationship or experience the benefits of such a relationship." (Pealer and O'Brien, 1985).

This same report went on to identify some of the barriers which people with learning disabilities may face in making relationships. They may be out of reach of relationships with people without disabilities because they live or work in segregated settings. They may not be able to go to places where they might meet and interact with others, often because they cannot afford to. They may have particular difficulties in communication in addition to their learning disability. They may lack confidence. They may, in the past, have experienced rejection by others.

WHAT THIS BOOKS SETS OUT TO DO

There is a need to overcome at least some of these barriers if the opportunities of people with learning disabilities for rewarding relationships are to be increased. It seems useful to try to identify what kinds of opportunities are most needed, what abilities, attitudes, or behaviours are important, and what barriers need to be removed to aid this process.

Our aim in this book is to point ways forward to help people with learning disabilities, who wish to do so, to widen their circle of acquaintances and develop friendships. In order to do this it was important for us to start from an understanding of how relationships develop among people without learning disabilities. We developed a number of key ideas about how best to help others to widen their circle of acquaintances and friends. Unfortunately, the limits of the project prevented us from dealing with the different expectations or behaviours which prevail within various ethnic groups within this country. Nevertheless, we have been able to draw some general conclusions and to make some specific suggestions and recommendations. We have included a discussion of resources which might be helpful to professionals and others working and living with people with learning disabilities.

Our first theme is that it is not possible to provide friendship, or to make friends, for other people. Because friendship cannot be made, but can only be chosen, we have paid particular attention to how people may make acquaintances, who may develop into friends. We have tried to highlight the breadth of people's social lives. We have emphasised that an individual's social life is not likely to be much improved merely by focusing on the use of leisure time. A social life during leisure time is but one part of someone's social relationships. Friends and acquaintances may also be made through education or work, amongst neighbours, and through close family or distant relatives.

A precondition for making friends is the motivation, the drive, and the desire for what friendship brings: intimacy, support or practical help, company, understanding, and warmth or "friendliness". Often these experiences are cemented by the expression of feelings. One of the circumstances about the lives of people with learning disabilities is that often communication about desires, wishes, expectations, and feelings has not been encouraged and fostered. It may even have been unwittingly discouraged over time. The encouragement of appropriate expression of emotions might be seen, therefore, as a backdrop to many of the other ideas in this book.

Acquaintances are made, relationships develop, and friendships are cemented through the activities we undertake with other people. Activities carry with them differing opportunities to meet new people or develop relationships with them. What appear to be similar jobs, for example, can provide vastly different opportunities for making relationships: compare solitary road sweeping with working as a member of a cleansing department truck team. A particular activity may provide differing opportunities according to the way it is used. Thus, keep fit may be pursued in an individual, competitive way, as it is by many men, or as an opportunity for socialising, as enjoyed by many women.

What we do with other people, and what we think about them, are both crucial to the process of meeting people and getting to know them better. Helping people to make acquaintances and find friends, therefore, often hinges on creating opportunities for them to meet others and to do things with them in the right social context. Such help is not only about *creating opportunities,* it is also about *supporting people* in making the greatest use of those opportunities. Two kinds of support may be needed. The first is by way of introduction and facilitation. The second is in the area of interpersonal skill. This book discusses the importance of interpersonal or social skill, as well as the limitations of social skill training in the way it has often been provided for people with learning disabilities.

Our approach does make one assumption which we should make clear at this stage. We share the view of Landesman – Dwyer and Berkson (1984) in their review of the published literature:

> "We know of no principles about social behaviour that appear unique to retarded individuals, nor are there any theoretical reasons that affiliative patterns should be guided by different factors in this population".

It is for this reason that we begin this book by finding out how acquaintanceships and friendships develop. We then apply those insights to consider how to help people with learning disabilities. We intend to provide not only food for thought, but food for action. The book therefore includes a chapter with a variety of ideas for action by parents, relatives, volunteers, and professionals of various kinds, as well as one on learning and training, and a section on resource materials which may be helpful.

It is a book with ideas to be drawn on. The issues are so wide and individuals' circumstances so varied that at many points the chapters offer different options, or highlight the same issues in more than one way. We hope this will enable readers to use the book in different ways.

REFERENCES

ATKINSON, D., WARD, L. *A Part of the Community: Social Integration and Neighbourhood Networks.* London: Campaign for People with Mental Handicaps, 1986.

ATKINSON, D., WARD, L. Friends and neighbours: relationships and opportunities in the community for people with a mental handicap. *In* Malin, N. (Ed.). *Reassessing Community Care.* London: Croom Helm, 1987.

BAYLEY, M. *Mental Handicap and Community Care.* London: Routledge & Kegan Paul, 1973.

BROWN, G., HARRIS, T. *Social Origins of Depression: a study of psychiatric disorder in women.* London: Tavistock, 1978.

COBB, S. Social support as a moderator of life stress. *Psychosomatic Medicine,* 1976; **38**:5, 300–314.

COBB, S. Social support and health through the life course. *In* Riley, M.W. (Ed.). *Aging from Birth to Death: interdisciplinary perspectives.* Boulder, Colorado: West View Press, 1979.

DEPARTMENT OF HEALTH AND SOCIAL SECURITY. *Better Services for the Mentally Handicapped.* (Cmnd. 4683). London: HMSO, 1971.

GREENBLATT, M., BECERRA, R.M., SERAFETINIDES, E.A. Social networks and mental health: an overview. *American Journal of Psychiatry,* 1982; **139**, 977 – 984.

HERON, A., MYERS, M. *Intellectual impairment: the battle against handicap.* London: Academic Press, 1983.

JONES, K. *Opening the Door. A Study of New Policies for the Mentally Handicapped.* London: Routledge & Kegan Paul, 1975.

KAPLAN, B. H., CASSEL, J.C., GORE, S. Social support and health. *Medical Care,* 1977; **15**:5, 47 – 58.

KING, R. D., RAYNES, N. V., TIZARD, J. *Patterns of Residential Care.* London: Routledge & Kegan Paul, 1971.

KING'S FUND CENTRE. *An Ordinary Life – Comprehensive Locally Based Services for Mentally Handicapped People. Revised edn.* London: King's Fund Centre, 1982.

LANDESMAN-DWYER, S., BERKSON, G. Friendship and social behaviour. *In* Wortis, J. (Ed.). *Mental Retardation and Developmental Disabilities, Vol. 13.* London: Plenum Press, 1984.

LYNCH, J. J. *The Broken Heart: the medical consequences of loneliness.* New York: Basic Books, 1977.

MALIN, N. (Ed.). *Reassessing Community Care.* London: Croom Helm, 1987.

OSWIN, M. *Children Living in Longstay Hospitals.* London: Heinemann Medical Books, 1978.

PEALER, J., O'BRIEN, J. *Personal Relationships for Persons with Developmental Disabilities.* Proceedings of a Conference on Informal Support. Columbus, Ohio: Ohio Society for Autistic Citizens, 1985.

RICHARDSON, A., RITCHIE, J. *Developing Friendships: enabling people with learning difficulties to make and maintain friends.* London: Policy Studies Institute/Social & Community Planning Research, 1989.

SHEARER, A. *Building Community with People with Mental Handicaps, their Families and Friends.* London: Campaign for People with Mental Handicaps and King's Fund Centre, 1986.

SOCIAL SERVICES COMMITTEE OF THE HOUSE OF COMMONS. *Community Care with Special Reference to Adult Mentally Ill and Mentally Handicapped People.* Second report, session 1984 – 5, Vol. 1. (Chairman, Mrs. R. Short.) London: HMSO, 1985.

THOMAS, D., KENDALL, A., FIRTH, H. *ENCOR – A Way Ahead.* London: Campaign for People with Mental Handicaps, 1978.

. . . a man, who lives on an isolated croft . . .

CHAPTER TWO

The experience of people with learning disabilities

THE CIRCUMSTANCES

People without disabilities usually have a variety of acquaintances and friends. Many could be said to have a rich social life. This is far less common amongst people with learning disabilities.

In an account of the lives of people with learning disabilities in the Highlands and Western Isles, Seed (1980) describes Murdo, an eighty-two-year-old man, who lives on an isolated croft with his sister, twenty-eight miles from the nearest village. The couple do not own a car and Murdo's winter activities go no further than walking round the croft and looking after a crippled sheep. In summertime his only regular visitors are professionals: the distict nurse and a local minister.

Perhaps it is not surprising that, in his geographical situation, Murdo should have a very small social network. The opportunity to develop a "rich" social life is simply not present. Yet in very many cases where the opportunities are present, the social lives of people with learning disabilities who live in the community are equally impoverished. Atkinson's (1985) survey of people living in the community in Somerset found, for example, that Geoffrey:

"has lost all contact with his family. He lives alone. He has no job. He has no friend and he is on bad terms with his neighbours".

Clearly, such a life does not deserve to be called a life as part of the community; much less a valued life as a part of the community.

Yet this situation, or something like it, is common enough for many people with learning disabilities who have grown up and left their families to live on their own or with support. Malin (1982, 1983) found in a survey of residents of group homes that over two-thirds would turn to one of the official support networks if they needed help, rather than to a friend.

The most comprehensive review of evidence about the friendships and social relationships of people with learning disabilities has been made by Landesman-Dwyer and Berkson (1984). They comment that a variety of descriptive studies over the past two decades have attested to the fact that friendships are amongst the most valued aspects of their lives. Edgerton (1967) and Edgerton and Bercovici (1976) highlighted the importance of personal relationships in the lives of people with mild degrees of learning disability who were attempting to live a "normal" life within their communities.

Moreover, various studies have shown that many people with learning disabilities do have very limited personal relationships, that frequently lack of opportunity for social contact is a major barrier to friendship and companionship, and that lack of appropriate teaching and learning opportunities contribute significantly to this. Landesman-Dwyer and Berkson (1984), in coming to this conclusion, describe the lack of companionship or friendship for sizeable numbers of people that has been demonstrated in a wealth of studies. More recent work supports this conclusion. For example, Zetlin and Murtaugh (1988) found that adolescents with mild learning disabilities had fewer friendships than their school peers, and these friendships were characterised by less empathy, less intimacy, and less stability than their peers' relationships. A substantial proportion of people nominated as "friends" by the adolescents with learning disabilities were relatives, such as cousins, which was not true of their peers.

These studies are generally consistent in showing that a substantial minority of adults, whether living with their own natural parents, in residential establishments, or on their own, lack close friends altogether or are regarded as having very poor social support networks. In one study, for example (Bell, Schoenrock, and Beusberg, 1981), telephone calls to friends only averaged close to one per week, visits to friends averaged less than twice per month, and contacts with neighbours averaged consistently less than one per week.

One effect apparent from the review by Landesman-Dwyer and Berkson (1984) deserves comment. Some studies have shown larger residences appeared to facilitate the formation or maintenance of friendships or companionships, whilst people living in smaller residences experienced more isolation. It appears that factors such as philosophy and attitudes in the running of particular facilities, as well as environmental constraints in terms of geographical siting, availability of transport, and people's individual financial circumstances, may often combine to restrict the opportunities of those living in smaller homes to meet people without disabilities. For example, residents may be discouraged from maintaining contact with friends outside the home, or may be restricted in their ability to invite friends or acquaintances to visit them at the home (Bercovici, 1981).

The effect of these kinds of staff or environmentally imposed restrictions is that people spend more time with their peers *within* the residence. Some studies have indicated higher rates of interaction between peers in larger residences than in smaller ones. For those living in large residences, however, contact with people who are not disabled may be very low. Campbell (1968) commented that the vast majority of hostel residents in that British study had *no* friends outside their immediate residence. It is important to be clear, therefore, that it is not small homes *per se* which restrict people's social opportunities, but the staffing, location, management philosophy, and staff attitudes which are likely to be critical in influencing the social opportunities of residents.

Thus, many people living in their local communities lead quite solitary lives. Gollay *et al.* (1978), in a broad survey of over four hundred people who had left institutions in the USA, commented:

"Some individuals functioned well – they were active in a variety of leisure activities and had many friends and satisfying social relationships. Others seemed to exist on the fringes of the domain – if they were active in leisure activities, these were usually solitary rather than social. They had few friends, even fewer romantic relationships, and often lived in residences which did not permit or encourage social independence".

Social isolation only becomes loneliness when the lack of friendship or companionship is noticed and missed. Most people, however, whether or not they have a learning disability, do value social contact and will experience loneliness if they are socially isolated. The evidence is that the social lives of very many people with learning disabilities are impoverished: they are indeed isolated.

Loneliness has been identified as a major problem experienced by many people who live in the community. For example, loneliness was stated to be a "big problem" by twenty-one per cent of the people surveyed by Gollay *et al.* (1978), it being reported as a problem more frequently amongst more able informants. This may reflect a perception of the difference between reality and expectations. Expectations are communicated by others to people with disabilities, who may also observe the situation of people without disabilities around them and on the media. Those who are more able may perceive more readily the difference between their own situation and that of others.

The barrenness in some people's lives is illustrated by the study in Dublin by McConkey, Naughton, and Nugent (1983). Their work illustrates the minimal contact many adults with learning disabilities have with others in their neighbourhood. There were, for example, only three groups of people – shopkeepers, bus conductors, and chemists – to whom more than half of the adults in the study had talked within the previous month. The very fact that these groups of people appeared so salient illustrates how impoverished were the adults' social lives as a whole. The authors concluded that:

> "community living is not a reality for most adults who are mentally handicapped ... only a minority ... have diverse and recent contact with others in their neighbourhood or city and even fewer have the regular companionship of a friend".

An earlier survey by McConkey, Walsh, and Mulcahy (1982) found that, of the adults with learning disabilities surveyed, over fifty per cent were not at work or attending a centre for training. Only forty per cent shared their leisure time with a friend, and forty-six per cent spent *all* their leisure time with their immediate family.

The authors' conclusion was that this hardly constituted community care, but this reflects a misunderstanding of the issue. These adults were being *cared for* within an ordinary local neighbourhood. In fact, they were being cared for in a way in which most care is provided: by women in their families. The point is that they did not have much of a community *life*. Their community – their own network of personal ties – was small. It is not the existence of physical care within a neighbourhood which is at issue. The question is whether those who are cared for in a community or neighbourhood are in any sense a *part* of that community. Most striking of all in the Dublin surveys (McConkey, Walsh, and Mulcahy, 1982; McConkey, Naughton, and Nugent, 1983) was the absence of friendship. With one exception – going to the cinema – friends rarely featured.

Richardson and Ritchie (1989a) have conducted the first major study in England of the quality of friendships developed by people with learning disabilities. They interviewed some sixty people, from two areas of the country, living in a variety of settings in the community including large staffed hostels, small staffed homes, independent flats and houses, and parental homes. They found that people living with their families generally spent most of their time with their parents or their brothers or sisters, who were often their only source of company. They comment strikingly on the restrictive effect which living within the parental home had had, in many cases, upon the relationships of the people surveyed. In contrast, people who lived in staffed accommodation were much more likely to spend their leisure time in the company of other people with learning disabilities, usually with other people who shared their house or hostel. Not surprisingly, paid staff were also an important source of company for them.

The overall picture which Richardson and Ritchie present is one in which people with learning disabilities, living either at home or in staffed accommodation, frequently led lives which were very constrained and limited socially. There were two notable exceptions to this pattern. People who lived in some form of housing network, often based loosely on a core and cluster model, reported that they visited each other's homes for meals, a social chat, or to join in some activity together. The most important exception, however, was that people who lived with a partner, or with one close friend of either sex, often found company amongst a much wider circle of people, and engaged in a wider variety of social activities. As Richardson and Ritchie comment:

> "The existence of someone both readily available and with whom the person felt comfortable, made it possible to extend further the sources of company".

Richardson and Ritchie (1989a) also found that some of the people they interviewed were able to derive intimacy from one of two kinds of relationship. Many had "special friends" with whom they chose to spend time, most of these people themselves having a learning disability, although some carers or paid staff were included in this category. A few people said that they had a partner with whom they could share some intimacy. The authors reported that people who had regular partners, whether or not they lived with them, had the greatest opportunities for making the kind of wide social circle which many people without learning disabilities enjoy.

Richardson and Ritchie's study emphasises that it was, almost exclusively, only people living independently in unstaffed accommodation who led full and varied social lives with a range of different kinds of activities and social relationships. Yet by contrast, some of the people living independently were the ones who led the most isolated and often lonely existences. The study documents vividly the isolation of many individuals living in staffed accommodation or their parental home. Apart from their immediate household or family, these people's lives were largely segregated from the lives of people without disabilities, and many appear to have experienced considerable emotional as well as social isolation.

Atkinson (1985) commented on how a number of her informants were merely observers of communities of which they were supposedly a part. Others referred to things they "used to do". Yet others had "got stuck" in particular roles or activities. It is notable that Atkinson (1986) emphasised the importance Richardson and Ritchie (1989a) later gave to the presence of one particular person, special friend, or partner as a door to wider social networks and opportunities. She highlights the efforts many people have made to "engage competent others" as a way of gaining advice, assistance, and support in making and maintaining relationships, as well as in other areas of life. Often such "competent others" have been social workers, whose role may encompass the functions of business contact, friend, authority figure, or close tie (Atkinson, 1989).

Some of the people in Atkinson's study were content to make the most of their relationships with other people with learning disabilities; others were not. Kaufman (1984) has noted that some people with learning disabilities are content with a limited social life, whether it be with other people with learning disabilities or with people who have no such disability. Many people, however, are not content with these situations, although they may find it difficult to change them. In particular, they often face severe problems in responding to the stigma they experience from others and are keenly aware of such stigma, as one recent study has shown (Jahoda, Markova, and Cattermole, 1988).

The British studies by Richardson and Ritchie (1989a) and Atkinson (1985, 1986) primarily involved interviews with people with mild or moderate degrees of intellectual disability. The kind of isolation described is often much more acute for those with severe learning disabilities. Recent examination of small projects designed to provide social integration for people with moderate or severe learning difficulties has emphasised these issues. Saxby *et al.* (1986) commented on the substantial use by the people in their study of shops, cafés, and pubs. But, once again, the results appear to highlight the poverty rather than the wealth of social integration. A study by de Kock *et al.* (1988) showed that levels of both family contact and contact with other people living and working in the community were higher for people with severe and profound learning disabilities living in small local homes than for those in larger units. Even so, they commented that despite the fact that increased participation took place in the community, social interactions with the public were of short duration and there appeared to be very few relationships which could possibly be described as friendship.

Another recent study (Firth, 1986; Firth and Short, 1987) noted that young people with severe learning disabilities who left hospital to live locally had most of their current contact with professionals, each other's relatives, and staff. They had few opportunities to make acquaintances or develop friendships, in comparison with the opportunities available to most people without such disabilities. Four kinds of relationship were actually available to them, namely:

relationships with their own family, and friends of their family;

relationships with staff, and relatives and friends of staff;

relationships with other household members, and their relatives or acquaintances;

relationships with professionals.

Only the first two of these, in reality, had much potential as sources of further relationships which might be age appropriate and relatively free of the dependence which may be a strong feature accompanying relationships with professionals (Atkinson, 1989).

Moreover, social contact with non-handicapped members of the community involved in such schemes can be exceedingly fragile. The study concluded that, despite much physical presence in the community, the greatest opportunities for the development of social relationships remained through the families of the young people themselves, and through the relatives and friends of staff. Furthermore, many of these opportunities depended crucially on the selection and training of the staff employed to help them, as Firth (1986) commented:

"One of the most valued kinds of relationships which Ann was able to develop was with the teenage children of the staff. Here valued non-handicapped members of the community of her own age visited often, and spent hours at a time, even whole days, either at the house or on outings. Here indeed would appear to have been one of the few real opportunities Ann had to develop a circle of relationships like those her non-handicapped peers would do at her age".

Staff may be crucial as people who can help to create opportunities for developing social relationships, but that so much depends on staff demonstrates the very tenuous social opportunities available to such young people (Firth, 1986; Felce and Toogood, 1988).

Landesman-Dwyer and Berkson (1984) also highlight the importance of opportunities for people with learning disabilities to meet acquaintances and make friends. In one of their studies, for example, twenty-six per cent of individuals had no opportunities to participate in *any* organised social activities within the community. Gollay *et al.* (1978) also concluded that:

"the opportunities for social experiences and for establishing social relationships appear to be inadequate for many retarded people living in the community".

Studies outside the British Isles and the USA, in Israel for example, have illustrated similar situations. A study by Reiter and Levi (1980) compared the social lives of adults with and without learning disabilities. Although most adults spent the majority of their leisure time in housebound activities such as watching television, those with learning disabilities saw themselves as having a major problem in terms of lack of friends and their difficulty in making them; whereas only a third of the adults without disabilities saw themselves as experiencing such problems.

It is important not to overlook the individual preferences of people with learning disabilities. As Malin (1982) commented:

"it should be recognised that mentally handicapped people living together in a group home may not need further help, nor desire further social contacts".

Many people with learning disabilities, although they do not have the opportunity, would like to leave the segregated world of mental handicap hostels and adult training centres. Others have clearly identified desires for companions or friends who do not have disabilities. Some do not feel the need for a social life outside the "handicapped world" (Atkinson and Ward, 1986; 1987).

Atkinson (1987) drew several conclusions from her accounts of the lives of people leaving hospital. One was that few admitted to having *no* friends. Some, she said, put a "brave face" on their predicament, minimising their isolation. Others extended the definition of "friend" to include neighbours or shopkeepers, who should perhaps be described more accurately as acquaintances. Some people referred to visiting professionals, such as social workers and nurses, as friends; where often the relationship was very far from reciprocal and was construed quite differently by the visitor (Atkinson, 1989). It seems that only a minority led what Atkinson calls a "full life".

Flynn (1989) has recently described, in an important and comprehensive study, the situation of eighty-eight people with learning disabilities living independently. She has highlighted many of the difficulties they face: financial, limited support, lack of jobs or education, lack of social opportunities, and victimisation. Her study is particularly valuable for the link she establishes between appearance and victimisation, the latter most frequently taking the form of intimidation by children and young people. Flynn has stressed the necessity for early intervention to model and correct abnormal posture, as well as the need to act on indications of victimisation. She has emphasised that more adequate preparation for people moving into independent living is required and has recommended particularly that:

"Training in assertion and self-presentation should be an integral part of preparation for independent living. Guidance in these areas should continue throughout people's placements . . .

. . . Training and guidance in interpersonal skills should precede and continue throughout placements. One way of accomplishing this is by using a role model/mentor . . .

. . . Support personnel need to be aware of the possibility that victimisation may be unreported as it is distressing and discrediting. They should be alert to such cues as changes in people's lifestyles and appearance, despondency, avoidance, and no money".

Flynn's study did not examine people's social relationships in depth, but she concluded that:

"it appears that most people have regular contact with individuals who may be described as friends. However, we must not lose sight of the fact that a number of people experience loneliness and isolation . . . In the interviews eighteen people did not mention contact with others. As a recipient of two marriage invitations and many requests for further contact with the people I met, I have to conclude that some people's networks are wanting".

Thus, many individuals with a learning disability have fewer opportunities to meet people, make acquaintances, and get to know people as friends than the rest of us. If the desire for friendship is strong, the opportunities or the finance may not be present. Where opportunities do exist, then a lack of social skill may sometimes frustrate them. Often, people have lived in situations which have discouraged them from expressing their true feelings, or even expressing their feelings at all. Such a combination of circumstances places many barriers in their way when it comes to finding and making friends.

THE BARRIERS

The many barriers that restrict the personal relationships of people with learning disabilities have been aptly described by Pealer and O'Brien (1985). Amongst the difficulties in the way of such relationships they list the following factors.

Getting to places to meet people or talk with them is often difficult. Access to transport may not be easy, and people may not have the ability to use transport or telephones, or to write letters without assistance from someone else.

Many people are *poor* and therefore cannot afford to travel to places, pay admission fees, or purchase refreshments. This limits their involvement in activities where it might be possible for them to form and sustain personal relationships.

Many people have difficulty *communicating with* or *being understood* by others. This makes relationships harder to sustain.

People are often *inexperienced* in forming relationships with people who are not disabled. They may have led lives that have been, in many ways, determined or dominated by others.

People may be *unsure of themselves* in relationships, partly because of their inexperience.

People may have experienced *rejection* by others and may have found ways of avoiding it. Such defences may not be easily overcome.

People without disabilities are often *unaware* of the importance of personal relationships for those with learning disabilities.

Professionalism may act as barrier, by defining people's difficulties in particular ways, by reinforcing low expectation of individuals, or by imposing interventions which may be very directive in character. Thus, lack of rewarding or close personal relationships may not be recognised by professionals as an issue. The way in which help with relationship issues is provided may be directive rather than facilitating.

People living in residential services may find that most of their relationships are with people who are *paid* to be with them. Turnover amongst such staff may be high, leading to the expectation as well as the experience that most personal relationships do not last and are disrupted when individuals move away.

People are rarely helped to find work alongside people without disabilities, even though the *work environment* is often one where relationships may be developed with people who are skilled at getting along with others.

People are often "out of reach" of relationships with people without disabilities because of the *segregation* of educational, vocational, and residential services.

People without disabilities frequently *assume* that those with learning disabilities will wish to find their friends only from amongst others with disabilities. This may or may not be true for any one person.

Segregation provides *"messages"* to people without disabilities about the worth of those with disabilities. These act as additional barriers.

Society values *images* that are young and beautiful. People with disabilities of any kind may thus be devalued and seen as being less worthy of getting to know.

Parents and professionals may have *low expectations* of people, or may be protective in ways which inhibit their relationships.

The opportunities which *family life* offers people to develop close personal relationships may contract as parents and other family members grow older.

Often, people have few opportunities to fulfil meaningful and valued *roles* within their own community. Without such roles they may appear less attractive to get to know than others within their community.

Some of these points require further explanation. Many are linked by two themes:

segregation, and the interpretation that people with learning disabilities are of less value than others; and,

the interaction of lack of abilities and low expectations by others, which reinforce each other and perpetuate factors that contribute to segregation.

Segregation of services provides a physical limitation on the opportunities people have to meet others without disabilities. The effects of segregation are possibly most pronounced in the educational field, because segregation at this point limits the opportunities young people have to learn from their more socially able peers. Whilst integration alone will not change the perceptions of non-disabled peers (Gottlieb and Leyser, 1981), if it is supported by public education, staff support, or skills coaching it can widen the opportunities of people with learning disabilities to form relationships with other young people.

Segregation of training services greatly restricts the opportunities for making relationships at work which may be extended outside the work setting. Other trainees in adult training or social education centres are unlikely to be involved in the variety of different activities and types of relationships outside work which commonly exist amongst a non-disabled work force. Moreover, segregated work and training congregates people, many of whom have particular difficulties in communicating, making it more difficult for them to either make close relationships or learn about each other's relationships.

People without jobs are usually poor. Poverty restricts people's ability to make and develop relationships. Many people with learning disabilities have little or no access to the use of a car for social purposes. Relatives or friends may offer lifts or provide regular transport for particular arrangements, but such help is no substitute for the freedom to be able to meet people, go to places, and maintain relationships with people who do not live close by which car ownership provides (Willmott, 1986; 1987). Moreover, journeying by public transport is not only time-consuming but expensive for those on low incomes. Transport aside, many sociable activities end up costing money, even if only to pay for a cake and a cup of tea after a walk in the park.

Lack of abilities and low expectations provide the second set of barriers to people's chances of developing relationships of their choice. The very real lack of abilities of people who have mild, moderate, severe, or profound learning disabilities clearly places obstacles in the way of experiencing such relationships. Yet others' expectations that they may not be able to cope socially, or may not appreciate particular social occasions, have an impact at two levels. First, people who are able to arrange or facilitate events, especially family members, may become unnecessarily protective of individuals. Second, individuals may come to see themselves as being more socially unskilled than they really are, or of less interest and worth in the eyes of others than they could be. They may then lose the initiative or the inclination to make or maintain relationships. They may learn expectations and patterns of behaviour in which people keep their feelings to themselves and the family "sticks together". Key people, such as relatives, may fear the emotional risks which other relationships may bring (Richardson and Ritchie, 1986,

1989a,b) and so consciously or unconsciously restrict opportunities for such relationships to develop.

Individuals with learning disabilities frequently experience rejection. The ensuing sense of stigma may have been experienced first during childhood, both in the street and in the school, and later in adult life. This stigma, and the fear which often underlies it, is fed by and compounds the segregation to which many people are subjected. Some contributions to stigma, such as appearance, may be directly altered by individuals. Others, such as the provision of homes for people in a building previously used for "deliquent youth", for example, can only be altered by changing the attitudes and practices of policy makers and decision makers. Many attitudes towards people with disabilities will only change slowly, as segregation itself is systematically reduced and people's successful integration in education, work, and community life is nurtured and supported.

These general attitudes combine with many others. People who find themselves the parents of children with learning disabilities often experience ambivalent emotions. As their children grow, natural protectiveness may combine with feelings of guilt, shame, or fear to increase the protectiveness of parents. Parents, especially those whose offspring have severe or profound disabilities, may be afraid of how their sons and daughters will behave. They may fear their own embarrassment. Social attitudes thus combine with personal fears to affect the upbringing and opportunities of young people with learning disabilities. A minority of parents respond with a challenge to themselves, and others, to accept them as readily as any other young person.

Expectations about age-appropriate behaviour play a powerful part in shaping parental behaviour towards children. There are strong pressures on parents of non-disabled children to expose them to certain risks and challenges from an early age: walking, climbing, playing alone, helping with cooking and household tasks; and, later, playing with other children, and playing out of sight of immediate supervision. These social expectations, that young people must be exposed to challenge and risk do not apply to parents of children with severe disabilities. For many of them there are no norms. So parents' natural protectiveness and lack of clear expectations can combine to bring up children who are, with the best of intentions, discouraged from exploration and experiment; who learn to stay close to parents, and hence fail to learn many of the basic skills of social interaction. Consequently, young people with profound disabilities may approach and hug any stranger, and those who are severely disabled may talk to anyone they meet as if to a household member. Without having learned how to behave appropriately with acquaintances or strangers, parents are understandably fearful for the risks their children may face if exposed to other, more able, sometimes spiteful, children. When their children become adults, parents may fear or deny their sexuality. Each may have a restrictive effect, through fear of sexual exploitation or through denial of their need to mix in age-appropriate ways with their peers.

Whilst there are many young people and adults who have grown up without these interacting limitations on their social lives, there are many who have. Where expectations have been high, opportunities may not have been present. Lack of social skills on the part of individuals or rejection on the part of others, may have frustrated such opportunities. Often, people may have had little encouragement to express their feelings about others, little chance to be seen as valued members of their community, and too limited an opportunity to learn from and model themselves on other people. Many do appear to want more opportunities for companionship and friendship than they have experienced.

How can these barriers be overcome? The next chapter will consider how acquaintances and friendships develop before turning to explore how such insights may be used.

REFERENCES

ATKINSON, D. With time to spare: the leisure pursuits of people with mental handicaps. *Mental Handicap,* 1985; **13:4**, 139–140.

ATKINSON, D. Engaging competent others: a study of the support networks of people with mental handicap. *British Journal of Social Work,* 1986; **16** (supplement), 83–101.

ATKINSON, D. How easy is it to form friendships after leaving longstay hospitals? *Social Work Today,* 1987; 15th June, 12–13.

ATKINSON, D., WARD, L. *A Part of the Community: social integration and neighbourhood networks.* London: Campaign for People with Mental Handicaps, 1986.

ATKINSON, D. *Someone to Turn To: the social worker's role and the role of front line staff in relation to people with mental handicaps.* Kidderminster: BIMH Publications, 1989.

ATKINSON, D., WARD, L. Friends and neighbours: relationships and opportunities in the community for people with a mental handicap. *In* Malin, N. (Ed.). *Reassessing Community Care.* London: Croom Helm, 1987.

BELL, N. J., SCHOENROCK, C.J., BEVSBERG, G.J. Change over time in the community: findings of a longitudinal study. *In* Bruininks, R., Meyers, C.E., Sigford, B.B., Lakin, K.C. (Eds.). *Deinstitutionalisation, and Community Adjustment of Mentally Retarded People.* Monograph Number 4, 195–206. Washington DC: American Association on Mental Deficiency, 1981.

BERCOVICI, S. M. Qualitative methods and cultural perspectives in the study of deinstitutionalisation. *In* Bruininks, R., Meyers, C.E., Sigford, B.B., Lakin, K.C. (Eds.). *Deinstitutionalisation, and Community Adjustment of Mentally Retarded People.* Monograph Number 4, 133–144. Washington DC: American Association on Mental Deficiency, 1981.

CAMPBELL, A. C. Comparison of family and community contacts of mentally subnormal adults in hospital and in local authority hostels. *British Journal* of Preventive Social Medicine, 1968; **22**, 165–169.

DE KOCK, U., FELCE, D., SAXBY, H., THOMAS, M. Community and family contact: an evaluation of small community homes for severely and profoundly mentally handicapped adults. *Mental Handicap Research*, 1988; **1:2**, 127–140.

EDGERTON, R. B. *The Cloak of Competence: stigma in the lives of the mentally retarded.* Berkeley: University of California Press, 1967.

EDGERTON, R. B., BERCOVICI, S.M. The cloak of competence: years later. *American Journal of Mental Deficiency*, 1976; **80**, 485–497.

FELCE, D., TOOGOOD, S. *Close to Home: a local housing service and its impact on the lives of nine adults with severe and profound mental handicaps.* Kidderminster: BIMH Publications, 1988.

FIRTH, H. *A Move to Community: social contacts and behaviour.* Morpeth: Northumberland Health Authority District Psychology Service, 1986.

FIRTH, H., SHORT, D. A move from hospital to community: evaluation of community contacts. *Child: Care, Health and Development,* 1987; **13**, 341–354.

FLYNN, M. C. *Independent Living for Adults with Mental Handicap: a place of my own.* London: Cassell Educational, 1989.

GOLLAY, E., FREEDMAN, R., WYNGAARDEN, M., KURTZ, N.R. *Coming Back – The Community Experiences of Institutionalised Mentally Retarded People.* Cambridge, Mass: Abt Books, 1978.

GOTTLIEB, J., LEYSER, Y. Friendship between mentally retarded and non-retarded children. *In* Asher, S.R., Gottmann, J.M. (Eds.). *The Development of Children's Friendships.* Cambridge: Cambridge University Press, 1981.

JAHODA, A., MARKOVA, I., CATTERMOLE, M. Stigma and self-concept of people with a mild mental handicap. *Journal of Mental Deficiency Research,* 1988; **32**, 103–115.

KAUFMAN, S. Friendship, coping systems and community adjustment of mildly retarded adults. *In* Edgerton, R.B. (Ed.). *Lives in Process: mildly retarded adults in a large city.* Monograph No. 6. Washington DC: American Association on Mental Deficiency, 1984.

LANDESMAN-DWYER, S., BERKSON, G. Friendships and Social Behavior. *In* Wortis, J. (Ed.). *Mental Retardation and Developmental Disabilities, Vol. 13.* London: Plenum Press, 1984.

McCONKEY, R. M., WALSH, J., MULCAHY, M. Mentally handicapped adults living in the community. *Mental Handicap,* 1982; **10:3**, 90–93.

McCONKEY, R., NAUGHTON, M., NUGENT, U. Have we met? Community contact of adults who are mentally handicapped. *Mental Handicap,* 1983; **11:2**, 57–59.

MALIN, N. A. Group homes for mentally handicapped adults: residents' views on contacts and support. *British Journal of Mental Subnormality,* 1982; **28:2**, 29–34.

MALIN, N. *Group Homes for the Mentally Handicapped.* London: HMSO, 1983.

PEALER, J., O'BRIEN, J. *Personal Relationships for Persons with Developmental Disabilities.* Proceedings of a Conference on Informal Support. Columbus, Ohio: Ohio Society for Autistic Citizens, 1985.

REITER, S., LEVI, A.M. Factors affecting social integration of non-institutionalised mentally retarded adults. *American Journal of Mental*

Deficiency, 1980; **85**, 25 – 30.

RICHARDSON, A., RITCHIE, J. *Making the Break*. London: King's Fund Centre, 1986.

RICHARDSON, A., RITCHIE, J. *Developing Friendships: enabling people with learning difficulties to make and maintain friends*. London: Policy Studies Institute/Social and Community Planning Research, 1989a.

RICHARDSON, A., RITCHIE, J. *Letting Go*. Milton Keynes: Open University Press, 1989b.

SAXBY, H., THOMAS, M., FELCE, D., DE KOCK, U. The use of shops, cafés and public houses by severely and profoundly mentally handicapped adults. *British Journal of Mental Subnormality*, 1986; **32**, 69 – 71.

SEED, P. *Mental Handicap: who helps in rural and remote communities?* Tunbridge Wells: Costello Educational, 1980.

WILLMOTT, P. *Social Networks, Informal Care, and Public Policy*. London: Policy Studies Institute, 1986.

WILLMOTT, P. *Friendship Networks and Social Support*. London: Policy Studies Institute, 1987.

ZETLIN, A. G., MURTAUGH, M. Friendship patterns of mildly learning handicapped and non-handicapped high school students. *American Journal on Mental Retardation*, 1988; **92**, 447 – 454.

. . . some people desire intimacy with one or two close friends

CHAPTER THREE

What does friendship provide
and how do friendships develop?

ACQUAINTANCE AND FRIENDSHIP: A PROCESS?

Almost all of us have many kinds of relationship: commercial, social, sexual, and familial for example. This book is concerned primarily with social relationships, and particularly with friendship and acquaintance. Its purpose is to examine how people with learning disabilities can be offered wider opportunities to develop personal relationships of their own choice. As a preliminary, this chapter explores how people *without* disabilities make acquaintances and friends. It is necessary to make clear the assumption behind this approach: that the principles that apply in respect of how relationships are made, sustained, and broken are no different for people with learning disabilities than they are for those without such disabilities. That assumption we share with Landesman-Dwyer and Berkson (1984).

People meet. They nod or say hello, respond, or comment as appropriate to the situation in which they find themselves. Very rapidly they make decisions about how far they might like to get to know each other. They do so on the basis of appearance, dress, gestures, and facial expressions – in particular, expressions of interest. They may think they would like to get to know one another better, or merely spend time together as "acquaintances". But as people spend time with each other, they get to know more about each other. Depending on the circumstances, on what people are engaged in, they may notice aspects of one another they were not aware of initially. Broadly speaking, the more time people spend together in some joint activity, the more they will get to know each other, and the more likely it is that they will grow to like each other, although this is by no means certain.

Getting to know people, therefore, is a process, much of which depends on circumstance. Some factors are within people's control; others are outside their control. Lack of money, degree of access to the use of a car, the fact, nature, or lack of employment or training, participation in segregated or integrated activities: all vitally affect the relationships each individual can make.

Much also depends on personal motivation: people's degree of interest in other people, their activities, and their feelings. To that extent, the desire to meet people and to make friends is the starting point for sociable interaction; and this is as true for people with learning disabilities as it is for anyone else.

Experiences also change people's expectations and goals. Many people with learning disabilities have led lives which are conspicuous for the absence of varied company, or of relationships which bring intimacy. As they begin to experience these the desire for company, or the desire for more close, trusting, "intimate" relationships, may grow.

Our framework sees every relationship as a process : from first meeting, through acquaintance, until sometimes developing into a friendship or partnership. Each relationship may be maintained, weakened, fragmented, or changed with time. We now attempt to consider and explain this framework.

"Friendship" has different meanings for different people. To some it means particularly close, special relationships: the kind they might have with only two or three people at any time. To others a "friend" is almost anyone whom they see repeatedly, with whom they share some activity or event, and with whom they are "friendly". Matthews (1986) discussed differing views of friendship, contrasting those held by people who are more selective with those of people who are less selective in their friendships. She recounted how the friendships of elderly people had developed through their lives, and distinguished three groups of people:

> those who desired intimacy with one or two close friends as a particularly high priority, and who perceived friendship in terms of a close relationship;

> those for whom the avoidance of social isolation was particularly important, who desired "company" through friends or acquaintances, and whose definition of friendship was broad;

> those who were "independent", for whom high levels of intimacy or socialisation were not a priority and who saw themselves as needing, and having, few friends.

As people vary widely in their views of what distinguishes friendship from other relationships, it is necessary for us to make some distinctions and clarify them here, so that readers will be certain about what we mean.

We have found Duck and Gilmour's standpoint (Duck, 1977, 1982, 1984, 1986; Duck and Gilmour, 1981a,b,c) the most helpful one in understanding and thinking about the development of relationships. They see relationships in terms of a process, with friendship forming through a process of acquaintance. They recognise that relationships are not static, but change with time; and that they require maintenance, else they will weaken, or break apart.

They also see relationships very much in terms of how each party thinks about and perceives the other. This emphasis on how people *think* about their relationships is one we have found particularly important. It is sometimes contrasted with viewpoints which emphasise people's behaviour or skill in relationships. The two viewpoints are not mutually contradictory, and we shall use both when appropriate. Nevertheless, we believe that how people behave is most easily understood if we also pay attention to how people think.

Duck (1977) uses the word acquaintance in a very particular way, and we shall follow that usage. Because he sees relationships in terms of a process, he uses the word *acquaintance* to mean *the process of getting to know someone*. Our *acquaintances* are *the people whom we are getting to know*. On this kind of understanding, therefore, friendship usually develops out of acquaintance. Only rarely do people become good friends on first meeting.

Some people see their friendships and their acquaintances as very different, and see themselves as having both acquaintances and friends. In a sense, there is some truth in this viewpoint: people often do make early decisions about whom they may want to become friends with, and whom they only want to know as acquaintances. Yet getting to know people is a process which may happen consciously or unconsciously, intentionally or unintentionally. It frequently happens that people who become friends already know one another, but not well, until some change of circumstances or desire brings the relationship closer. At other times people who thought they were becoming friends drift apart.

Often we know, and make a conscious choice, early in a relationship whether we want it to develop into a friendship or not. Our viewpoint is that, despite this, getting to know someone else is always a process. Acquaintance is the first step, which may be accomplished very quickly or very slowly. Friendship and a close relationship may follow if the wish, the opportunity, and the supports are present.

WHAT DISTINGUISHES FRIENDSHIP?

So, what are the features of friendship? It does not seem particularly helpful or useful to try to define terms like "real" or "true" friendship. But it does seem helpful to describe certain features which distinguish different relationships from one another, and which help to define friendships and distinguish them from other relationships.

Duck (1977) described friendship as "a special case of liking". This emphasis is echoed in the aspects of helpful personal relationships highlighted by psychotherapists such as Rogers (1961) and Truax and Carkhuff (1967) as warmth, empathy, and genuineness. "Warmth" has sometimes been specified as "unconditional positive regard", which stresses the non-judgemental nature of the relationship, and its strength even when one person may be expressing thoughts or feelings to someone which would elicit very negative and judgemental reactions from most other listeners.

Others have highlighted different aspects of relationships which constitute friendship, such as commitment, choice, and persistence, as well as the subjective experience of empathy in intimate relationships. Empathy may be inferred in relationships between people who cannot communicate with words. It is demonstrated by behaviour appropriate to the feelings the other person may be experiencing.

Relationships such as acquaintance and friendship can differ in various ways.

The extent of *choice* in relationships may be strongly influenced by the number of people an individual knows.

Relationships, including friendships, may be more or less one-sided at any point in time. The degree of *reciprocity* in what is said, in who contacts whom and how often, may vary between one relationship and another.

There may be different degrees of *commitment*. How much time will a person give? How available is one person to the other?

The amount of actual help given by each party in a relationship varies enormously. In some friendships *mutual assistance* is the cornerstone of the relationship; yet, for example, neighbours may help each other often but not consider each other as "friends".

The degree of a person's *trust* in the other's loyalty, confidence, judgement, or reliability will all distinguish one particular relationship from another.

Some relationships lapse if they are not constantly *renewed*. Others seem almost to strengthen in such adversity, because other features of the relationship may be highlighted, emphasising how close two people are.

The degree of *intimacy* in different relationships varies, and may vary in one relationship over time. The degree of *empathy* may vary likewise. Many people regard intimacy as an essential characteristic of friendship. Men and women may view friendship differently in this respect. It is common, particularly amongst men, to regard other people as good friends even when there is little intimacy, if they are seen as reliable sources of help in time of need.

The existence of relationships across different *settings* is another way in which they vary. Some relationships may be largely confined to one setting, such as the workplace, the club, or the Women's Institute. Others manifest themselves in many settings.

Relationships differ in the *frequency* of actual contact between the people involved.

Views of what characteristics distinguish friendship vary widely amongst different cultures, different social classes, different age groups, and especially between women and men. We will discuss some of these differences and confusions shortly, but for clarity's sake, we will put forward our own views first.

We take the view that the following four characteristics most usefully distinguish friendship from other relationships – from acquaintance, from colleague, from companion, from situations of infatuation or mere admiration, and from relationships which are primarily those of family, relative, or neighbour.

Choice distinguishes friends from colleagues, companions, or people who are thrown together by force of circumstance. It can also distinguish friends from relatives. Some people, however, do choose to regard particular relatives as friends because of the nature of their contact with each other. Some relatives, therefore, may also be chosen as friends.

Friendship is a *mutual* process. This distinguishes it from admiration or infatuation, and from situations where dependence is central to the relationship.

Commitment distinguishes friendship from relationships which are insincere, unreliable, shallow, temporary, or superficial. This may be judged by the priority people give to a relationship when there are other possible ways of spending their time, by the inconvenience or discomfort they are willing to endure, and the time they will give in order to maintain the relationship.

Persistence distinguishes friendships from temporary or short-lived relationships, and from some very close and intimate, perhaps sexual, relationships which do not persist.

There is one more characteristic which clearly distinguishes some friendships from others: *intimacy.* Intimacy in close friendship has much in common with intimacy in other close relationships, such as those between family members, or between partners or spouses. The needs met by close friendships are often very different from the needs met by less intimate friendships. Hence, we shall give particular attention to some features of close relationships at various points in the subsequent discussion.

Choice has a central place in distinguishing friendship from other relationships. The range and types of opportunities for making relationships which people experience will therefore have an important impact on their ability to develop the friendships and close relationships of their choice. Personal attitudes, motivation, and skills are also fundamental to the kinds of relationships people make. We shall therefore explore friendship, and how friends are made, with both situational and personal factors in mind.

WHAT NEEDS DOES FRIENDSHIP MEET?

Friendship may be said to meet a number of very different kinds of need, such as the need for company, for intimacy, for self-esteem, for self-identity, for help, and for advice. Richardson and Ritchie (1989) have distinguished three broad functions for "social support" which in their view includes friendship. These are:

the provision of company;

the establishment of a sense of rapport or intimacy; and,

the provision of practical help.

The first two of these functions closely complement the distinction made by Weiss (1975) between two different types of isolation, social isolation and emotional isolation, meaning the felt absense of company and of intimacy.

Duck (1977, 1986) based his approach on Kelly's (1955) *personal construct theory*. Kelly's approach sees people as having hypotheses about other people which are constantly tested, evaluated, and changed in the light of experience. The beliefs and values, or "constructs", people have about themselves are validated by comparison with others' views, perceptions, and behaviour. Duck, therefore, sees friendship as a fundamental way of people sharing, clarifying, and strengthening their beliefs and values about themselves and the world, with others who share their values.

Our own view, based on this approach, is that friendship fulfils essentially two functions:

providing opportunities for people to share feelings and viewpoints, especially those linked to deeply held values, with others who share similar assumptions and values;

providing opportunities for people to clarify and confirm beliefs and feelings about themselves.

We can separate this second function into two components: that of people checking out beliefs about themselves and testing and confirming their self-identity; and that of people confirming their feelings and values of themselves as individuals and building and sustaining self-esteem. Our analysis may be summarised by saying that friendship or other close positive relationships:

provide people with opportunities to share and confirm important feelings and values;

enable people to develop, define, and express their personal identity as individuals; and,

enable people to build and sustain personal self-esteem.

Sustaining self-esteem, as well as being a function of friendship, is often a necessary precondition if people are to develop effective relationships with others. More precisely, self-confidence is a crucial element in forming and maintaining friendships. (Self-esteem is used here to mean people's personal judgement of their own worth and acceptance of themselves (Burns, 1979); self-confidence to mean the behaviour people show to others in a particular situation.)

It appears from this perspective that one of the main purposes of friendship is to provide opportunities for the kind of exchanges which enable friends to show empathy for each other and communicate warmth to each other. Such exchanges will often take place within the context of some degree of intimacy; although the degree of intimacy may be slight and brief, as between men or women busily engaged in some other activity.

If this is so, then the provision of *company* is not necessarily a function of friendship. Company can be provided, and often is, by acquaintances. There are some common situations, such as pubs, bars, cafés, and restaurants, as well as journeys, trips, and most leisure activities, which it is well recognised that many people will avoid unless they have company; but the company of acquaintances may be perfectly adequate for those purposes.

Rephrasing these themes, the needs which friendship meets may be described as:

providing non-judgemental warmth and understanding, or empathy;

developing and confirming self-identity; and,

raising and sustaining self-esteem.

The first of these functions appears almost synonymous with the provision of intimacy, as described by Richardson and Ritchie (1989). Yet our analysis differs from theirs in that we view the provision of self-identity and self-esteem as essential functions of friendship, and see the provision of company as something able to be fulfilled by acquaintances as well as by friends.

If people's individual needs for company, and for warmth and understanding, are not met, then they may suffer from isolation. As

. . . enable friends to show empathy for each other and communicate warmth

already stated, two very distinct kinds of isolation have been distinguished by Weiss (1975):

social isolation, being the absence of company or an engaging social network; and,

emotional isolation, being the absence of intimacy or close emotional attachments providing warmth and understanding.

We view both these forms of isolation as being linked to the absence of different kinds, or combinations, of relationship. Social isolation reflects the absence of both friendships and acquaintances. Emotional isolation specifically reflects the absence of friendships or other close relationships.

The experience of *loneliness* can derive either from social isolation, or from emotional isolation. But loneliness is an experience suffered by individuals. Social or emotional isolation of itself does not imply that people will experience loneliness. People differ in the extent to which they wish to have wide, or frequent, social contacts. They differ in the number of intimate relationships and the degree of intimacy they need, particularly at different times of their lives. Their needs and expectations may change from time to time throughout life. Weiss (1975) argues that people's experiences of loneliness, whether from social or emotional isolation, are not generally related to their degree of isolation but rather to changed or changing circumstances: geographical move, change of job, loss of partner, friends, or family members, or changing relationships in school, work, or personal life.

Loneliness may be experienced in different ways, according to the need which is not met. Weiss (1975) distinguished these differences thus:

"the loneliness of emotional isolation is strongly reminiscent of the distress (emptiness, anxiety and apprehension) of the small child who fears he has been abandoned by his parents. On the other hand, the loneliness of social isolation (is) like the (aimlessness), boredom, feelings of exclusion and the feelings of marginality of the small child whose friends are all away".

People who do not expect to experience friendship or close relationships, or who have not in the past had these experiences, may not feel loneliness in the absence of social or emotional attachments. However, there is much to suggest that many people with learning disabilities do feel lonely, even when they have not been led to expect that they will make close friendships (Richardson and Ritchie, 1989).

Some people do not seem to mind, or may even seem to prefer, being relatively isolated, both socially and emotionally. For others, the presence of adequate rapport or intimacy with at least a few people is of particular importance. For yet others it is company, the avoidance of social isolation, which is most significant. As Matthews (1986) has suggested, people may seek many friends, or a few very close friends, or they may regard themselves as independent, not acknowledging close friends and not experiencing any feelings of loneliness.

But for those who are not satisfied with their situation, what contributes to it, and what factors may alleviate or change the situation? If we are to understand the situation of people with learning disabilities, and help when necessary to change it, then we must consider such issues.

People's beliefs about themselves have a powerful impact on their behaviour. The belief that they are "incapable" of finding or making friends, is not helpful, and needs to be changed if loneliness is to be overcome. A feeling of lack of control over the situation is also often a key feature of loneliness. Thus, allowing elderly people to choose when volunteers visit, for example, can have a significant impact on their feelings of loneliness, without even altering the number or length of visits they receive.

In later chapters we shall consider the situations and opportunites, and the personal attributes, motivations, and skills which may help friendship develop. Environment has a great impact on whether people become and remain isolated. But individual attributes undoubtedly influence people's vulnerability to isolation, their capacity to overcome it, and the extent to which they experience loneliness in consequence.

Considering individual attributes and personal situations directs attention to different issues and suggests different remedies to isolation. Broadly, the latter suggests the need for approaches that might make available a richer social world; whereas the former suggests attention be paid to individual motivation and skill, and to education in particular.

We shall pursue two issues, focusing in turn on individual attributes and situational factors. The first will consider what enables people to develop a wide range of acquaintances and friendships. The second will explore what it is that promotes the development of rapport and intimacy.

HOW DO FRIENDSHIPS FORM AND DEVELOP? A PROCESS OF ACQUAINTANCE

The previous discussion emphasised the distinctions between the extent of acquaintance and friendship, and the closeness or intimacy of relationships. Here we return not to the distinctions between acquaintance and friendship, but to the continuity between them. Degrees of liking, rapport, and intimacy separate acquaintances from friends, and friends from close or very close friends.

Sometimes close friendships, or close emotional or sexual relationships, develop rapidly between people who meet for the first time, or between people who have met previously but whom some circumstance has now thrown together. Other friendships develop gradually over weeks, months, or years, out of acquaintance. Very close friendships may develop this way, more or less slowly. Longstanding emotional and sexual relationships between spouses or partners have often developed over a period of time, frequently between people who had already known each other for a considerable period, either as acquaintances or friends. The transition from non-sexual to sexual relationships is usually fairly marked because of the distinctive nature of the latter, but changes in the emotional closeness of such relationships may not proceed at the same time or pace.

Most often friendships – whether or not they are intimate, "special friendships" – develop irregularly, at a speed determined by events which draw the parties together and the personal inclinations of the particular individuals involved.

The viewpoint on the development of acquaintance and friendship which we find most useful and which we draw upon (Duck and Gilmour, 1981; Duck, 1986) is that each relationship passes, usually imperceptibly, through a series of steps from initial introduction through a *process of acquaintance.*

This approach suggests strongly that close friendships are likely to be found more easily when people have at least a few acquaintances. As one of the features of the lives of people with learning disabilities is that they often do not have very many acquaintances, we place particular emphasis on the development of such relationships, out of which close friendships may form.

Some people do become friends almost overnight: occasionally people meet, perhaps while on a long journey or on holiday, spend time together, and become close friends straightaway. Usually, however, people meet one another at least two or three times before initial liking grows into friendship.

What is common in both of these situations is the process of people *getting to know* each other better as time progresses, and testing out each other's attitudes, values, and behaviour as they do so. This exchange may be by way of gossip, for example, about the neighbours next door, the new arrivals to the street, or a friend's manner of dress. But it is important for people to be able to do this, and confirm whether their own values are shared by others. Generally, the relationships which become closest are those between people who share many of what they consider to be the most important values.

Duck (1977) places much emphasis on the consequences of the initial impressions and perceptions people gain about each other when they first meet. This leads us to conclude that proper introductions may be vital in helping people with learning disabilities to develop a number of acquaintances some of whom might later become friends. Later on we shall explore how the idea of providing proper introductions can be extended into a concept of enabling and supporting people's choice and development in relationships.

WHEN IS A FRIENDSHIP NOT A FRIENDSHIP? THE INFLUENCES OF GENDER, AGE, SOCIAL CLASS, AND CULTURE

Gender, age, social class, and culture all affect people's relationship patterns. Equally important, these factors influence how people *think* about their relationships.

Gender differences

There is little doubt that men and women see friendship in differing terms. It is more debatable whether there are consistent differences in the way they conceive of friendship. One view is that women typically see emotional intimacy as a key element in a relationship of friendship, whereas men include relationships which are based primarily on company, on being together, and on doing things together with other men. Such a view undoubtedly has an element of truth: some men and women do see their friendships in these ways. What is striking, however, is the difficulty that any mixed group of men and women have in agreeing on anything about this issue: not merely as to what differences exist, but as to whether any consistent differences exist at all between the way women and men conceive of friendship.

The research suggests that there are consistent differences in the ways men and women behave. For example, Willmott's London study (1987) showed that same-gender friendships are more common than cross-gender friendships: men tend to have more men friends and women more women friends. Friends whom people saw alone were almost exclusively same-gender friends, though women and men differed in this behaviour. In Willmott's study women more often saw their (women) friends alone, but men more often saw their (men) friends in wider company.

Willmott ascribed much of this difference to the differing roles of women and men, particularly amongst couples with a woman caring at home for dependent children.

Class and cultural differences

Gender, age, class, and culture all interact in their effects on relationship patterns. For example, it is striking that the gender differences just referred to in Willmott's study were accentuated amongst working-class couples, where relationships with friends were often almost entirely segregated by gender.

Stereotypes confound discussions of gender and class differences. Allan's (1979) discussion of friendship, with it distinction between working-class "mateship" and middle-class friendship reflects real differences in friendship behaviour, but has reinforced a stereotype of the working-class male whose contact with his friends is at work and at the club. Some men do maintain their friendships in this manner. For some, these relationships meet their need for company, for some they meet their need for intimacy, and for some they meet both needs.

Cultural patterns of behaviour are changing fast. Willmott (1986, 1987) has documented how greater material resources, in particular car ownership, have dramatically altered working-class patterns of sociability, enabling relationships to be more easily sustained over greater distances, and making working-class friendships less dependent on work, family, and neighbourhood connections. Nevertheless, some of Allan's (1979) findings about class differences in relationships in the 1970s were still true for some people in Willmott's studies: more working-class male relationships were confined to particular settings (work, pub or club, football team) than was true for women or for the middle class. Working-class people were more likely to invite friends of both sexes to their home for a meal than they were in the past, but class differences remained.

Perhaps the most striking difference remaining was people's perception of what constitutes friendship. A few of Willmott's male working-class informants held to the view that a friend is "someone you meet for a drink". This view epitomises the stereotype held by many people about how men view friendship, but many men do not view friendship in this way. Nevertheless, Willmott (1987) concluded that:

> "this study . . . seemed to confirm the finding from other research that women's ties with friends are different – 'closer', more intense and more important to them – than those of men".

What underlined these differences in friendship patterns, Willmott argued, were differences in role. It seemed that women often adopted a role as social organisers, not just for themselves but for their families and friends: they made arrangements, and telephoned or wrote to friends and relatives. Underlying this, we believe, lies a broader difference between the thinking and behaviour of many men and women about their relationships. This is that women are socialised not only to care for others, but also to care about them. It appears to us that this manifests itself as a more frequent concern amongst women to nurture, maintain, and develop acquaintances and friends than is often present, consciously or unconsciously, in the thinking and behaviour of men.

It is this difference in thinking about relationships which we wish to emphasise. It is a difference – if exaggerated – between a viewpoint which assumes that friendships simply exist or happen, and a viewpoint which assumes that friendships are ever-changing relationships which require to be nurtured actively by the individuals involved. We hold, in essence, to the latter view.

Age and friendship patterns

People's perceptions of what friendship is all about, their own particular needs, their upbringing and social class, all affect how their friendships will actually develop over time during their lives. The research with children and young people which has attempted to disentangle "stages" of friendship has shown that, as children grow up, their understanding of what friendship is about changes and develops (Dickens and Perlman, 1981; Firth and Rapley, 1987). Young children see friendship very much in instrumental terms – how enjoyable and rewarding the relationship may be. As they develop they usually come to see friendship as involving commitment, loyalty, and shared values. Those are the kinds of abstractions to which adults will usually refer when describing close friendships, particularly long-lasting ones.

Despite the differences in language use and in the level of thinking about relationships, however, the processes underlying friendship formation remain in essence similar at different ages. For young children, adolescents, or adults, friendships are formed and chosen with people who in some way allow them to share, clarify, and strengthen the way that they see themselves. Even in the one-way admiration or infatuation of young children for older role-models, or of adolescents for their hero or heroine, there is the need to be with, or become like, others who epitomise what those young people would like to value in themselves. Ambivalence and ambiguity often exist between self-perception and ideal self-image. Nevertheless, acquaintances and friends at all ages provide, confirm, and define people's own identities.

As people grow older it often becomes easier for them, and for others, to perceive their particular relationship needs. These needs may often not be met, but people usually become clearer and more articulate about their preferences as they grow older. We have already referred to Matthews' (1986) distinctions between elderly people who desired intimacy, company, or independence. Such preferences interact with people's social class and upbringing.

One recent study of changing friendships over time amongst elderly women (Adams, 1987) suggested that many women in higher social classes often contracted their overall network of friends with age, developing and cherishing a few close relationships; whilst many middle-class and working-class women saw old age as a chance to explore new relationships not previously possible because of the constraints of children, spouses, and jobs. Whilst some constraints are released in retirement from employment or family work, old age often brings physical constraints in terms of reduced mobility, ill-health, reduction in the number of roles performed, and less financial resources. Older people, even if they "reinvest in friendship", are likely to lose friends through death, ill-health, or reduced mobility (Brown, 1981; Dickens and Perlman, 1981; Lowenthal, Thurner, and Chiraboga, 1975).

The loss of a spouse through separation or divorce in middle life will frequently lead to social and/or emotional isolation for one of the partners. The loss of a spouse through bereavement at any age often leaves the widow or widower not only extremely emotionally destitute, but often socially isolated as well. This may occur through a combination of broken ties previously maintained through the lost spouse, acquaintances and relationships weakened during a period of withdrawal in bereavement, and loss of self-confidence and changed patterns of activity. For elderly or very elderly people such processes may be compounded by the loss of other elderly friends, physical infirmity, and an implicit or explicit belief that they would rather join the spouse who has died.

To these difficulties in maintaining friendships in old age must be added the constraint some elderly people feel about forming cross-sex friendships. There are, of course, fewer elderly men than elderly women. Even so, Adams (1985) has argued that culturally perceived barriers to friendships with men, amongst women brought up around the turn of the century, are a significant constraint on their social relationships: "People would talk".

Expectations about behaviour have changed enormously over the century through which today's elderly people have lived. Material changes, such as the telephone, car ownership, and changing patterns of wealth and social habits, are altering the stereotypes about relationships of individuals of all ages and all social classes. Yet amongst the most significant changes are the changes in people's perceptions of what their relationships ought to bring, what they might be expected to enjoy, and whether their relationships meet their needs for different kinds of friendship.

STAGES OF FRIENDSHIP, OR A PROCESS OF DEVELOPMENT?

Some of the most important changes in perceptions about friendship to which we have referred occur in childhood, adolescence, and early adulthood. Many people working with children believe it is helpful to see them as developing through distinct stages in their relationships. A corollary of this for some is that people with severe learning disabilities cannot develop beyond certain stages, and cannot show "true" friendship. We dispute this.

The link between such stages and intellectual and chronological development is a convenient and attractive one for developmental psychologists. Yet such links are not straightforward: at times the fit is extremely uneasy. Developments in relationships may be more usefully seen as a result of growth in individuals' personality, confidence, social skills, and security, than as a consequence of intellectual development.

Is intellectual development necessarily linked with the ability to form friendships? Many researchers have demonstrated the link between children's own conception or understanding of friendship and their increasing intellectual powers as they grow older (Dickens and Perlman, 1981). This should not be confused with stages of friendship as such. For example, Selman (1981) has linked stages or types of friendship with

*. . . from first meeting . . . each relationship may be
maintained, developed, or changed with time*

developing stages of intellectualising about relationships. He puts forward five stages of friendship: momentary playmates; one-way assistance; fair-weather cooperation; intimate relationships; and autonomous and interdependent friendship.

These levels may appear sophisticated. They are an attempt to link cognitive development with the development of friendship in a set of stages in the tradition of Piaget (Flavell, 1963). Yet, on closer examination, Selman's description of the limitations of intimate relationships, for example, stresses the possessiveness of the two-person clique. This suggests difficulties in confidence or security rather than the lack of cognitive abilities.

There are, indeed, different stages in the nature and conceptualisation of relationships as children grow up. This does not imply that children of particular intellectual abilities are only capable of certain kinds of relationship, even though their perception and description of their relationships may be limited by their intellectual powers. Moreover, such views of young people's relationships as limited and linked to stages of intellectual development may seriously belittle the quality of their relationships with other people. Even very young children without speech show consistency in their preferences, amongst both children and adults, and these can be related to the attitudes and behaviour of others towards them.

The ability or inability to describe a friendship does not determine its existence. People's conception of friendship (like love) is coloured by the limits of their experience of it. That some children, some adults, and some adolescents may be very free with the use of the term "friend" does not mean that the label is not meaningful for them. Nor should the use or misuse of the word be confused with the presence or absence of friendship as we have defined it. Many people, of all ages, confuse temporary feelings with more lasting emotional ties. A third party may often be needed to help identify the true nature of a relationship.

Evidence that exists from others' observations suggests that intellectual ability is not correlated in any simple way with the ability to form friendships. Gollay et al. (1978), in their study of people living in the community, reported that the frequency of friendships did not vary with degree of learning disability. Bell, Schoenrock, and Bevsberg (1981) also found no relationship between number of close friends and intelligence quotients in their study of people leaving hospital to live with their families, in community residential facilities, or on their own. Landesman-Dwyer and Berkson (1984) report that the level of disability of the people they studied did not relate to friendship choices or to other measures of social behaviour. The single exception to this finding was that people with profound disabilities, who did evidence a wide variety of social behaviour, failed to distinguish what was appropriate behaviour in different situations.

Clearly, people without the necessary intellectual (and, particularly, linguistic) abilities cannot think, analyse, and control their social behaviour to respond most appropriately to changing social situations. But there is no evidence to suggest that severity of intellectual disability is linked in any simple way with the capability to maintain relationships which others would describe as friendship.

Conceiving friendship development in stages or levels carries with it the danger of specific expectations: thus, friendships which have not "reached stage three" may not be considered "real" friendships. This danger is particularly pronounced in the context of people with learning disabilities, for whom the parallel understanding and ability to describe friendships may not be present.

Many adult relationships of an everyday kind could be categorised according to Selman's (1981) stages of one-way assistance or fair-weather cooperation. Thinking of many relationships at work, surely these are not developmental stages in friendship. They are, rather, *types of relationship*. If these stages are rethought, in terms of types of relationship, they may offer useful insights.

As far as we are concerned the elements of choice, reciprocity, commitment, and permanence in time remain friendship's defining characteristics. These are all aspects of relationships which may be demonstrated by people with profound disabilities and able academics, by young toddlers and elderly grandparents. People with profound learning disabilities may not be able to develop friendships which involve understanding each other's needs for dependence and interdependence. But they may be able to develop friendships with a high degree of intimacy and reciprocity in terms of non-verbal behaviour. The elements of choice, reciprocity, persistence, and commitment (as judged by attention and concentration) may all be present.

To recap. We do not think it useful to conceive of stages of friendship. We do not think it useful to conceive of a hard and fast distinction or boundary between acquaintance and friendship. Following Duck (1977), we see the one develop from the other through a step-by-step process over time. We do not think it is particularly helpful or useful to try to define terms like "real" or "true" friendship. We do believe it may be helpful for people to describe how close they feel to each other. But this is only one variable describing any friendship or relationship.

We hold to the view that the ability to form close relationships is not determined by intellectual ability or cognitive development. Developmental psychologists have then to offer us not a sequence of stages in friendship, but some different categories of relationships. To paraphrase Selman (1981) we might describe these categories thus:

brief acquaintance or cooperation;

one-way or mutual (but temporary) assistance;

relationships involving reciprocity over time;

relationships involving shared intimacy;

relationships – whether at work or at home – which have withstood the test of time and where both parties acknowledge some need for dependence as well as acknowledging each other's independence.

It can be said that young people generally become less egocentric in their friendships as they grow older. As Duck (1986) has put it:

"The focus shifts from 'me and what you can do for me' to 'you and what we can do together' to 'us and how we can help one another to grow as people'."

As this quotation illustrates, it is primarily through the development of personality rather than intellectual ability that these changes take place. Moreover, people with severe or profound learning disabilities may be very capable of developing relationships we would define as friendships; even if our understanding of these relationships may not be shared by them, or *vice versa*.

SKILLS IN MAKING RELATIONSHIPS

Making relationships which develop beyond brief acquaintance demands certain conditions, such as motivation, opportunity, confidence, and skill. Richardson and Ritchie (1989) describe some of these as "components" of friendship.

The first precondition is motivation: without the desire to develop a relationship, no relationship is likely. In practice, people do not always wish to develop relationships: either because they wish to remain isolated; or because they have sufficient company or intimacy through existing relationships; or because of ambivalence about what relationships may bring – hurt as well as pleasure, rejection as well as acceptance.

People's motivation towards relationships is greatly affected by past experience. Those who have experienced repeated or traumatic rejection themselves may openly reject people who offer friendship or may demonstrate extreme ambivalence, evident perhaps as implicit or explicit "testing" of new relationships. People who have not experienced friendship (perhaps during long institutional lives) may have developed protective ways of coping so that they feel they no longer need friendship.

Self-confidence is an important attribute in making relationships. It may vary from hour to hour, from day to day, or from one year to the next. It, too, is fundamentally influenced by people's past experiences, as well as by such physiological factors as tiredness and lack of sleep, and by people's perceptions of their personal situation and of others' views of them. In particular, self-confidence derives from family relationships and friendships. As we emphasised earlier, one of the main purposes of friendship is to build and maintain self-esteem, which sustains self-confidence in behaviour.

Self-confidence is needed at every point: in making, keeping, and nurturing friendships; in deciding to go out to work or to some social activity; in the process of greeting someone, responding to them, and parting; and in sustaining contact over time. All this depends not only on people's self-perception, but on their perception of how other people see them. The ability of people to infer how others might see them is a skill. As with piano-playing, some individuals are able to become more skilled than others. Like piano-playing, the skill acquired also needs learning to develop fully.

There are many other skills involved in maintaining relationships. Many of them involve thinking, particularly thinking about other people and how they might be feeling. Knowing how long to stay when visiting an acquaintance, or how much eye contact is appropriate with a possible girlfriend, can be seen as skills, in the sense that they are behaviours that are learned and practised either unconsciously or consciously. The "social skill" approach stresses that these facets of interaction can be taught and learned in the same kind of way, in principle, as riding a bicycle, sailing a boat, or driving a car.

Some of the skills are about observation. Some of the skills are about communicating. Some skills involve interpreting what is seen or heard, and making appropriate decisions about how to respond. These thinking skills involve judgements about other people's mood, attitude, and motivation. Various other skills are also needed for people to be able to decide how best to handle the social situation they are in. It is the exercise of these skills in combination which may be called "social skill".

Some of the skills involved in getting along with others are not simple, however, and require considerable ability to think through situations. Spivack and his colleagues (Shure and Spivack, 1978; Spivack, Platt, and Shure, 1976; Spivack and Shure, 1974) have researched extensively some of the skills involved in avoiding or resolving conflict. Their work has highlighted the importance of individuals being able to think about alternative courses of action and to consider the various possible responses other people might make.

This perspective reminds us that many skills are acquired from childhood, through a combination of observation, imitation, practice, and feedback, as well as through conscious planning and rehearsal. People who have difficulties in social relationships, or in making friends or acquaintances, lack opportunities to learn social skills in these ways.

Often, people with learning disabilities have not been able to learn the skill of expressing feelings clearly to other people. This presumes an attitude on their part: that it is acceptable to express their feelings to others. Unfortunately, the experiences of some people with learning disabilities have not encouraged them to expect that their feelings will be welcomed, or taken into account by others.

A lack of social skills, therefore, may be a barrier to making friends. Nevertheless, many people who are not very skilled in this area are able to make close and rewarding friendships. Moreover, social skills training is not a panacea which will allow all people with learning disabilities to develop the relationships they would wish for. Issues of confidence, choice, attitude, opportunity, and motivation may all be more important – quite apart from the sheer complexity involved in teaching some of the skills that are employed in forming close or long-term relationships.

THE DEVELOPMENT OF CLOSE FRIENDSHIPS

What is known about how close friendships develop? Most of the academic research which has been done on relationships has focused on their formation, probably because researchers have found it easier to examine these early stages. There has been a vast increase in research interest in the topic of personal relationships over the last fifteen years, as a recent edited collection by Perlman and Duck (1987) testifies. Writing in that volume, Perlman and Fehr (1987) emphasise that relationships between individuals are not static, but are constantly changing. Not only do the relationships themselves change, but so do the ways that the people involved think and feel about them. People may like someone, intend to get acquainted, and find that close friendship develops. Or they may hope, wish, or strive for a close friend, a confidante, or a sexual partner, but then change their expectations and settle for an acquaintance.

Although this viewpoint sees the processes of getting to know people as fundamentally similar at every stage – clarifying how far values, attitudes, and beliefs are shared with other people – Duck and his colleagues (Duck and Gilmour, 1981a,b,c; Duck, 1982, 1984) have emphasised additional factors which contribute to the success or failure of close relationships. People do not generally sit down and discuss their attitudes or values directly. They discuss other people and they talk about events which have happened, and their feelings about them. Beliefs, attitudes, and values are explored indirectly, through situations and feelings about them.

As friendship develops, people generally come to rely on that relationship for more than confirmation of their own feelings and beliefs. Close friends rely on each other for many personal emotional needs, which are different for each individual. Skill is required in the ability to understand and respond to other people's needs. People with little experience or skill in personal relationships, including people with learning disabilities, are at risk of damaging or losing friendships by failing to meet others' needs, or by inadvertently breaking some common rules about close relationships, such as those identified by Argyle and Henderson (1984), listed in Box 1.

Many people, with and without learning disabilities, are poor at expressing their feelings well to others, or may be particularly reluctant to do so. For them friendship may progress well initially, only to stagnate, falter, or break down as the relationship develops over time and as more intimate issues and feelings are explored. As Duck (1981) commented:

> "Unfortunately, there is little evidence . . . (from research, to throw light on) this possibility . . . and social skill literature focuses at present mostly on the management of those superficial social encounters in which many . . . people also feel . . . uncomfortable".

Relatively little is actually known about how intimate relationships develop, but shared values appear to be at the basis of relationships with a high degree of intimacy and emotional attachment. As one informant put it to Robert Weiss (1975), she was unable to make friends in the

---

Breaking the following "rules" was believed by young people to have contributed to the loss of a friendship with someone "who had once been a good friend but is no longer"

Do not be jealous or critical of their other relationships

Do not discuss with others what is said in confidence

Do not criticise them in public

Do offer help when they need it

Do show them emotional support

Do stand up for them in their absence

Do trust and confide in them

Do not nag them

Do show positive regard

Do respect their privacy

Avoid taking up just as much of their time as you feel like

Do be tolerant of their friends

Do repay debts or favours

Do try and make them happy when you are together

Do share news of successes with them

**BOX 1. Some "rules" about friendship, adapted from
Argyle and Henderson (1984)**

locality to which she had moved because, quite simply, she said: "They have nothing in common with me".

Intimate or close relationships, therefore, appear to require three ingredients from the people involved:

a desire for intimacy or closeness in the relationship;

shared values; and,

understanding or "rapport" with each other.

Our own view is that, besides these individual or personal attributes, there are also some common *situations* which may help to bring people together into relationships which are closer than they might otherwise have been. Situations which involve sharing with others are likely to bring people closer. Shared feelings, shared concerns and anxieties, shared adversities, shared pleasures, or even sharing a great deal of time together: all may bring people into closer relationships with each other. Sharing – values, feelings, problems, joys – is a vital ingredient of friendship. As friendship develops or deepens, more and more feelings and experiences may be shared between the people involved.

Something which is not always recognised is that the sharing of experiences can provide the starting point for close friendships. Certain kinds of shared experiences – particularly adversity – may impel people to share many feelings, thoughts, and values which otherwise they might not have done. Out of this friendship may develop, as a mutual commitment which lasts beyond the particular circumstance which initiated it.

Any shared experience which brings people closer together may foster the development of friendships, including close friendships. The experience of joining in action on a common concern (self-help groups, self-advocacy groups, tenants' associations, residents' associations, or religious or moral campaigns) may foster friendships between those engaged in it (Bulmer, 1986). Various shared activities may function in this way, especially if the activities are of a kind which encourages the sharing of emotional issues, such as drama, or artistic, religious and sporting activities.

We would summarise by saying that close relationships involving a degree of intimacy may be promoted by a number of different kinds of situations, including:

spending a great deal of time together;

common action over shared concerns (self-help, campaigns);

activities which involve sharing feelings and emotions (drama, and artistic, religious, or sporting activities);

situations of common adversity.

DIFFICULTIES IN FRIENDSHIPS AND CLOSE RELATIONSHIPS

The process of getting to know someone may proceed in either direction: relationships may become stronger, or they may drift or break apart.

Friendships are not totally positive: all bring with them times when feelings of anger, hurt, depression, or boredom seem to be uppermost. Often these difficulties occur because friends have not understood each other's needs sufficiently or they have not done enough to meet them. Often, people's expectations are different. Some people may expect to lean heavily on others, perhaps seeing them daily and pouring out their troubles until they feel overwhelmed.

Less has been explored or written about why relationships fail to deepen or develop, or why they break down. Nevertheless, we can again trace some personal factors and some situational issues which may contribute.

Argyle and Henderson (1984) described fifteen "rules" which they found applied to friendships (see Box 1). When these are not followed by one of the parties the friendship may be damaged: the other party may feel hurt, or offended, or angry. If this happens repeatedly, the friendship may break up rapidly, as in a row, or may gradually weaken and dissolve. On the other hand, apologies or compensations of one kind or another may help to repair the friendship, if the damage is not too great.

It is people's feelings and beliefs about a relationship which are altered when a friendship is damaged or threatened. Friendships can continue for years with almost no actual contact (perhaps the occasional Christmas or birthday card) provided both parties still believe the relationship holds the trust, commitment, or intimacy they value. If these valued features are damaged, however, tact, effort, time, or all of these will be needed to sustain and repair the relationship.

There are various other factors which may also lead to changes in relationships, or their dissolution. Divergence of interests, especially as individuals grow older, is a common reason why friendships weaken or lapse – particularly so amongst children and young people (Harvey *et al.*, 1982). Situational factors may lead to close friendships becoming weakened. Whilst very close friendships usually withstand long separations of geography or time, and do not necessarily require frequent contact, less secure friendships may often suffer somewhat if people become separated. This is particularly true amongst children and adolescents. Separation is also likely to be a problem for people who find it difficult to write, or to use the telephone, or who cannot afford to travel or find journeys to visit difficult.

Break-ups of very close relationships or partnerships, for any reason, are particularly upsetting. It is worth stressing that all the emotional force of a divorce or separation can occur in people who have had no sexual relationship but have lived together, sharing a house or flat. Such a break-up, arising through personal factors, typically proceeds through

Stage	Concerns	Repair work
Dissatisfaction with relationship	"Can't put up with this"	What is wrong? What are strengths and weaknesses in relationship?
Dissatisfaction with other person	Chiefly with other's faults	How does each person perceive the other?
Confrontation	Expression of conflict	What is the best form for the relationship?
Publication or social phase	Support from others; confirmation of own viewpoint	Help hold parties together, or, help save face
Getting over it	Self-justification	Support (perhaps with tactful attention to what went wrong?)

BOX 2. Stages in the break-up of close relationships, adapted from Duck (1986)

several stages (Duck, 1986). Recognising these stages, summarised in Box 2, may help others to assist friends to understand what is happening and to repair, alter, or break the friendship as they wish.

The feelings of people who experience one loss or separation will often adversely affect the strength of their other relationships. The effects on their life, and hence on other relationships, may be compounded by one or more of the following events (Jones *et al.*, 1985):

loss of a close friend or relative through death, move, or other circumstances;

geographical mobility;

new situations (including new jobs, education, or training);

unemployment, low income, and lack of transport;

spending much time alone (especially mealtimes, weekends);

spending little time with relatives or others;

little participation in social or educational activities;

lowered self-esteem and initiative.

These factors may thus initiate a vicious circle of social isolation, psychological withdrawal, emotional isolation, and loneliness in some people. Moreover, through their effects on mood, self-esteem, and initiative, these factors make it more likely that some people will lose the intimacy and closeness of the relationships they do retain. Often, as Weiss (1975) has illustrated, one single event – such as a move of house or, for someone with a learning disability, leaving home, hostel, or hospital – may be sufficient to set this chain of circumstances in motion.

REFERENCES

ADAMS, R. G. People would talk: barriers to cross sex friendships for elderly women. *The Gerontologist,* 1985; **25**, 605–611.

ADAMS, R. G. Patterns of network change: a longitudinal study of friendships of elderly women. *The Gerontologist,* 1987; **27**, 222–227.

ALLAN, G. *A Sociology of Friendships and Kinship.* London: Allen and Unwin, 1979.

ARGYLE, M., HENDERSON, M. The rules of friendship. *Journal of Social & Personal Relationships,* 1984; **1**, 209–235.

BELL, N. J., SCHOENROCK, C. J., BEVSBERG, G. J. Change over time in the community: findings of a longitudinal study. *In* Bruininks, R., Meyers, C. B., Sigford, B. B., Lakin, K. C. (Eds.). *Deinstitutionalisation, and Community Adjustment of Mentally Retarded People.* Monograph No. 4, 195–206. Washington DC: American Association on Mental Deficiency, 1981.

BROWN, B. B. A lifespan approach to friendship. *In* Lopata, H. Z., Maines, D. (Eds.). *Research on the Interweave of Social Roles: Friendship.* Volume 2. Greenwich, Connecticut: JAI Press, 1981.

BULMER, M. *Neighbours: the work of Philip Abrams.* Cambridge: Cambridge University Press, 1986.

BURNS, R. B. *The Self Concept: theory, measurement, development and behaviour.* London: Longman, 1979.

DICKENS, W. J., PERLMAN, D. Friendship over the life cycle. *In* Duck, S., Gilmour, R. (Eds.). *Personal Relationships 2: Developing Personal Relationships.* London: Academic Press, 1981.

DUCK, S. W. *The Study of Acquaintance.* Farnborough: Gower Press, 1977.

DUCK, S. W. Toward a research map for the study of relationship breakdown. *In* DUCK, S. W., GILMOUR, R. (Eds.). *Personal Relationships 3: Personal Relationships in Disorders.* London: Academic Press, 1981; 1–29.

DUCK, S. W., GILMOUR, R. (Eds.). *Personal Relationships 1: Studying Personal Relationships.* London: Academic Press, 1981a.

DUCK, S. W., GILMOUR, R. (Eds.). *Personal Relationships 2: Developing Personal Relationships.* London: Academic Press, 1981b.

DUCK, S. W., GILMOUR, R. (Eds.). *Personal Relationships 3: Personal Relationships in Disorders.* London: Academic Press, 1981c.

DUCK, S. W. (Ed.). *Personal Relationships 4: Dissolving Personal Relationships.* London: Academic Press, 1982.

DUCK, S. W. (Ed.). *Personal Relationships 5: Repairing Personal Relationships.* London: Academic Press, 1984.

DUCK, S. W. *Human Relationships.* London: Sage, 1986.

FIRTH, H., RAPLEY, M. *Making Acquaintance*. Morpeth: Northumberland Health Authority District Psychology Service, 1987 (revised 1989).

FLAVELL, J. H. *The Developmental Psychology of Jean Piaget*. London: Van Nostrand Reinholt, 1963.

GOLLAY, E., FREEDMAN, R., WYNGAARDEN, M., KURTZ, N. R., *Coming Back – The Community Experiences of Institutionalised Mentally Retarded People*. Cambridge, Massachusetts: Abt Books, 1978.

HARVEY, J. H., WEBER, A., YARKIN, K., STEWART, B. An attributional approach to relationship breakdown and dissolution. *In* Duck, S. W. (Ed.). *Personal Relationships 4: dissolving personal relationships*. London: Academic Press, 1982.

JONES, W. H., CALVERT, C. W., SNIDER, R. L., BRUCE, T. Relational stress: structures and events associated with loneliness. *In* Duck, S., Perlman, D. (Eds.). *Understanding Personal Relationships*. London: Sage, 1985; 221–242.

KELLY, G. A. *The Psychology of Personal Constructs*. New York: Norton, 1955.

LANDESMAN-DWYER, S., BERKSON, G. Friendship and social behaviour. *In* Wortis, J. (Ed.). *Mental Retardation and Developmental Disabilities, Volume 13*. London: Plenum Press, 1984.

LOWENTHAL, M. F., THURNER, M., CHIRABOGA, D. *Four Stages in Life*. San Francisco: Jossey Bass, 1975.

MATTHEWS, S. H. *Friendships Through the Life Course: oral biographies in old age*. London: Sage Publications, 1986.

PERLMAN, D., DUCK, S. W. *Intimate Relationships*. London: Sage, 1987.

PERLMAN, D., FEHR, B. The development of intimate relationships. *In* PERLMAN, D., DUCK, S.W. *Intimate Relationships*. London: Sage, 1987; 13–42.

RICHARDSON, A., RITCHIE, J. *Developing Friendships: enabling people with learning difficulties to make and maintain friends*. London: Policy Studies Institute/Social and Community Planning Research, 1989.

ROGERS, C. *On Becoming a Person*. London: Constable, 1961.

SELMAN, R. L. The child as friendship philosopher. *In* Asher, S. R., Gottman, J. M. (Eds.). *The Development of Children's Friendship*. Cambridge: Cambridge University Press, 1981.

SHURE, M. B., SPIVACK, G. *Problem Solving Techniques in Child Rearing*. San Francisco: Jossey Bass, 1978.

SPIVACK, G., PLATT, J. J., SHURE, M. B. *The Problem Solving Approach to Adjustment: a guide to research and intervention*. San Francisco: Jossey Bass, 1976.

SPIVACK, G., SHURE, M. B. *Social Adjustment of Young Children: a cognitive approach to solving real life problems*. San Francisco: Jossey Bass, 1974.

TRUAX, C. B., CARKHUFF, R. *Towards Effective Counselling and Psychotherapy*. Chicago, Ill: Aldine, 1967.

WEISS, R. *Loneliness: the experience of emotional and social isolation*. London, Mass: Massachusetts Institute of Technology Press, 1975.

WILLMOTT, P. *Social Networks, Informal Care and Public Policy*. London: Policy Studies Institute, 1986.

WILLMOTT, P. *Friendship Networks and Social Support*. London: Policy Studies Institute, 1987.

. . . Joining a club can make people first and foremost members of the club they choose . . . but someone else (may need) to accompany them to help the process . . .

CHAPTER FOUR

The role of leisure in social life

SOCIAL LIFE AND LEISURE TIME

Every interaction we make – from purchasing a newspaper at a newsagent's, to the many social contacts we may make in our work time (whether paid work, education, training, or job seeking), to the exchanges with fellow spectators at a football match or with fellow students at night class, or with our family or flat mates, or with acquaintances over a cup of tea or at the pub – forms part of our social life.

For most people, some parts of this social life are more important than others. For people with many friends and acquaintances, the daily chat with the newsagent, greengrocer, or someone at work may be of little importance. Yet for those who have very few friends and acquaintances, a brief social exchange with the greengrocer or the postmistress can be of great importance, and the feeling that there are one or two people at work whom they can talk to over a cup of coffee one day may be greatly valued. Some people's social life revolves around visits, calls, news, and information exchanged between members of their family and they may value this. Thus, people's social lives extend throughout all aspects of work, leisure, family, and household.

Leisure is probably best defined in terms of the activities and time available to people when they do not "have" to do something else. The mother who looks after children at home may feel she has precious little or no leisure time, even in the evenings. The hard-working members of many community organisations may likewise feel they have little or no leisure time available to them. Tending the garden is leisure for some, for others a chore. Certainly leisure is not merely to be equated with the absence of paid work. Some people choose to spend their leisure time in activities shared with other people. Others prefer more solitary activities, such as reading, drawing, gardening, walking, or listening to or playing music. It is clear that social lives and leisure lives are not the same thing.

Yet, in trying to help people with learning disabilities, social relationships and leisure time are often confused. Some writers quite rightly stress the role that leisure and recreation may have as potentially powerful ways of extending the social relationships available to them (Lyons, 1986). But unfortunately there are some staff in statutory and voluntary agencies who see leisure and recreational activities as the *only* route to offering people wider social lives. There is, moreover, the risk that agencies may respond to newly identified needs by providing a new "service". It is easy for organisations providing residential and support services for people with learning disabilities to try to meet their social needs through the provision of organised leisure and recreational activities. To do so misses the point, however, and greatly limits people's opportunities to make the relationships they might choose.

Many people with learning disabilities enjoy an extensive social life, and are busy in their leisure time. Yet others lead very impoverished social lives and have very limited, often solitary, leisure activities. The social isolation of many people with learning disabilities living in residential accommodation in the community was well documented by Tyne (1978). He described the leisure activities of many people as conforming largely to a "TV in the evenings" pattern, and commented that the adults he met frequently led "curiously unstimulating lives". Surveys since then have confirmed Tyne's findings (McConkey, Walsh, and Mulcahy, 1981; McConkey, Naughton, and Nugent, 1983; Richardson and Ritchie, 1989). Cheseldine and Jeffree (1981) surveyed adolescents with severe learning disabilities and found that they largely participated in solitary, passive, and family oriented activities when not in education. They commented on three particular reasons for this:

some parents had become the sole providers of both care and recreation and had thus unwittingly restricted the opportunities of their sons and daughters;

some adolescents had difficulty in developing friendships with other adolescents in the locality;

some adolescents lacked specific skills, which limited their choice of leisure activities.

McConkey and his colleagues (1981) also found that most of the leisure activities of the two hundred adults in their survey in Dublin were passive and solitary in nature, such as watching television, or listening to the radio or records. Nearly half of their sample did not take part in any activity outside of the family.

It appears, therefore, that:

neither the leisure nor the social lives of many adults with learning disabilities living in the community can be described as "rich";

their leisure activities are often solitary or family centred; and,

leisure activities, of themselves, do not appear so far to have provided many people with learning disabilities with a rich social life.

This third conclusion seems hardly surprising in the light of what is known about where people find their friends. Willmott (1986, 1987) has shown that people without learning disabilities meet their friends through many sources. The most common source of new friends is through work. People's immediate neighbours provide the second source of new friendships. Leisure interests are third in importance (Willmott, 1986). If all those who form people's present network of friends are included, leisure activities appear even further down the list as a source of friends, because many friends were met in childhood, often at school, and have remained close friends since (Willmott, 1987).

HOW CAN LEISURE ACTIVITIES BE USED TO MEET PEOPLE AND MAKE FRIENDSHIPS?

There is little evidence so far to suggest that leisure activities, on their own, provide a good way of extending the social lives of people with learning disabilities. Merely meeting other people does not necessarily lead to relationships that will be kept up subsequently. Moreover, it seems unlikely that deliberate, specialised attempts to provide "leisure activities" for people will achieve greater opportunities for a variety of social relationships unless some very specific circumstances are met. In particular, there is a danger that some people may find their leisure time so full of programmed activities that they have little time left to spend with people they would choose.

Leisure activities will not provide increased opportunities for social relationships unless they are shared with others in situations which make it likely that social contact will extend beyond the activities themselves. For example, on schemes where volunteers accompany students with disabilities in and out of school settings, or take companions who are disabled on leisure and sporting outings, there is a possibility that personal friendships may develop between some volunteers and their disabled companions. Yet such projects offer little opportunity for wider social contact, unless specific efforts are made to foster it. Positive attitude changes may take place amongst the non-disabled people participating, but it is uncertain to what extent friendships do develop out of such initiatives.

Nevertheless, "befriending" or "special friend" projects can offer valuable social opportunities to people with learning disabilities which they would otherwise have been denied (Walsh, 1985; Voeltz 1982), and can allow them to try out new activities and to increase the variety of experiences about which they can later communicate.

Frequently, what people with learning disabilities chiefly lack is an introduction to the situation. Someone may be needed to introduce them to the new activity and possibly to guide them, not only in the activity itself but in the social relationships surrounding it.

McConkey (1983) and his colleagues noted that it was opportunities rather than capabilities that were most needed to extend people's social lives. Gathercole (1981) has stressed the importance of developing opportunities: he sees the role of the leisure volunteer as being an enabler of activities and relationships. The same theme comes out of the work of Felce and Toogood (1988).

Leisure is not simply a gateway to a richer social life. The issue is *how* leisure is used. If personal relationships are to be made easier through leisure activities, leisure time will need to be used in such a way as to focus attention on a joint interest above and beyond the issue of learning disability. Joining a badminton, bell-ringing, or philatelic club can make people with learning disabilities first and foremost members of the club they choose, not people with disabilities. But if joining a club is to lead to new friendships, then the opportunities created must be used. If people are not themselves sufficiently outgoing, assertive, or socially persuasive to make the most of these opportunities, it will be important for someone else to accompany them to help the process.

People with learning disabilities do not always have to be the receivers of help. They can sometimes be the providers of assistance. In certain situations, by acting as volunteers in helping others directly or indirectly, their role as helpers may facilitate social interaction. Something straightforward, like handing round the drinks at a coffee morning, for example, is a very good way of getting to know people.

The important point is that it is in *shared* activity that there is scope for not only making but developing relationships. Watching television indiscriminately may restrict social life because little time is left for other activities. Attending to specific programmes may be helpful, as far as providing topics for conversation (Dallas or Coronation Street, the News, or documentaries). Watching specific programmes *with someone else* who has the same interest, however, may be an excellent way of sharing an experience, talking about it, and getting to know each other better in the process.

Thinking about leisure as *the* way to develop relationships, therefore, is putting the cart before the horse. If our goal is to help people with learning disabilities to meet people and find opportunities to make friends, then their activities need to be shared with others – whether they be work, training, religious, educational, social, sporting, household, or leisure activities. It is important to remember that, in many of these activities, it will often be very helpful for an acquaintance or a companion to accompany them, at least for a time, to help in the process of making relationships.

REFERENCES

CHESELDINE, S. E., JEFFREE, D. M. Mentally handicapped adolescents: their use of leisure. *Journal of Mental Deficiency Research*, 1981; **25**:1, 49–59.

FELCE, D., TOOGOOD, S. *Close to Home: a local housing service and its impact on the lives of nine adults with severe and profound mental handicaps.* Kidderminster: BIMH Publications, 1988.

GATHERCOLE, C. E. *Leisure Volunteer's Guide.* A supplement to: *Residential Alternatives for Adults who are Mentally Handicapped.* Kidderminster: BIMH Publications, 1981.

LYONS, M. Students as buddies: a proposal for smoothing the path towards a broader life experience through recreation. *Occupational Therapy*, 1986; April, 111–114.

MCCONKEY, R., WALSH, J., MULCAHY, M. The recreational pursuits of mentally handicapped adults. *International Journal of Rehabilitation Research.* 1981; **4**:4, 493–499.

MCCONKEY, R. M., NAUGHTON, M., NUGENT, U. Have we met? Community contact of adults who are mentally handicapped. *Mental Handicap*, 1983; **11**:2, 57–59.

RICHARDSON, A., RITCHIE, J. *Developing Friendships: enabling people with learning difficulties to make and maintain friends.* London: Policy Studies Institute, 1989.

TYNE, A. *Looking at Life – in Hospitals, Hostels, Homes and Units for Adults who are Mentally Handicapped.* London: Campaign for People with Mental Handicaps, 1978.

VOELTZ, L. M. Effects of structured interactions with severely handicapped peers on children's attitudes. *American Journal of Mental Deficiency*, 1982; **86**, 380–390.

WALSH, J. *Let's Make Friends.* London: Souvenir Press, 1985.

WILLMOTT, P. *Social Networks. Informal Care and Public Policy.* London: Policy Studies Institute, 1986.

WILLMOTT, P. *Friendship Networks and Social Support.* London: Policy Studies Institute, 1987.

. . . involvement in activities brings contacts with other people through whom new acquaintances and friends can be made . . .

CHAPTER FIVE

Putting ideas into practice – what kind of help?

"I can offer no method for ending loneliness other than the formation of new relationships that might repair the deficit . . . And I think this solution ordinarily is not easy."
(Robert Weiss, 1975)

THE ISSUES SO FAR

As part of the preparation that went into this book, a variety of literature was examined for the ideas presented here. Some of this material is described in Chapter 12.

The first theme which became evident to us from this material is the importance of relationships in the maintenance of people's physical, as well as mental, health and quality of life (Atkinson and Ward, 1986; Beigel, McCardle, and Mendleson, 1985). Writers such as Brown and Harris (1978) and Weiss (1975) have highlighted the particular importance that relationships involving trust, confiding, and intimacy may have in maintaining people's physical and mental wellbeing. These conclusions may seem obvious. Nonetheless, the circumstances of many people with learning disabilities described earlier, indicate that these issues need reiterating.

Recent shifts in thinking, towards an acceptance that community care is not only possible but is desirable for people with learning disabilities, began with broad policy statements (Independent Development Council, 1984; King's Fund Centre, 1982; Malin, 1987). Latterly there have appeared an increasing number of contributions which have begun to bridge the gap between desirable policy and the achievement of high quality community services. Books and materials – such as those by Cooper and Hersov (1986), Hopson and Scally (1980), Mansell *et al.* (1987), the Open University (1986), and Shearer (1986) – offer guidance on service planning, thinking about individuals' lives and circumstances, and specific issues such as self-advocacy.

Yet, until recently (Richardson and Ritchie, 1989), there has been no overview of the issues that need to be considered in helping people with learning disabilities maintain, develop, and exercise choice in their relationships. As it is our hope to provide in these pages one such overview, it is appropriate to review briefly the themes of this book so far, and the issues to be addressed.

The first distinction to be emphasised has been that between social isolation or lack of company, and emotional isolation or lack of intimacy.

Second, considerable emphasis has been placed on the fact that people's social lives are not limited to "leisure", but extend throughout their days and nights – through family, education, and work as well as leisure time.

Third, we have emphasised that friendship develops, however quickly or slowly, out of acquaintance. We have used the term "acquaintance" specifically (following Duck, 1977) to mean that process of getting to know someone, and getting to know that person better, through which relationships must pass to reach the shared understanding and trust of friendship. Thus, we include as acquaintances all those people who are known slightly, or known fairly well, but who are not regarded as "friends".

Fourth, we believe that the principles behind the learning of relationship skills and the manner in which relationships are started, developed, maintained, and fall apart, are in no major way different for people with learning disabilities than they are for people without such disabilities (Landesman-Dwyer and Berkson, 1984).

We have stated that choice is integral to friendship. Helping people with learning disabilities to make realistic, informed choices is therefore one important component in any approach which seeks to help them to develop the friendships they want. A number of ideas are put forward in Carle (1986), but we see self-advocacy as having a particularly important role to play in building self-confidence and experience in expressing views and choices (Williams and Shoultz, 1982).

The following chapters discuss some general issues of concern to those endeavouring to help people make friends and acquaintances. They explore in more detail what could be done to help foster opportunities for people with learning disabilities to meet others, what attributes and skills might help this process, and what might help close relationships to develop from initial acquaintances.

Chapters 6, 7, and 8 explore in depth what can be done in four areas, namely:

providing opportunities for acquaintances to develop;

personal attributes and abilities which help in making acquaintance;

circumstances which may facilitate closer relationships;

attitudes and skills which might foster closer relationships.

These are illustrated in Box 3 to show the type of opportunities and personal attributes required to encourage the development of relationships ranging from acquaintance to intimacy.

THE ROLE OF SERVICES IN FRIENDSHIP AND COMPANIONSHIP

First, we wish to emphasise that more "services" on their own are not the answer to people's needs for social and emotional contact. There are many things that services can do, such as providing people with opportunities and helping them make use of the chances their lives offer. Services of this kind, which aim to offer advice or which use staff or volunteers to help people take part in activities and meet other people, have much to offer. But services which aim to "provide friends" may overlook the fact that friends are people we *choose* from those we know. Companionship may, or may not, develop into friendship.

Providing a companion will only meet someone's need for rapport, intimacy, and emotional attachment if these qualities actually develop between the two people: if the companions become friends. Moreover, if someone does develop a close relationship with a companion, there is a risk that feelings of distress, disappointment, and loss will be experienced if the companion fails, for whatever reason, to maintain contact.

Friends usually not only like, but care about, each other. They care *about* rather than *for* each other. Friendship may not exclude caring for someone in time of need, but it is the commitment, the caring *about* the other, which is central to the relationship (Allan, 1983). Schemes and services can contract people to care for someone. They cannot in the same way engage people to care about someone. Friendship should not be confused with relationships which are about providing care. One may develop from the other in the course of a relationship, but services and schemes need to be clear about which it is that they are primarily aiming to provide.

Payment also affects the nature of relationships. Who pays whom in a relationship has major implications, both for control of the relationship and for the images and status of the people involved. The status of an individual who chooses to pay someone as a companion has been a valued one in our society, even if it is uncommon and now somewhat dated. But to have a third party pay someone else to be a companion to you, when you do not choose the person who is thus employed, and do not initiate or terminate the contract, is not a valued position in which to be.

Wertheimer (1983) and Allan (1983) have both emphasised the danger of confusion between the volunteer relationship and friendship. Allan comments:

"there are (limits) in the relationship between volunteers and those in need of support. Volunteers cannot be regarded as directly equivalent to friends even though part of their role may be that of 'befriending' an otherwise isolated individual".

Allan goes on to suggest that having strangers provide services for people on a regular basis without payment will lead to an indebtedness on the part of recipients which they will be in no position to repay. This issue is not straightforward, in that the rewards volunteers gain may be intrinsic and not necessarily apparent to the receivers. He comments that, "in such cases it may be particularly inappropriate to dress the volunteer relationship up as simply one of a (groundless) friendship". His suggestion is that it is often more appropriate to give recipients some control on the relationship through a payment. Recipients of support who are able to pay volunteers' expenses themselves, and then have this cost refunded by a suitable scheme or service, would be in a position of greater control and greater esteem. Moreover, in this context it would still be possible for the helping relationship to transform into one of friendship: people could determine for themselves when to use and when to terminate the formal paid arrangement.

DEVELOPING SKILLS AND OPPORTUNITIES

The different approaches to helping people with learning disabilities form relationships with people they like each have their strengths and weaknesses. One kind of approach emphasises helping them to improve their personal skills. These social skill or personal help strategies, which focus on intrinsic factors and encourage individuals to change aspects of themselves, have two major strengths. First, if change is seen as a long-term process, the benefits can last for life. Second, both growth in the person and changed relationships are indeed attainable through social skill or personal helping strategies.

For people to change their ways of relating to others, however, is often an extremely difficult task, even with help from others. Expectations may be unrealistically high. If people are unsuccessful in the short-term in achieving some major changes, then they may even be blamed or punished for their inability to learn sufficiently quickly.

There are two reasons why much social skill teaching is unsuccessful, or achieves only small and short-lived success. One is that it often focuses on very particular skills in a classroom setting, often not the skills that might be most crucial in real, day-to-day settings. The second, more important reason, is that it often neglects to consider what the people

Type of relationship	Opportunities	Personal attributes
ACQUAINTANCE, COMPANY	Varied leisure and vocational activities	Having things to talk about
	Doing practical things together in small groups	Age appropriate appearance
	Citizen advocacy	Having the skills to join activities with others
	Work in integrated settings	Helping other people
	Education and further education	Appreciating others' experience
	People who help and "enable"	Acquisition of social skills
	Providing help for other people	Confidence
	Having a confident companion	Self-esteem
		Self-identity
	Spending time with people you like	Choosing to share pleasures, hurts
	Privacy	Expression of feelings to others
	Someone to share feelings with	Offering help when needed
	Religious activity	Trust; keeping confidences
	Groups sharing a common cause	Willingness to do favours
	Self-help groups	"Dating" skills and sexual education
CLOSE RELATIONSHIPS, INTIMACY	Availability of counselling on sexual issues	

BOX 3. Some of the ingredients needed to enable the development of relationships

being taught *think*: what they think about other people; whether they can see others' point of view; whether they can think of different ways of behaving. This kind of learning takes time. It is often best taught to people by someone who is close to them, gently and repeatedly.

Even when people have learned new skills, they are of little use without opportunities to practise them. People need to be able to compare their own performance with that of others more competent than themselves, and to receive some constructive and positive feedback afterwards.

A second approach to helping people with disabilities is to emphasise the opportunities they have to learn, and to make relationships. This focuses attention on practical possibilities, on helping people rather than teaching them. It concentrates on things people do together, which we believe are vital to the development of friendships. This approach also maximises the chances people have to learn through experience, which is how most of us make mistakes and learn about relationships.

Yet focusing on opportunities can lead to neglect of the degree of support people may need. Different people behave very differently in the same situation. Some people are shy; others, though far from shy, put other people off unintentionally by their behaviour. Advice, guidance, help, and teaching about appropriate ways of behaving are often required for people who do not have the necessary attitudes and abilities to think through and use the right social skills unaided. Providing models of appropriate behaviour may not be sufficient for those who fail to notice the relevant cues: for them, guidance and tutoring may be needed.

Involvement in activities and groups has the advantage that it generally brings people into contact with a wealth of other people through whom new acquaintances and friends can be made. Such a strategy offers possibilities for one introduction to lead to another, thereby enabling a branching and growing web of relationships. Yet this process, too, may take a long time, and it neglects the need to learn ways of maintaining and nurturing relationships. It is important to be aware of this if disappointment and discouragement are not to ensue. However, most people have a number of arenas in their life where such development is possible, such as work, leisure activities, hobbies, or adult education.

Thus different professional models have in the past adopted approaches which seek to maximise the presence of people with learning disabilities in the community, or have sought to treat their problems, overcome their difficulties, or teach new skills in the course of step-by-step habilitation or rehabilitiation programmes. These differences of approach are now beginning to be overcome, through the combination and integration of each with the other.

Projects which seek to support people's choice in and opportunities for making relationships ought at least to consider their need to develop personal social skills and *vice versa*. Any project is limited. Yet published accounts of schemes which provide direct teaching of social skills to people with learning disabilities generally give little priority to helping to provide continuing opportunities in which to develop those skills. It would be refreshing to see schemes adopt a systematic approach to providing new opportunities for meeting people and support this by helping people with disabilities to learn the specific attitudes and social skills they need to make the most of those opportunities to develop relationships of various kinds.

REFERENCES

ALLAN, G. Informal networks of care: issues raised by Barclay. *British Journal of Social Work*, 1983; **13**, 417–433.

ATKINSON, D., WARD, L. *A Part of the Community: social integration and neighbourhood networks*. London: Campaign for People with Mental Handicaps, 1986.

BIEGEL, D. E., McCARDLE, E., MENDLESON, S. *Social Networks and Mental Health. An Annotated Bibliography*. London: Sage Publications, 1985.

BROWN, G., HARRIS, T. *Social Origins of Depression : a study of psychiatric disorder in women*. London: Tavistock, 1978.

CARLE, N. (Ed.). *Helping People to Make Choices: opportunities and challenges*. London: Campaign for People with Mental Handicaps, 1986.

COOPER, D., HERSOV, J. *"We Can Change the Future". Self-Advocacy for People with Learning Difficulties: a staff training resource*. London: National Bureau for Handicapped Students, 1986.

DUCK, S. W. *The Study of Acquaintance*. Farnborough: Gower Press, 1977.

HOPSON, B., SCALLY, M. *Life Skills Teaching Programmes No. 1*. Leeds: Life Skills Associates, 1980.

INDEPENDENT DEVELOPMENT COUNCIL. *Next Steps: an independent review of progress, problems and priorities in the development of services for people with mental handicap*. London: Independent Development Council, 1984.

KING'S FUND CENTRE. *An Ordinary Life*. London: King's Fund Centre, 1982.

LANDESMAN-DWYER, S., BERKSON, G. Friendships and social behavior. *In* Wortis, J. (Ed.). *Mental Retardation and Developmental Disabilities Volume 13*. London: Plenum Press, 1984.

MALIN, N. (Ed.). *Reassessing Community Care*. London: Croom Helm, 1987.

MANSELL, J., FELCE, D., JENKINS, J., DE KOCK, U., TOOGOOD, S. *Developing Staffed Housing for People with Mental Handicaps*. Tunbridge Wells: Costello, 1987.

OPEN UNIVERSITY. *Mental Handicap: patterns for living (Course P555)*. Milton Keynes: The Open University, 1986.

RICHARDSON, A., RITCHIE, J. *Developing Friendships: enabling people with learning difficulties to make and maintain friends*. London: Policy Studies Institute/Social and Community Planning Research, 1989.

SHEARER, A. *Building Community – People with Mental Handicaps, their Families and Friends*. London: Campaign for People with Mental Handicaps and King's Fund Centre, 1986.

WEISS, R. *Loneliness: the experience of emotional and social isolation*. London, Mass.: Massachusetts Institute of Technology Press, 1975.

WERTHEIMER, A. *Leisure*. London: Campaign for People with Mental Handicaps, 1983.

WILLIAMS, P., SHOULTZ, B. *We Can Speak for Ourselves: self-advocacy by mentally handicapped people*. London: Souvenir Press, 1982.

*... links between existing friends and new acquaintances ...
can be vital in establishing relationships when people may find
interaction stressful ...*

CHAPTER SIX

Meeting people and making friends: opportunities and activities

WHERE TO START?

How do most people learn how to get along with others, get to know them, and make friends? For most people this involves a great deal of trial and error, much of it whilst young enough not to think consciously about what is being practised and learned. That trial and error requires opportunities: opportunities to observe, imitate and interact with peers of the same age through childhood, adolescence, and adulthood. Learning to make and sustain friendships requires many such experiences over a long period of time.

The experience of being with other people serves two purposes. Each such experience involves a social relationship of some kind in itself, but it also allows observation and learning about the behaviour and experiences of others.

In this chapter we focus on the different ways in which people get to know other people, and how different settings influence that process. One of the main themes of the chapter is that it is through *doing things with others* that relationships are strengthened. We will start by looking at introductions to new people and situations, and will go on to explore the kind of opportunities which might allow relationships to become closer.

Weiss (1975), discussing social isolation, that is, the lack of company, comments:

"The problem ... is to ... (find) ... a group or network of adequately attractive and congenial others, and manage to stay in touch with at least some of its members long enough to establish ... oneself".

Weiss discusses three strategies through which people may be able to overcome social isolation:

meeting new people through those they have already met;

meeting new people through joining new activities or organisations, or drawing on special services;

meeting people in similar situations to themselves, through joining specialist organisations or self-help groups.

The first approach, Weiss argues, has the major advantage in that there are "links" between existing friends and the new acquaintances which make it easier to share information, and develop trust. These links can be vital in establishing relationships through the initial stages, when people do not know each other well and may find interaction stressful. Box 4 illustrates one way in which people can gradually get to know new people through existing contacts.

Unfortunately the situation for many people with learning disabilities who want to make friends is that they do not know many people in the first place, or do not know them well enough to join their social circles. Joining activities or organisations where they are, initially, strangers may therefore be the only way forward. This strategy does sometimes have one

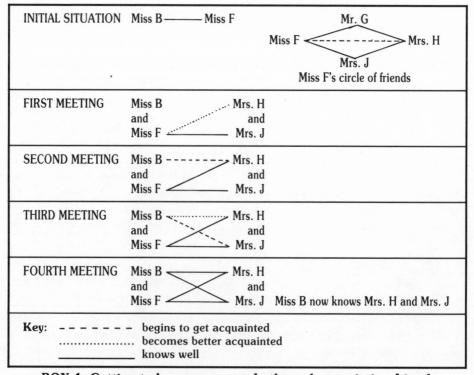

BOX 4. Getting to know new people through an existing friend

advantage: it is often possible for people to capitalise on their status as a newcomer and so be introduced to a wide variety of new people.

Besides groups which cater for particular leisure interests or hobbies, many localities have various groups whose members meet to help each other over common concerns. Tenants' groups and residents' associations, for example, are active in many areas.

In the last two decades there has been a proliferation of voluntary and community groups in many urban localities; ethnic organisations, self-help groups, and campaigning organisations can be found in many areas. Some groups aim specifically to help promote friendships amongst their members. For example, family centres and family groups may be run by local authorities or by voluntary organisations. Their aims vary. Some try to help individuals and families who are in need of mutual support to overcome social isolation, to gain skills and confidence, and to make new friends. Bringing people together over a common cause, however, whether or not overcoming social isolation is an explicit aim, does promote social contact which can lead on to personal friendships. A sense of mutual adversity is one factor that is likely to draw people into closer relationships with each other (Bulmer, 1986; Willmott, 1987).

Weiss (1975) does warn of one possible pitfall for people who adopt the strategy of joining groups whose members are in a similar situation to themselves: that their social world may be inward-looking and segregated from others. Extending a network to meet other new people in the future may then prove difficult.

These, then, are the different ways in which people – whether or not they have a learning disability – can try to avoid or overcome social isolation. People with disabilities who use any of these "strategies" may require some assistance from others, especially initial introductions and support. We shall return to this shortly. Yet, whatever the approach, relationships are made (or broken) through doing things with others.

Richardson and Ritchie (1989a) identified three main ways in which the people they interviewed had extended their social circles:

Attending integrated day activities. Activities which took people outside segregated settings played a key role for some people. Examples included attending a college for one or two days a week, visiting community social centres, and doing voluntary work.

Carers' encouragement. Some residential care staff or key workers had encouraged people to take up new forms of activity where they had met new people. Some parents had also fulfiilled this role. For example, one father had helped his daughter to join a local choral society which had become a source of new relationships for her.

A close friend or partner. We commented earlier on how the existence of a partner or close friend could often prove critical in helping people to go to new places and meet new people. Such close friends or partners can be helpful in three ways: by bringing with them a range of social relationships which they already possess; by providing a stimulus for social activity; and, most important of all, by carrying out the role of a confident companion.

SOURCES OF FRIENDS AND ACQUAINTANCES

Some people's social lives revolve around work. Others' revolve around their upholstery classes. Some revolve around the contact that they have with their neighbours or their relatives. For a few, minority or ethnic interests provide the focus. It is worth exploring the many different contexts which provide possibilities for people to make acquaintances and friends. These include:

family and relatives;

the home or household;

professionals;

existing friends;

neighbours;

work or other roles an individual may have;

education or further study;

common interests, hobbies, or leisure activities;

membership of clubs and organisations.

There is not much evidence to date about where people, with or without learning disabilities, first meet those who become their friends and acquaintances. Patterns vary. Elderly people, for example, tend to find more of their friends from amongst their neighbours. As already mentioned, one major survey of people without disabilities (Willmott, 1986) concluded that work, neighbours, and leisure interests were the three most common sources of new friendship for the adults in their sample (see Box 5).

FRIENDS AND RELATIVES

Relatives are customarily distinguished from friends, but it is how people think about and see situations which is important. Sometimes someone in a family may demonstrate a particular empathy with, and trust, and commitment in another family member, thus becoming both a friend and a relative. The family, especially the extended family, should not therefore be underestimated as a source of acquaintances and friends.

"How did you first meet him or her?"			
MEN	*Per cent*	**WOMEN**	*Per cent*
Work and spouse's work	32	Neighbours and former neighbours	31
Neighbours and former neighbours	20	Work and spouse's work	27
Clubs, churches, and leisure interests	19	Clubs, churches, and leisure interests	11
College, school, etc.	10	Through relatives	10
Through relatives	9	College, school, etc.	7
Through existing friends	6	Through children	6
Through children	2	Through existing friends	4

BOX 5. Most common sources of recently met friends, adapted from Willmott (1986)

The commitment that family members usually feel towards each other can also be valuable in that relatives may provide introductions to other people, and may offer information, advice, and help about ways of meeting people and joining organisations or activities. Perhaps most significantly, because of these ties of obligation which attach to family relationships, relatives can be approached and asked for help with introductions or information, even though they may not be able to give of their own time.

Some people with learning disabilities describe family members as their only friends. Sometimes, this is by choice. Often, however, it is not through choice; they simply have not had the opportunity to meet sufficient other people to exercise a choice. They may wish to have other friends, but do not have them.

Families can often be a very useful source of friends and acquaintances. Frequently, however, families unwittingly restrict the opportunities of their younger members to broaden their social networks. Very real concerns about exploitation, for example, may lead some families to attempt to provide for all the needs of their members who are disabled within the family network. This may pose problems, both for the people with disabilities and their families. Other families, aware of the issues involved in "letting go", make great efforts to help broaden the friendship networks of family members with learning disabilities. It is important, however, that people outside the family are sensitive to these concerns, especially those of parents about the welfare of their son or daughter (Richardson and Ritchie, 1989b).

HOME, HOSTEL, OR HOSPITAL: MAKING AND BREAKING CONTACTS

The households in which they live may provide opportunities for acquaintance and friendship for some people at certain stages in their lives: students and young people, for instance, often share flats together. Living with others may be important for some people, simply because it provides opportunities to meet and get to know each other's friends and acquaintances. Richardson and Ritchie's research (1989a) demonstrates strikingly that this is indeed so.

The role of staff

For people with learning disabilities moving out of hospital into the local community there may be additional, and slightly different, issues (Felce and Toogood, 1988; Mansell *et al.*, 1987).

Often the potentially most enduring and rewarding contacts they are likely to make with other people will be through the staff of their new homes, and their friends and relatives. Many of these opportunities, therefore, will depend on the selection and training of the staff who are employed to work in "resettlement" schemes (Firth, 1986). It is possible to select staff who have good local knowledge, and ready access to local organisations and activities.

Staff employed in houses of this kind have a potentially crucial role to play in this respect. They are members of a local community and they are members of different networks themselves. They have families and friends whom they may be more or less likely to encourage to meet the people with whom they work. It seems of paramount importance to employ and encourage staff who will encourage their own families and friends to make contact with the people they serve.

What are the factors to look for in staff selection? A job description which highlights the importance of helping people to develop acquaintances and relationships might be helpful. What is more likely to be helpful is information about the range of friends and contacts potential members of staff have. Their involvement in leisure or other community activities, such as church or Round Table, may be particularly relevant. So too is their attitude to encouraging their own friends and contacts to visit and develop relationships with people leaving hospital.

Effects of being moved

Maintaining valued relationships which provide emotional or social support when leaving one place for another is important if the effects of loss through separation, as described in Chapter 2, are to be avoided. Richardson and Ritchie (1989a) document the fact that, for the people they interviewed who had moved out of a hospital or hostel, some friendships had not survived. They comment that sometimes this was "because no-one had helped to keep the contact going . . . the lack of any opportunities to meet and the difficulties of writing or telephoning to keep in touch had often meant a lost friendship or connection".

Heller (1982) and Braddock and Heller (1985) have reviewed the effects of involuntary resettlement. Braddock and Heller have suggested that the effects of resettlement depend on three kinds of factors: individual characteristics (age, sex, physical health); cognitive mediators (how the individual is prepared); and environmental characteristics (location, physical comfort, number and familiarity of co-residents).

Heller (1982) concluded that the aged were particularly vulnerable, both because of the direct effects of relocation on friendships and adjustment of daily living patterns, and because of the more generalised insecurity a move may induce for some. As might be expected, people whose physical health was poor had greater difficulty in adjustment following a move. Relocation of elderly people within institutions was less disruptive when their relationships with staff, peers and family could all be maintained. The documented consequences of relocation have included long-term grief reactions (affecting forty per cent of people in one study), physiological changes, higher accident rates, drug use and, in some studies (especially amongst the elderly), higher mortality.

Braddock and Heller have taken the view that three features are crucial if resettlement is not to lead to ill consequences: an improved quality of environment in the new setting; avoidance of disruption to social relationships; and the degree to which people are prepared psychologically for the change, through preparatory counselling, visits prior to the move, and realistic information about the new setting. Special efforts may therefore be needed, both before and after the move. Time, energy, and money may be required for visits, letters, telephone calls, and the sending of photographs and birthday, Christmas, or holiday cards. Assistance with transport arrangements may be particularly important in helping people maintain friendships. Gollay *et al.* (1978) reported that when contact with friends is broken once people have left institutions, the most frequent reason is transportation problems.

Perhaps the most worrying finding from studies of people being relocated from institutions is that from the work of Landesman-Dwyer (Landesman-Dwyer and Berkson, 1984): that amongst people with severe and profound disabilities, those most "passive" in their social behaviour were the most vulnerable to the negative effects of relocation. Although they had shown less ability to intitiate social relationships with others many had clear ties to other individuals (staff or residents). When these ties were broken, their social interaction became reduced in consequence. Unlike people who were more able to initiate contact, they not only did not "replace" their broken relationships, but they were at especial risk of being overlooked and ignored by others.

Particular efforts need to be made by staff to identify real friendship networks which may exist between people living within long-stay

. . . select staff who have good local knowledge, and ready access to local organisations and activities . . .

hospitals. All too often staff perceptions of "friendship" are at some variance with those expressed by people with learning disabilities themselves. Whilst sharing a bedroom on a ward for twenty years may have allowed a relationship to develop, it is not a guarantee, or even a reliable indicator, that the people involved are "friends". They may have found their friends elsewhere, however, and staff should recognise this. Staff may also need to adopt a positive approach to supporting existing sexual relationships when thinking about future living arrangements for people moving out of hospital. People who have moved out with their chosen friends have been shown to do better in terms of their sociability and overall adjustment than people who have been separated from their friends.

NEW HOMES: FEATURES OF A NEIGHBOURHOOD

A particular issue is worthy of attention by those engaged in helping people move from hospital to community. Moving home to a new locality can break many ties and lead to social and emotional isolation for people with or without learning disabilities. There is evidence (Weiss, 1975) that areas with low population density, and which are to some extent geographically isolated, may present especial difficulties to the social integration of newcomers. City suburbs and estates can be particularly unsuitable places to move to, unless people already have some connections in the immediate locality upon which they can rely. Such neighbourhoods are often particularly poor in the variety of opportunities and activities available locally. Relatively poor access to other localities (excepting the city centre) by public transport often compounds this problem. We have already emphasised the importance of the cost, as well as the time required, if visiting acquaintances or friends means lengthy bus journeys.

People who move to neighbourhoods like these are therefore particularly likely to be at risk of emotional isolation and loneliness unless luck or circumstance allows them to find close friends easily. Maintaining existing friendships may become very difficult in such circumstances.

The King's Fund Centre (1988) has made some specific recommendations for features of a neighbourhood which are important to consider when selecting new homes for people with learning disabilities and has described what may help in getting to know, and becoming known in, a new neighbourhood.

RELATIONSHIPS WITH PROFESSIONALS

Some people with learning disabilities experience a relationship with a professional as a friendship. Such relationships may meet their individual needs for a close relationship or emotional attachment, and the professional may be the only person available with whom an intimate exchange of feelings and experiences can take place. Such relationships may be mutual, with both people deriving from them much that is of value to them personally. In some such situations there is a genuine commitment on both sides which lasts beyond the termination of the professional relationship itself. In these circumstances professionals can be sources of close friendships for people with learning disabilities.

The nature of such relationships, however, is not always clear to either party. Each may have a different perception of the relationship. This can cause great distress and loss, if the professional moves away or professional responsibility ends for some reason, if the "client" has perceived the relationship as friendship but this has not been understood by the professional. We may all experience loss if friends move away and are lost to contact. But the hurt is much more pronounced if we interpret this to mean that the "friend" never was a friend really, and betrayed us by allowing us to think otherwise.

Atkinson (1989) has described a variety of roles and relationships which may develop between social workers and their clients. She has highlighted a number of different kinds of role: the social worker as a business contact; as informal official; as "the big gun"; as a threat; as a friend; or as a close tie. This latter kind of role may involve particular difficulties for the professional. Atkinson quotes one social worker's description of the ambivalent feelings and conflict that might be involved:

> "In Geoffrey King's situation the close tie evoked feelings of ambivalence, described by the social worker thus: 'It is an ambivalent relationship. He is very dependent on me for help, advice and support, but resents this dependency, too. It's a bit like a marital relationship – I'm the most important person in his life, and the person closest to him, and I get the most abuse, too! But I have stood the test of time, I've been with him through all his troubles, and I've never been disloyal'".

Professionals, on the other hand, can experience discomfort when people appear to become "overdependent" upon them. Such situations pose difficulties, and may not always be readily foreseen. They require careful consideration. Sometimes people become dependent on a professional because the nature and limits of the professional relationship were not made sufficiently clear initially. Sometimes however, for one reason or another, people's upbringing or life history leads to them having particularly strong needs to become very dependent on others. Such needs are not easily met. It may be helpful to involve a number of different individuals who can each help to meet such needs, but each of whom is clear about the potential demands upon them, and each of whom has some support to help them cope when these demands become particularly great or threaten to overwhelm them.

Some people, with or without learning disabilities, do demand enormous amounts of time and energy from the few close friends they have, so much so that their relationships are frequently threatened. These patterns of relating to others, sometimes involving dramatic "testing out" behaviour, usually have their origins in experiences which have led to insecurity. They may not be easy to change. It may be important for others to spell out clearly to such people just how much they are available, and to keep clear limits on the type and extent of their involvement. It may be especially important to avoid taking on undue, unnecessary, or inappropriate responsibility for people's lives in this situation. Professionals and others can easily become "drawn in" in a way which makes a total escape from the relationship the only eventual coping strategy. Such cycles of involvement and rejection only lead to further harm by increasing people's insecurity.

It is important, therefore, for professionals to understand clearly the nature of such relationships from their own point of view, to communicate this to their clients, and not to raise false expectations or misunderstandings which may cause people great distress subsequently.

GETTING TO KNOW OTHERS THROUGH EXISTING FRIENDS

Richardson and Ritchie (1989a) reported that, for the people with learning disabilities whom they interviewed, one of the most effective ways of meeting new people and getting to know them better was through people they already knew, especially partners or other close friends. Many people without learning disabilities will have met most of their present friends this way.

Getting to know people is often easier in small groups. Joining a friend to spend time with one or two other people is a good way to get to know others. On the whole, the smaller the group, the easier this process is likely to be. We suspect, though there is little evidence, that the optimum size group for each person to be able to join in, while not being "pressured" to listen and respond continually, may well be three, or perhaps four, people. This may also be the optimum size for maximising the intimacy and feelings shared between people who are getting to know each other well. Couples do offer the greatest opportunities for intimacy, but pose enormous strains on each other if the two people have not already got to know each other somewhat in a "safer", less threatening group.

Box 4 (see page 84) illustrates this process. Groups of three to four people may be helpful because:

going with a friend means newcomers can either just talk with them, or talk "through" them to the group if they wish;

it is easier for people to start relating to strangers when they are with someone they already know quite well;

conversation or interaction often pauses between two people, but with three or four people, interaction and conversations often proceed more smoothly;

the person who knows everyone can often help the others get to know each other by talking about things they all have in common;

small groups of people may be less likely to provoke anxiety in some individuals:

in small groups it is generally possible to join in with anyone, whereas larger groups may "split up" and leave individuals isolated.

Larger groups, of five or more people, can also be useful as a way of making acquaintances, joining a group of people who are already mutual friends, or being included as someone "new" into an existing group of friends. These larger groups, however, do not generally make it easy to develop intimacy, trust, and other qualities of a closer relationship.

There is one important exception to this. Larger groups of people who are engaged in some project, such as environmental conservation, building a theatre set, or camping, often allow smaller groups to work together and get to know each other. In these circumstances the sense of common purpose and the comparatively long periods of time spent together may actually help to draw people closer together.

NEIGHBOURS AS FRIENDS

Neighbours – people living in the same street – may be a major source of friends and social life. This is particularly true for people whose lives do not give them many other opportunities for social contact. It is frequently people who are elderly, or unemployed, or who for financial or other reasons do not have transport, who find the immediate neighbourhood becomes a particularly important source of friendship.

The problems that can arise for people with disabilities in attempting to initiate acquaintance with neighbours should not be underestimated (Mills, 1988). Leyin (1988) has discussed the difficulties there may be, especially if service providers somehow feel obliged to enter a "negotiated" move, by consulting the neighbours in advance of people taking up residence. Whilst, as Mills (1988) vividly illustrates, these difficulties may be very real, the literature suggests that a very "low key" approach, relying on the "development of neighbourly contact in a more natural way through individual contacts" (Leyin, 1988) is the best strategy. The work of Atkinson and Ward (1987) and Atkinson (1988) has shown that people with learning disabilities can and do develop strong relationships with their neighbours.

There are particular skills in judging how best to become acquainted with neighbours. Clearly, these vary enormously from one part of the country to another. One approach which may be useful for people moving to a new locality, is to meet neighbours when first arriving. Another is to follow up this initial contact with offers of help or small gifts at suitable opportunities.

WORK AND EDUCATION AS SOURCES OF ACQUAINTANCE

Work is one of the two most common sources of close friends for people without learning disabilities, and a major source of acquaintances for many people. Many people who eventually become good friends meet initially through work, or are friends of people who work together. Lunch, coffee, or a drink after work are all social events that provide opportunities not only to get to know people from work better, but to meet new people.

A paid job, a training centre work experience scheme, or voluntary work may fulfil this function for some people with learning disabilities. Nevertheless, the segregation of work and training services remains, for many people, one of the major barriers in reaching a wide range of opportunities to make new relationships. We stressed in Chapter 2 how mixing together many people who do not find it easy to broaden relationships and take them outside of the work setting may perpetuate their social isolation. Adult training and social education centres have the additional disadvantage that the homes of the people who use them may be widely scattered geographically, and reliance on social services department or voluntary society transport for attendance each day makes social contact of an informal nature difficult outside work time.

Adult education, by contrast, can provide many opportunities for meeting people with and without learning disabilities. Shearer (1986) has described some of these, such as the *Gateway 2* and *Link* courses run by Kingsway Princeton College and Camden Social Services in London.

ORGANISATIONS, INTERESTS, AND SOCIAL WORLDS

Formal membership of a club or oganisation is, perhaps, the only thing which a third party can confer on people, which may help them widen their social circle. Different kinds of opportunities for social life come with different kinds of organisations. If one of the main aims of joining is for people with disabilities to meet other people, then it will be important for them to join an organisation whose members are likely to be of roughly the same age and who share some of the same interests.

Bishop and Hoggett (1986) have listed a variety of different types of leisure activity in which contacts can be made. It is worth considering:

sports;

arts (music, drama, dance, painting);

crafts;

hobbies;

social and religious activities and associated organisations such as church organisations, womens' institutes, and ethnic groups;

educational opportunities with a leisure component (such as cooking, or dance).

There are many organisations or activities – bell ringing is a good example – which it is possible to join without any prior knowledge or skill in the subject at all, though often some information or interest beforehand makes social interaction easier. It is easier for people to talk to others about ballroom dancing or angling if they have at least a little idea of who's who and what's what in the ballroom world or the angling world. So it may be helpful to join what may be called the "social world" of dancing or angling first. By this is meant those activities which people do, largely on an individual basis, through which they join in a wider group of enthusiasts, for example, watching particular television programmes, buying or borrowing specialist magazines, window shopping and studying catalogues, or going to watch dancing or angling events. These are all good ways to find out something about the activities before joining a club or doing these things personally.

Many people with learning disabilities participate in very few such "social worlds", yet it is one way in which other people often experiment with a variety of interests before making greater commitments in time, money, and energy.

Often the act of joining an organisation provides the ideal opportunity to ask to be introduced to other members, or to engage a helpful ally to make some introductions. Most organisations feel a responsibility to make new members welcome, introduce them, and include them in social events or conversation. Often this opportunity passes if it is not taken up at the start. Much, of course, will depend upon the particular organisation. A Citizens' Band radio enthusiasts group may involve much introduction and conversation, but it may not involve the right kind of social contact for some people. In many other organisations it may be necessary to "get oneself introduced" soon after joining.

Sometimes opportunities are limited by lack of awareness of what is available. Bishop and Hoggett (1986) listed a huge variety of leisure activities around which, to their knowledge, local clubs or societies had been organised. This list, reproduced in Box 6, may offer ideas for people in need of inspiration or suggestions.

THE IMPORTANCE OF SHARED ACTIVITY

A task or activity shared with another person allows a relationship to develop. A shared task makes this much easier than just sitting down

Basketball	Microlights	Military modelling
Old-time dancing	Harmoniums	Modern sequence dance
Chess	Netball	Computers
Cats	Ballroom dancing	Rowing
Aerobics	Guitars	Film and video
Orchestras	Whist	Folk dance
Football	Keep fit	Wives groups
Lapidary	Judo	Squash
Table tennis	Wrestling	Subaqua sport
Skittles	Athletics	Sailing
Beekeeping	Brass bands	Weight-lifting
Meditation	Caving	Motor scooters
Antiques	Handball	Handicrafts
Hockey	Darts	Bird watching
Toy dogs	Metal detectors	Choirs
Aquarism	Volleyball	Slimming
Fishing	Parascending	Boxing
Morris dancing	Orienteering	Aikido
Tennis	Rat fancying	Drama
Flower arranging	Computer games	Light opera
Bridge	Point-to-point	Lace making
Gardening	Family histories	Softball
Fuchsias	Lacrosse	Macrame
Windsurfing	Climbing	Yoga
Railway preservation	Local history	Bowls
Allotments	Industrial archaeology	Gymnastics
War games	Hang-gliding	Shove-ha'penny
Cricket	Numismatics	Upholstery
Wine	Naturalism	Silk-screen printing
Philately	Snooker	Oil painting
Photography	Mums and toddlers groups	Rifle & pistol shooting
Horse riding	Clocks	Model railways
Canoeing	Practical conservation	Cycling
Women's Institutes	Vintage motor cycles	Whippets
Skating	Swimming	Dress-making
Mouse fancying	Leek growing	Canal preserving
Caged birds	Aero modelling	Pigeon racing
		Model boats

BOX 6. Leisure activities around which clubs, societies, or organisations may be available locally, from Bishop and Hoggett (1986)

"talking" or "being together". So, although it may seem in some senses obvious, we wish to stress this point:

Relationships with other people are developed through doing things with them.

. . . the sharing of experience can provide the starting point for friendship

Such possibilities present themselves in all kinds of situations – in the church group, political organisations, talking about a holiday, cooking a meal, doing the washing up, or talking about the lives of mutual friends and acquaintances. It is perhaps because doing things with other people is such an important means of establishing relationships with them that leisure activities are often seen as providing one way of widening the social circle of people with learning disabilities. Further education, community projects, or work itself, however, can all provide the shared activity which is the basis for forming a relationship. Moreover, each activity may provide a new relationship. Each new relationship brings possibilities of new things to do, potentially leading in turn to more relationships.

DIFFERENT ACTIVITIES – DIFFERENT OPPORTUNITIES

Different activities offer different opportunities. Some activities are useful for meeting new people, whilst others provide good situations for maintaining and developing relationships.

Careful thought needs to be given to which activities provide which kinds of opportunities if people's needs and expectations are to be met. The opportunities presented by each activity will vary according to each individual's skills, circumstances, and the support available. The illustration provided in Box 7 may be helpful in suggesting, encouraging, or choosing particular things people may like to do.

Good activities for forming relationships are those where people are likely to meet others with some of the same interests as themselves. Clubs, societies, and regular activities based around a particular interest may be good ways to meet new acquaintances. For instance, folk dancing, keep fit, religious and political activities may offer such opportunities.

Getting to know people better is often helped by doing something together which:

is practical

so that there is something to be done,

with something to talk about,

with plenty of time,

but without any obligation or "pressure" to talk or interact;

is done in a small group

so that there is opportunity to interact first with one person then another,

with opportunities for others to join in and help the flow of interaction,

which is small enough to get to know everyone, at least a little;

Activities likely to offer opportunities for making new relationships (some also appear below)	
Folk/old-time dancing	Historical society
Workshop and religious activities	Keep fit, yoga
Rambling with a Ramblers Club	Railway enthusiasts' club
Bingo	
Singing, acting, dancing	Pub-quiz
Membership of social clubs	Football supporters' club
Political activities	Outdoor course/events (eg canal
Adult education (all kinds, including especially practical skills, eg embroidery)	renovation)

Activities likely to offer opportunities for developing existing relationships	
Gardening	Rambling, hill walking, climbing
Decorating	Watching television programmes (where there is shared interest)
Window shopping	Visiting friends
Church and religious social activities	Inviting friends to visit
Snooker, pool, or darts	Folk/old-time dancing
Going to cinema, concerts, theatre (if relationship already established)	Social clubs
	Disco dancing (with friends/ partner)
Outdoor events (eg environmental conservation)	Visiting museums (with acquaintances)
Singing, acting, dancing	Visiting pubs (with acquaintances)
Horse-riding (with acquaintances)	Political activities
Shared hobbies or classes (eg pottery, making lampshades, flower arranging)	Going out for a meal
	Camping
	Holidays

Activites unlikely to offer opportunities for making or developing relationships	
Spectator sports (alone)	Shopping
Cycling (alone)	Weight training
Swimming (alone)	Modelling, carving (unless through classes, etc)
Visiting libraries	
Photography (unless through a club)	Collecting (unless through local club)
Dominoes	Jigsaws
Knitting/sewing/embroidery (unless through classes/clubs)	Keeping common pets such cat, dog, rabbit

BOX 7. Types of opportunities that can be provided by different kinds of activities

is sufficiently quiet

so that it is possible to see, hear, and listen to each other, and to be seen, heard, and listened to by others;

is not competitive

so that people can help each other,

and admire, praise, encourage, or laugh about and enjoy each others' efforts;

allows informal interaction between people

so that people can pursue their conversations, ideas, or ways of doing things without disrupting what others want to do.

Box 7 illustrates a variety of activities with these features, such as gardening and many other household tasks, indoor or outdoor activities from window shopping to playing pool, and a variety of practical hobbies or studies, ranging from rambling and flower-arranging, to political activity.

CHOICE

Opportunities for people with learning disabilities to take a helping, providing role within some of the situations already discussed are particularly likely to allow relationships to grow, through the often greater equality of such relationships. Valued work roles, for example, may be particularly helpful in this respect (King's Fund Centre, 1984; Porterfield and Gathercole, 1985).

Mutual choice is an essential aspect of friendship. If choice is seen as important in people's relationships, then helping to make possible a number of different opportunities will be one key to enabling people with disabilities to make the friends they choose. Opportunities allow choices, although there may be difficulties in helping people to exercise choice. Helping people with learning disabilities to make meaningful, rational, but personal choices may present a challenge. A recent pamphlet by Carle (1986) has highlighted some of the issues. For example, a vicious circle may develop, whereby limited opportunities and experience lead to little confidence in making decisions. This, in turn, can lead to "bad" decision-making and the perception by others that people are unable to make appropriate decisions.

To help overcome this vicious circle it is suggested that people need assistance to help them understand the options and make realistic assessments. Citizen advocates can help people learn to express their views, or can communicate them on their behalf (Sang and O'Brien, 1984). Alternatively, participation in self-advocacy may help people develop self-confidence, as well as learn from the experiences of others.

THE ROLE OF A THIRD PARTY: INTRODUCTION AND FACILITATION

A third person can play a crucial role in introducing people to each other, as Richardson and Ritchie (1989a) have illustrated.

Frequently people are introduced to each other by someone they already know, who does much more than a formal introduction; who eases the relationship along. They may then meet at a friend's house, or at some event on one, two, or more occasions, with the mutual friend, before the relationship takes off on its own account. Those who might fulfil this enabling role for people with learning disabilities include:

relatives;

friends;

neighbours;

volunteers;

professionals;

prominent or active members of local clubs;

friends, acquaintances, or contacts of the above people.

Such people can also act as "role models", demonstrating appropriate skills and behaviour which people with learning disabilities may be able to observe and imitate, especially if the relevant skills and behaviours are discreetly pointed out.

Creating opportunities will often be about fostering this kind of introduction, this kind of enabling process. One example of such a process is the *Outreach* club described by Shearer (1986); another is Lyons' (1986) approach to facilitating relationships, through leisure activities. Approaches of this kind may require the provision of considerable support for the enablers if they are to carry through their role without being either overintrusive, or insufficiently helpful and supportive. Thought may need to be given, according to prevailing circumstances, to such issues as suitable events, possible conversational topics, and cues about social or interpersonal skills.

Attention may need to be paid to determining realistic commitments and time scales, as well as to providing encouragement for enablers, if these kinds of approach are to work as well as possible. Shearer (1986) for example, describes how *Outreach* volunteers were initially concerned that in moving out from their social club to accompany young people at yoga classes or roller skating, they might lose the club, and their own role within it. In the event, the experience of volunteers at the club was that this change of role brought greater rewards for them as well as for the young people they were helping.

THE CONFIDENT COMPANION

There is a different and distinct role for a third party, which may be more easily filled by visiting friends, relatives, or acquaintances, as well as by interested others, such as advocates or staff. That is, quite simply, the "confident companion" or "competent companion" (Atkinson, 1986): the person who is at ease in a situation and thereby can ease the introductions, smooth the conversation, and help the farewells or arrangements to meet again. It is a straightforward and generally well understood role, which anyone who is confident in a given situation can perform. It does not involve the preparation and careful attention to detail which is required of enablers.

EMOTIONAL ISOLATION AND THE SEARCH FOR A CLOSE RELATIONSHIP

Weiss (1975) concludes his book on loneliness with the following pertinent comments on the situation of people lacking close relationships:

"I would think it poor strategy to attempt to deal directly with the loneliness of emotional isolation by putting great energy into 'finding someone'. It would be more useful to accept that one's loneliness may last for some time . . . Yet it seems . . . that there is something constructive one can do: direct one's energy to projects, friendships, groups one cares about. This is not quite advising that one keep busy, although there is something to be said for that advice too. Rather it is advising that one develop relationships with others, engagements with activities, memberships in networks . . .

Then it may well happen that a potential attachment figure will be encountered in connection with these social activities. And because it will then be someone who is within a *milieu* in which one also has 'membership', the many problems of attachments outside of social contexts will be avoided".

We entirely agree with Weiss, that building up a range of different things to do with other people is more effective than "searching" for a close relationship. It is, however, worth offering some ideas on the kinds of opportunities, activities, and situations which might help an acquaintance develop into a closer relationship.

First, we believe it may be very helpful for people to have *someone else* to whom they can turn, or whom they see in any case, with whom they can share their emotions and feelings about others. It is far easier for them to develop trust and build a relationship of any kind with one person if they have a "confidante" of some kind with whom to share some of those experiences. Such a person might or might not know their other friends and acquaintances. Sometimes such a person might accompany them as part of a small group, of three or four perhaps, for a sociable event. Such a person will also be ready to share feelings.

We have already talked about the effects of different *numbers of people* in a social situation. The process of moving from acquaintance to friendship, and on to a close relationship, will be aided by meeting initially as part of a small group of three or four people, who already know each other reasonably well. Only when trust and evidence of some mutual commitment develops is it likely to be helpful for two people to start meeting or doing things together without the others. Close friendships can often develop spontaneously in this way, although when one person is seeking a possible sexual relationship, then spending time alone with someone else too early in the relationship is likely to impose strains on the social skills of both individuals. People without disabilities often find this stressful, especially young people or those who have not built up their self-confidence. People with learning disabilities, whose self-confidence is not high and whose social skills are not versatile and well practised, may find one-to-one situations particularly difficult to cope with.

Third, it is often not realised just how important *privacy* can be for some people at certain times if they are to have the opportunity for relationships to develop and deepen. Many people with learning disabilities have less opportunity than the rest of us to have some privacy with their friends and acquaintances, at the time and in the manner of their choosing. Many residential establishments, for example, offer little opportunity for two people to spend time together in comfort, without frequent intrusion. People living with parents, or living with others in hostels or group homes, may only have their bedrooms in which to seek privacy unless others "make room" in some way or other to give them a little privacy when it seems indicated.

We have commented earlier that some kinds of situations do more readily throw people together into closer relationships. These are often situations where there is some *common concern* or sense of adversity (Bulmer, 1986; Willmott, 1987), such as is found in:

self-advocacy groups;

other self-help groups (eg tenants' associations);

campaigning groups concerned with neighbourhood or political issues (eg saving a community centre);

religious or moral campaigns.

Working with other people in activities of this kind may provide opportunities to get to know people. The expression of feelings about the issues may lead naturally to closer friendships and emotional attachments may develop. Alternatively such relationships may be fostered by making arrangements to meet in some other, perhaps more intimate, situation.

Having made the acquaintance of people in one of these situations, getting to know them well is helped by:

spending a good deal of time with someone;

doing things which involve physical exertion in a group or team;

joining in a common cause over some issue, particularly if the cause involves religious, political, or social values;

working closely with someone whilst helping others who are in need;

watching or participating in events that have a strong emotional content.

In Box 8 we have listed some situations and activities which we think may foster the sharing of feelings and values. Some of these activities may be undertaken by people with severe or profound learning disabilities, who have no verbal means of communicating. Certain of these activities prompt, by their nature, a concern for feelings or values. Others involve spending lengthy periods of time with other people, thus allowing time for trust and mutual understanding to develop. Some involve a sense of adversity within a group, which may bring people together. Finally, some involve physical exertion – or even exhaustion – which often leads people to pay particular attention to caring about one another.

Sharing prolonged periods of time together allows feelings about each other to emerge readily, and so may also allow irritation and anger to surface. Camping and other kinds of holidays, for example, may pose particular strains. They can readily break up relationships where there is a lack of trust, commitment, or social skill. Arrangements of this kind may need careful thought.

Watching and talking about films or television programmes with a strong emotional content

Self-help groups, self-advocacy groups, and organisations of people who share a common cause, such as tenants' or residents' associations

Helping others in need – either individuals at a time of need or distress, or through voluntary work

Watching drama, dance, theatre

Team sporting activities

Rambling, hill climbing

Outdoor courses and events

Camping and other kinds of holidays

Shared religious activities or experiences

BOX 8. Activities likely to encourage the sharing of feelings and values

ISSUES FOR PEOPLE WITH PROFOUND LEARNING DISABILITIES

Are the issues in this chapter any different for people with profound disabilities than for other people? The issues and approaches are indeed relevant, even if some of the means and examples discussed earlier are not. The functions of acquaintance and friendship have been described as meeting people's needs for company, and for mutual understanding, and for sustaining self-identity and self-esteem. These needs are more likely to be met if they can join in doing things with other people, however profound their disabilities. The ways to get to know people well which were listed at the end of the last section apply particularly for people with profound or multiple disabilities.

The activities which interest people who are profoundly disabled are as individual as they are for anyone else. The kinds of leisure activities distinguished by Bishop and Hoggett (1986) – sports, arts, crafts, hobbies, social, religious, or educational (cooking, dance) – all present opportunities for people with profound disabilities. Often they will not be able to participate along with others in an organised group, but they may be able to do so informally. Many of the physical activities listed in Box 6 offer possibilities, if only for participation or learning at a very simplified level.

Such activities can be undertaken either for their own sake or as ways in which to spend time and get to know other people. Individuals' preferences and participation will be tapped to the extent that other people pay attention to them: to their motivation, their concentration, their ability, their mood, and their attitude. Paying attention to and responding to people's preferences enables them to develop their self-identity, as walkers, or dog lovers, gardeners, or rock concert fans. Preferences and choice express self-identity. Satisfaction in chosen activities, and pleasure at being with chosen people, expresses self-esteem.

Friendship involves people in chosen relationships with others whom they prefer to be with. Most people, however profound their disability, can express preferences for individuals by their behaviour. When those individuals in turn reciprocate with a real attempt to understand the feelings, wishes, excitements, and disappointments of the person who is disabled, friendship ensues. Such friendships are possible for everyone, with the possible exception of people who have been deprived of relationships of warmth throughout their lives, or a few with a particular additional disability such as autism.

Some people may establish such friendships within the family, and with family friends and neighbours. Others may find that educational or vocational settings can bring contact with people who can provide this interest, understanding, and support for their personal identity and worth. Some people may need the involvement of outsiders to provide them with company, and to act as enablers in introducing them to clubs, groups, or new activities. All the remarks made earlier on the role of enablers apply equally when they are involved with people who have profound learning disabilities.

A particular responsibility, however, rests on other people who seek to help those with profound disabilities, whether they are professionals, acquaintances, or friends, to portray those individuals in as positive a manner as possible, both in initial presentation (Richardson, Koller, and Katz, 1985), introductions (see Box 18, Chapter 9), and subsequently. Roles such as helping, participating, choosing, and purchasing, all emphasise the person's social value. So do descriptions which convey that the more able person is accompanying, assisting, or making possible the chosen actions of the person who is disabled, rather than conveying that the more able person is in control. Such socially valued roles help other people to pay attention to the person who is disabled, speak and look to that person rather than the companion for communication, and thereby get to know the person a little better as an individual. More social opportunities may be opened up as a result.

Formalised involvement of helpers may bring particular benefits for some people. Schemes of the kind described by Walsh (1985) or Lyons (1986) involve volunteers as companions. Citizen advocates (Sang and O'Brien, 1984) should be able to negotiate for wider social opportunities for people, and can often act as companions themselves. Potentially, citizen advocates have several important roles: they may spend time with people with disabilities, help introduce them to a variety of activities and other people, and attend to, and inform other people of, their preferences. They can help to ensure that other people take account of people's preferences for spending time in particular activities or with particular individuals. There is insufficient evidence available as to whether citizen advocacy leads to extended networks of other relationships for people with disabilities. There is however much experience of citizen advocacy having led to strong, individual relationships between advocates and the individuals for whom they act.

REFERENCES

ATKINSON, D. Engaging competent others: a study of the support networks of people with mental handicap. *British Journal of Social Work*, 1986; **16**, supplement, 83–101.

ATKINSON, D. *Someone to Turn To: the social worker's role and the role of front line staff in relation to people with mental handicaps.* Kidderminster: BIMH Publications, 1989.

ATKINSON, D., WARD, L. Friends and neighbours: relationships and opportunities in the community for people with mental handicap. *In* Malin, N. (Ed.). *Reassessing Community Care*. London: Croom Helm, 1987.

ATKINSON, D. Moving from hospital to the community: factors influencing the life style of people with mental handicaps. *Mental Handicap*, 1988; **16**: 1, 8-11.

BISHOP, J., HOGGETT, P. *Organising Around Enthusiasms*. London: Comedia Publications, 1986.

BRADDOCK, D., HELLER, T. The closure of mental retardation institutions: implications. *Mental Retardation*, 1985; **23**, 222-229.

BULMER, M. *Neighbours: the work of Philip Abrams*. Cambridge: Cambridge University Press, 1986.

CARLE, N. (Ed.). *Helping People to Make Choices: opportunities and challenges*. London: Campaign for People with Mental Handicaps, 1986.

FELCE, D., TOOGOOD, S. *Close to Home: a local housing service and its impact on the lives of nine adults with severe and profound mental handicaps*. Kidderminster: BIMH Publications, 1988.

FIRTH, H. *A Move to Community: social contact and behaviour*. Morpeth: Northumberland Health Authority District Psychology Service, 1986.

GOLLAY, E., FREEDMAN, R., WYNGAARDEN, M., KURTZ, N. R. *Coming Back – the Community Experiences of Institutionalised Mentally Retarded People*. Cambridge, Mass.: Abt Books, 1978.

HELLER, T. The effects of involuntary residential relocation: a review. *American Journal of Community Psychology*, 1982; **10**, 471-492.

KING'S FUND CENTRE. *An Ordinary Working Life*. London: King's Fund Centre, 1984.

KING'S FUND CENTRE. *Ties and Connections: an ordinary community life for people with learning difficulties*. London: King's Fund Centre, 1988.

LANDESMAN-DWYER, S., BERKSON, G. Friendships and social behaviour. *In* Wortis, J. (Ed.). *Mental Retardation and Developmental Disabilities. Volume 13*. London: Plenum Press, 1984.

LEYIN, A. What shall we tell the neighbours? *Mental Handicap*, 1988; **16**:1, 11-15.

LYONS, M. Students as buddies: a proposal for smoothing the path towards a broader life experience through recreation. *Occupational Therapy*, 1986; April, 111-114.

MANSELL, J., FELCE, D., JENKINS, J., DE KOCK, U., TOOGOOD, S. *Developing Staffed Housing for People with Mental Handicaps*. Tunbridge Wells: Costello, 1987.

MILLS, J. An uncaring community. *New Society*, 1988; February 20-21.

PORTERFIELD, J., GATHERCOLE, C. *The Employment of People with Mental Handicap*. London: King's Fund Centre, 1985.

RICHARDSON, S. A., KOLLER, H., KATZ, M. Appearance and mental retardation: some first steps in the development and application of a measure. *American Journal of Mental Deficiency*, 1985; **89**, 475-484

RICHARDSON, A., RITCHIE, J. *Making the Break*. London: King's Fund Centre, 1986.

RICHARDSON, A., RITCHIE, J. *Developing Friendships: enabling people with learning difficulties to make and maintain friends*. London: Policy Studies Institute/Social and Community Planning Research, 1989a.

RICHARDSON, A., RITCHIE, J. *Letting Go: dilemmas for parents*. Milton Keynes: Open University Press, 1989b.

SANG, B., O'BRIEN, J. *Advocacy: the UK and American experiences*. London: King's Fund Centre, 1984.

SHEARER, A. *Building Community for People with Mental Handicaps, their Families and Friends*. London: Campaign for People with Mental Handicaps and King's Fund Centre, 1986.

WALSH, J. *Let's Make Friends*. London: Souvenir Press, 1985.

WEISS, R. *Loneliness: the experience of emotional and social isolation*. London, Mass.: Massachusetts Institute of Technology Press, 1975.

WILLMOTT, P. *Social Networks, Informal Care and Public Policy*. London: Policy Studies Institute, 1986.

WILLMOTT, P. *Friendship Networks and Social Support*. London: Policy Studies Institute, 1987.

. . . learning by experience – by observing, by talking, by joking, and by listening to others' experiences . . .

CHAPTER 7

Meeting people and making friends:
attitudes and skills

INTRODUCTION: THE INTEREST, THE CONFIDENCE, THE SKILLS

Motivation and choice are needed if people are to make and keep successful relationships. The desire to make acquaintances, the wish to have friends, choose them, and keep them, must all be present if the barriers presented by finance, lack of opportunities, lack of self-confidence, disappointment, and personal embarrassment or hurt are to be overcome.

Self-confidence is essential if we are to be able to approach people, maintain and renew contact with those we have met before, and develop and nurture relationships with people who are, or might become, close friends.

Other abilities are essential to the maintenance of good relationships. Many of these can be learned, consciously or unconsciously. Some non-verbal "skills" can be learned by observation and imitation, deliberately or unwittingly, from family, from peers, and from television and film stars. Others are very difficult to learn simply by observation and imitation, such as the thinking skills needed to foresee the effects of personal behaviour on others and skills of anticipating the likely feelings and reactions of other people. These abilities are usually learned in childhood and adolescence, by demonstration, explanation, and feedback: feedback which often takes the form of humour, teasing, or sarcasm. Adults, both at home and in school, spend much time and trouble with young children to explain some of these basic principles, one way or another:

"You must think of other people . . ."

"What would *you* think if she did that to you?"

"Look, you've hurt him, now . . ."

"You're not the only pebble on the beach . . .".

People with learning disabilities do not always receive the same emphasis on learning to think of others. This is partly because the people with whom they spend time are often also disabled in their personal relationships, and partly because, for them, such learning often needs to continue throughout adolescence and into early adulthood, a time when people with learning disabilities may have few friends and acquaintances to point out the issues.

We will now consider in turn the issues of motivation and choice, self-confidence, and personal abilities and social skills.

MOTIVATION AND CHOICE

Man is a social animal. A few people voluntarily choose to restrict their social existence by living a life of retreat. Most do not. People generally choose individuals with whom to spend their free time, within choices made and limited by circumstance. Yet some people withdraw largely or totally from social contact, not because of circumstance but because of mood, or motivation. People who are depressed, for example, may avoid opportunities for social contact, may allow existing friendships to slacken or be interrupted, or may not show the confidence or ability to make the relationships they would like. "Cognitive" therapy, or help with the way people think and feel, is becoming widely used with people without learning disabilities who are depressed or who experience emotional isolation or loneliness (Young, 1982).

Some people with learning disabilities choose to live a life largely independent of other people. They are few. Some choose to live within the "handicap world" and make their relationships largely with others with learning disabilities. Others choose to live outside the "handicap world" altogether (Atkinson, 1987; Atkinson and Ward, 1987).

Individuals' motivation to enter relationships of any kind, from casual acquaintances to companionship or friendship, may be drastically affected by their past experiences, especially hurts and humiliations, recent or distant. Changing the actual opportunities, helping to build people's confidence, offering them opportunities to discuss relationships, or "merely" listening to their history (Ryan and Walker, 1985), may all change people's interest in finding and developing personal relationships.

Most people without learning disabilities choose to have friends, and most people with learning disabilities would like to have friends (Atkinson, 1987; Richardson and Ritchie, 1989). But there are some people who clearly demonstrate by their actions that they would like to make different kinds of relationships, who nevertheless actively resist help of any kind. They may reject not only "organised" help from a group or professional, but even the simple opportunities that friends, workmates, or family may tender. There is no easy solution to such a reluctance to accept help except the gentle, patient provision of opportunities. There are few people, it seems, who do not want to have friends.

SELF-CONFIDENCE

Everyone's ability to relate effectively to others is vitally affected by their degree of self-confidence. Moreover, changes in this condition, from minute to minute and day to day, can affect their interactions from moment to moment or person to person. One brief rebuff can lead to withdrawal from the next encounter. Tiredness, or some perceived failure, can lead to avoidance of social contact with others and, hence, to loss of further social validation and social reinforcement. Thus, the growth of self-confidence, or the loss of it, can become a self-perpetuating process. Self-confidence is critical in finding, maintaining, and developing friendships, which in turn sustain self-esteem. It is needed to cope successfully with many experiences, such as responding to failure, to teasing, or to being left out, which are essential for getting along with others (see Box 9).

Richardson and Ritchie (1988, 1989) reported that many of their informants had overcome a major barrier by strengthening their own self-confidence:

> "Although there are other social skills that might be helpful, none were mentioned with the force of a need for confidence or feeling a sense of worth" (Richardson and Ritchie, 1988).

Atkinson (1989) has commented on the role social workers and other support staff can play in building self-confidence.

Warm, positive, and accepting relationships are one vital contribution to self-esteem and self-confidence. This probably means more than the warmth, empathy, and genuineness likely to be received from one or two professional staff who may stay in people's lives for a year or two at most. For people with learning disabilities it usually has more to do with the nature of day-to-day relationships with those with whom they live and work, although professional help can be a vital ingredient for some people at some times of their life.

The importance of one close, *valuing* relationship cannot be overestimated.

Much self-confidence is a result of past experience, especially during childhood, and lack of self-confidence through adverse early upbringing is not easily overcome. Nevertheless, helping people to build up an account of the past which they can relate with some confidence (Ryan and Walker, 1985) may be critical in allowing them to face aspects of the present with confidence. Citizen advocacy may have a role to play here, by providing relationships with people whose job is to get to know, understand, and speak up for the individuals' interests.

Listening:	Do you pay attention to someone who is talking and make an effort to understand what is being said?
Introducing yourself:	Do you become acquainted with new people on your own initiative?
Introducing other people:	Do you help others become acquainted with one another?
Giving a compliment:	Do you tell others that you like something about them or their activities?
Apologising:	Do you tell others that you are sorry after doing something wrong?
Knowing your feelings:	Do you try to recognise which emotions you are feeling?
Expressing your feelings:	Do you let others know which emotions you are feeling?
Understanding the feelings of others:	Do you try to figure out what other people are feeling?
Dealing with someone else's anger:	Do you try to understand other people's angry feelings?
Expressing affection:	Do you let others know that you care about them?
Sharing something:	Do you offer to share what you have with others who might appreciate it?
Helping others:	Do you give assistance to others who might need or want help?
Using self-control:	Do you control your temper so that things do not get out of hand?
Responding to teasing:	Do you deal with being teased by others in ways that allow you to remain in control of yourself?
Dealing with being left out:	Do you decide whether you have been left out of some activity, and then do things to feel better about the situation?
Standing up for a friend:	Do you let other people know when a friend has not been treated fairly?
Responding to failure:	Do you figure out the reason for failing in a particular situation, and what you can do about it, in order to be more successful in the future?

BOX 9. Useful skills for getting along with others, adapted from Goldstein (1981)

Self-advocacy can have a dramatic and positive effect on self-confidence. By its nature it is designed to help people with learning disabilities to voice their concerns and interests and gain confidence. Much self-advocacy takes place through groups, almost all of which are run within adult training centres (Crawley, 1988). Self-advocacy groups can help individuals to gain self-confidence in both small and large social groups, and in various degrees of informality and formality.

People can also be helped to build up their confidence, both in advocating for their own interests and in more personal interactions, without the use of groups. Small, one-to-one activities can be used which give people a sense of their own importance as individuals, whether through experience or achievement.

One of the most powerful sources for generating self-confidence is the demonstration that people are of value to others. Helping others, therefore, can offer much that will facilitate the growth of confidence. It is unfortunate that services have, in the past, so frequently denied people with learning disabilities the opportunity to take on the helping role, and that normalisation concepts have often had only limited impact on the roles they can take within local communities.

PERSONAL ABILITIES AND SOCIAL SKILLS: LEARNING, TEACHING, THINKING

How do we learn to get on with others and make friends? We learn to communicate our respect and warmth, our understanding of others, and our openness toward them. We do this through a host of largely unconscious social "skills" about relating to other people. How do we learn all this? Some aspects come naturally with an attitude of warmth and openness toward others. Other aspects are learned quite unconsciously, by observing others. How unconscious this process usually is can be illustrated by noting how habits about eye contact or facial proximity vary between different cultures. The Chinese, for example, avoid prolonged, direct eye contact in most friendly, sociable interactions. Americans, on the other hand, use it to convey openness and honesty. These social skills, therefore, are learned by observing and copying others, and changing our behaviour in the light of others' reactions. Occasionally (especially in childhood and adolescence) other people give us hints or advice about specific points. These skills are important.

Especially important are the experience and skills needed to judge and interpret what other people are thinking and feeling. Young people who are effective at making and maintaining friends are likely to have more detailed and more accurate perceptions of their peers than those who are less good at making relationships. The skills and habits of being aware of others and their likely thoughts and feelings are incubated during childhood by parents and nursery teachers, and during adolescence and adulthood by peers' remarks and behaviour.

It might be expected, therefore, that social skills education would concentrate on helping people with learning disabilities to appreciate the likely thoughts and feelings of others. This kind of approach is central to the work of Shure and Spivack (1978) and others who have followed them (Cartledge and Milburn, 1986) in solving problems by thinking about other people and their likely reactions. The methods used may be called the *cognitive* approach to social skills.

Unfortunately, most social skills education has developed from a different, behaviourist tradition. This has often led to less concentration on the likely feelings, thoughts, and actions of other people and an over-emphasis on the spoken word, tone, and non-verbal behaviour of people with learning disabilities. This *behavioural* approach has often employed relatively didactic methods of learning. Teaching social skills through behavioural training programmes and social skills training groups has become very popular.

Much has been made in the past two decades of the value of social skills training and its possible contribution for people who have difficulties in relationships. Some workers, however, see it as part of a mechanistic, almost impersonal approach, which over-emphasises behaviour at the expense of feelings, thoughts, attitudes, values, and beliefs. Why is this?

What is meant by "social skills"? The term is used to mean different things in different contexts. Some people use it to mean social competence – cooking, shopping skills, the use of public transport, and so forth. We use the term in the narrower sense of the skills of social interaction – looking, listening, talking with others – and the other skills involved in social exchanges, like deciding when to initiate contact and when not to. Social skills, in the sense of interpersonal skills, are clearly essential to the process of acquaintance and finding friendship.

The model of "skill", social skill, comes from the behavioural and occupational traditions of psychology, which express the viewpoint that the subtleties of human interaction can be analysed and taught, like the skills of other human endeavours – driving cars, climbing mountains, or writing job applications, for example. Argyle (1983) pioneered this approach to human relationships, and has made a major contribution to the understanding of the way people interact. This approach to the analysis of relationships has had far reaching consequences for our understanding of how to help people with relationship difficulties. However, the "skill" model emphasises issues which may distract from the approaches which we regard as most helpful.

Are social skills most usefully conceived of as bits of behaviour? Is it important to consider the way people *think* about others in relationships?

What is the most effective way to learn the social skills of behaving and thinking? Is it by teaching and training, or by observation and demonstration ("modelling") in natural settings, learning from others and from personal experience?

The traditional behavioural social skill approach (Argyle, 1983; Trower, Bryant, and Argyle, 1978; Wilkinson and Canter, 1982) answers to these questions are these:

to focus on behaviour;

to teach individual skills carefully and systematically.

The approach we offer to these issues is different on both points, even though we do greatly value the contribution the social skill approach has made. Our views are that we should:

consider the ways people *think* as being at least as important as the ways they behave;

emphasise learning by experience – by observing, by talking, by joking, and by listening to others' experiences, for example, as much as from teaching and training.

This can perhaps best be illustrated by saying that, potentially, the more relevant guidance and coaching anyone can receive, the better. A constant attention to issues to do with relationships and others' thoughts and feelings during childhood and adolescence, at school or out of school, can only be of benefit.

Yet the key is *relevance*. Much social skills training, as practised currently, is not particularly high on relevance, and focuses on small elements of social behaviour rather than on the *attention* and *thinking* processes ("cognitive" skills) which underline that behaviour.

It should be said that this criticism does *not* apply to social skills teaching for people with profound learning disabilities, whose lack of verbal communication and understanding precludes approaches which focus on thinking processes.

THINKING ABOUT OTHERS AND EXPRESSING FEELINGS

Shure and Spivack (1978) have argued that it is not so much specific skills which people need to make relationships, but ways of thinking which can help them to decide how to behave. This approach is complementary to traditional social skills approaches: emphasising the more generalised thinking processes involved. Shure and Spivack stress a number of processes which people must master if difficulties in relationships are to be overcome effectively and appropriately. These are to be able to:

understand a *sufficient vocabulary*, including words describing people's feelings;

understand that *others' wishes and feelings* may differ from their own and to have some idea how to find out what these are;

think of *alternative* things to do in any particular social situation;

think of *some possible consequences* of each of these actions – how other people may react;

evaluate these consequences and make a choice as to what they will do.

An appropriate readiness and ability to communicate feelings and emotions to others so they do not remain hidden or bottled up, only to burst forth in inappropriate behaviour at a later time, should be added to this list.

The emphasis in this approach is strongly on helping people learn for themselves what are the best courses of action, rather than to teach any "right way". A small illustration is provided in Box 10. The approach has

---

THE BASIC SKILLS

- Understanding words describing people's feelings
- Recognising others' wishes and feelings may differ from one's own
- Being able to find out what others think and feel
- Being able to think of alternative things to do in situations
- Awareness of different ways others may react
- Ability to choose a sensible word or action in consequence

AN ILLUSTRATION

Specific problem: Child reciprocates hurting or grabbing behaviour.

Questions to encourage problem-solving communication:
  1   How did it make you feel when _____ (hit) you?
  2   OK, you felt (mad)
  3   What happened when you (hit) him back?
  4   After child answers, say: (Hitting) is one thing you can do. Can you think of something different to do that will make you feel happy?
  5   After child answers, say: That's a different idea. Is that a good idea? What might happen if you try that?

**BOX 10. Teaching problem-solving techniques with children
from Shure and Spivack (1978)**

been built up in a series of curricula for children and adolescents by Camp and Bass (1985) and by Bass and Camp (1981, 1985a,b) called the *Think Aloud* programme. Cartledge and Milburn (1986) have also elaborated on these themes in a text which will be useful to those planning social skills teaching.

The importance of this approach has already been emphasised. Its implications vary widely according to the individual abilities of the people who need help. People with severe learning disabilities may need to be helped to learn the meanings and use of words or signs for feelings and emotions, and to be encouraged to pay attention to others' needs. At the next level of sophistication, the focus may need to be on other people – on their wishes, their thoughts, their feelings. At a third level it becomes possible to focus on the processes of interaction: on alternative things to say or do, how others might react to these, and how to choose what to say or do.

All these areas may require a consistent focus over a period of several years if lasting change is to be achieved by individuals in their relationships. We believe the skill areas set out above provide a clear overall framework for learning about relationships. More detail is provided, for those who wish it, by Shure and Spivack (1978), Camp and Bass (1985), Bass and Camp (1981, 1985a,b), and Cartledge and Milburn (1986).

The appropriate expression of emotions is not amongst the six core skills areas emphasised by Shure and Spivack, but is equally important. Attention, enquiry, and recognition of people's feelings is a good way to encourage them to become aware of emotional states and to communicate them. Cartledge and Milburn (1986) discuss approaches to teaching people awareness and expression of emotions, and refer to a number of American programmes for teaching appropriate skills including, for example, the *Boiling Point List* for assessing situations that provoke angry feelings. This lists a variety of circumstances rated on a scale from "does not anger me at all" to "I get extremely angry in this situation", thus:

"when your friends do something without you";

"when someone borrows something of yours and breaks it";

"when you are unjustly accused of something";

"when someone causes you to get in trouble";

"when you do something good and no-one notices".

Cartledge and Milburn refer to three curricula designed for American educational settings, which specifically cover emotional awareness and expression (Dinkmeyer, 1973; Dupont, Gardner, and Brody, 1974; Elardo and Cooper, 1977). They have a number of common themes:

sense of self-identity, and development of self-esteem
including the ability to identify positive attributes, assets, and strengths as well as to identify and accept negative attributes, limitations, and imperfections;

awareness and expression of feelings
including recognising feelings, using words to label them, and using non-verbal as well as verbal means to express emotion;

awareness of the feelings of others
including inferences from verbal and non-verbal behaviour, and social expectations about emotions appropriate to specific situations;

awareness of complexities in emotional expression
including the recognition that feelings change over time, and that emotions in self and others may be mixed.

In fact, most of us learn many of our "cognitive" social skills from observation, from listening to others' experiences and learning from them, by practice, and by paying attention to the feedback underlying the jokes and teasing to which we are subject.

Learning through opportunities to experience and observe relationships, including those of competent and less competent models in the flesh and on television, is significant for most people in enabling them to refine their social skills. Yet much of this is based upon certain fundamentals learned early in childhood, taught by parents and others. Those fundamentals are about:

paying attention to other people;

foreseeing what other people might think or feel;

listening to other people;

understanding what other people regard as important.

Many people with learning disabilities have not learned these fundamentals by the time they become adolescents or adults. They may therefore need much more explicit hints, advice, guidance, teaching, or coaching than their peers.

This teaching, however, needs to be relevant. It needs to address the basic skills, not merely the superficial skills of appearance, eye contact, facial expression, and verbal response, if the nature of people's relationships is to change.

We have argued earlier (Chapter 3) that learning of social skills requires at least four ingredients:

observation of both competent and coping models;

imitation of appropriate behaviour;

opportunity for practice;

feedback on performance.

Most of those ingredients can be provided in natural settings rather than formal training sessions. Observation needs to include watching people manage, and "just" cope, whether peers or television actors. Correct imitation will only take place if attention is given to appropriate aspects of behaviour: hints, cues, and comments may be needed to draw attention to relevant aspects of other people's behaviour. Practice implies opportunity; much has been said elsewhere about this. Feedback can be given in many forms, but sarcasm, teasing, and criticism are often counterproductive as feedback because the recipient may "shut off" and reject not only the giver, but the message.

We wish to stress that *all* these ingredients can be offered through "natural" situations as easily as through structured teaching, if parents, staff, or others are alert and motivated in two respects:

a need to be aware of the issues;

a need to be prepared to use the opportunities provided.

All learning takes time. Perhaps one of the strongest arguments for buttressing formal coaching with informal learning situations is that learning can generally take place over a longer period of time through informal situations outside formal classroom teaching.

The next section examines the "cognitive" approach and its focus on thinking skills in a little more detail.

OTHER KEY ATTRIBUTES AND ABILITIES

There are numerous skills which many people who have difficulties with social interaction may never be able to master successfully. We have tried, therefore, to highlight some of the skills and issues which are important in enabling people with all degrees of learning disability to make acquaintances and friends. Box 9 has illustrated some skills (adapted from Goldstein, 1981) which are useful in getting on well with others. Boxes 12 to 14 (Chapter 8) will illustrate further attitudes and skills which can be important in making, developing, and maintaining personal relationships.

A major pre-requisite for natural, positive relationships with others is appearance. Attention may need to be given to posture, gait, dress, decoration (such as jewellery, rings, badges), hair, cosmetics, and accessories such as spectacles or hats. Flynn (1989) has highlighted how unusual physical appearance stigmatises people living independently in the community and is strongly linked to their victimisation. Goffman examined the processes behind stigmatisation over two decades ago (1963). It is important to note that, although many physical features of

. . . awareness and expression of feelings . . .

appearance may not be changeable in adult life or may require major surgery, there is usually much that can be achieved through dress, hair styles, and decoration.

Tall men, for example, may need to attend to dress and social skills to avoid appearing threatening. People with profound intellectual disabilities require attention to be paid to very particular issues. Appearance and gait are of especial significance. Anything particularly unusual in these two areas is likely to exacerbate any social difficulty or embarrassment experienced by others who are not used to communicating with people who do not speak. Perhaps of equal impact, however, is their manner of introduction or greeting. Hugging is rarely appropriate except between people who know each other well, and is often very off-putting to those who are not expecting to be hugged. Teaching people to shake hands and maintain an appropriate distance instead are, therefore, important skills. Attention to other aspects of age-appropriate and culture-appropriate behaviour may be necessary, particularly distinctions between behaviour which is acceptable within the home situation and that required in public. Facial expressions and mannerisms can be particularly distinctive and can draw attention to people's "difference" from others. Helping them to correct unusual non-verbal facial behaviour and responses presents great difficulties because of the problems of providing feedback that will be understood. It may help to work on one important non-verbal habit at a time over a long period, perhaps a year or so. Mirrors, role play, and video recordings may also be helpful. Lack of facial response to others and antagonistic expressions, such as grimaces, are likely to be of greatest significance, but other features such as tics, nose picking, or teeth grinding may be important to some individuals (Flynn, 1989; Richardson, Koller and Katz, 1985).

People who do use language, an issue which is rarely stressed, need opportunities for a wide variety of different activities, pleasures, and experiences as a basis for conversation, to provide something to talk about. It is almost impossible for people to pursue any acquaintance beyond the most simple introductions unless they can establish some event, relationship, or experience to communicate about with another person. Variety of experience, most particularly variety of recent experiences, is what we draw on when establishing contact with others. The effects of restricted experience on the ability of people with learning disabilities to make even basic acquaintances, and to maintain such relationships, is often woefully unappreciated. Experience or, at least, information about the kinds of activities others may engage in may be critical in enabling people to strike up conversations with them.

The importance of significant experiences, and the need for a variety of them, may be better appreciated by considering how important "story telling" is in even fairly casual conversation, both with people who are relative strangers ("Once, when I was . . .") and with people whom we know well or with whom we spend much of our time. Over use of one or two such stories or experiences, however, can be particularly annoying to people who are told them repeatedly.

It is easy to forget the importance of understanding the meanings of words that describe people's feelings, if conversation is to progress towards some degree of shared intimacy. Hence, another important piece of preparation for some people is to learn the meanings or nuances of a variety of such words.

It is often underestimated how socially difficult it is for people to introduce themselves to others; and how easy things can be made by a good introduction from someone else. Even the most socially competent of us can find ourselves in social difficulty when we are not introduced to someone and, for some reason, it seems either inappropriate or socially difficult to remedy this for ourselves. The skill of being able to introduce themselves clearly, or to get others to introduce them, is very important for people with learning disabilities in making the acquaintance of people whom they have not met before.

In developing relationships, some people effectively dominate others in such a way that they wish to escape. Friends, acquaintances, and carers may need to give each other feedback on whether someone's conversation is too intimate or insufficiently personal to hold the interest of another person and not drive that person away. These problems are mentioned because some individuals with few social contacts are frequently rejected by people who might otherwise have become their closest friends because they feel overwhelmed by their demands, by impositions on their time, or by the over-personal nature of their enquiries (see also Box 1 in Chapter 3, and Box 15 in Chapter 8).

People may not always regard getting to know others as something that they are particularly motivated to do. Reference has already been made to the three "types" of people identified in Matthews (1986) study, some of whom were considered "independent".

Whilst respecting people's choice to be independent of close personal relationships it may be worthwhile to explore whether this is a valid "choice" on their part, or the effect of what may have been a lifetime of exclusion from the experience of relationships. Such exploration may be especially necessary for people whose behaviour presents particular difficulties for others, or for people with severe learning disabilities and other impairments. Pointing out and demonstrating to them the benefits of social interaction, possibly over a long period of time, may be one way to approach this issue.

Another kind of difficulty arises when people who lack self-confidence, or feel depressed or unhappy, do not have the necessary motivation or drive to sustain them through making new acquaintances or going out to join a new activity where they are strangers. It may be sufficient to prompt such action and make sure it is rewarded. Alternatively, it may be necessary to tackle their state of depression or lack of self-esteem more directly before trying to improve their social situation or social abilities.

If existing friendships are not to be threatened, then Argyle and Henderson's (1984) rules (Box 1, Chapter 3) suggest that keeping confidences, not being jealous of others' friends, not taking up too much of a friend's time, and respecting friends' privacy are all of great importance.

WHAT TO TALK ABOUT

Another critical issue for many people is that of what it is, and what it is not, appropriate to discuss in conversation. This can be a subtle issue, dependent on whom people are talking to, in what situation, and how long they have known them. At a basic level it might be helpful for them to learn some very simple rules. One such rule might be not to be the first to ask or talk about other people's or their own private family life. Many people find being questioned about their private lives much more threatening and off-putting than similar questioning about their work, their leisure, or what they have been doing recently. Box 15, at the end of the next chapter, provides material which may be helpful in discussing what it is appropriate to talk about, with whom, and when.

One of the chief difficulties people face is the lack of suitable topics to talk about. Trower, Bryant, and Argyle (1978) usefully summarised different areas of conversation which can be tried (or mixed) according to circumstances. We have adapted these as follows:

People
> information, questions, or "gossip" about people who may be known to you or to the other person;

Events
> anything you or the other person have been involved in recently in the past, is involved in at present, or may be planning for the future, and the people you or they have met as a result;

Activities
> things you or the other person may have been doing at home, work, socially, or in leisure, and people thus met;

Shared topics
> things you may have in common with each other, such as being "here", places you both may know, things you may both have seen or done, subjects of general interest to both of you (hi-fi, cars), or people you both know;

General topics
> public information of one kind or another, such as news, gossip, the weather, sport, personalities in the news.

Rehearsing things to talk about, and practising conversation in each or any of these topic areas, can be valuable for some people who have difficulty starting or maintaining conversations.

Trower, Bryant, and Argyle (1978) suggest that questions asked of others can usefully proceed from the general to the specific, and then to questions about feelings ("How are things going?"; "Do you get very exhausted and fed up?"; "What do you like most about what she is doing now?"). This may be a difficult skill for many people with learning disabilities to follow. Asking questions about other people and their lives, rather than telling people about themselves, is, however, important if other people are to find the interactions interesting and rewarding. Asking questions encourages others to talk, to become engaged: but only if the questions are not too private. The list of topics given in the next chapter (see Box 15) might provide some guidance.

HOW CAN SUCH ABILITIES BE LEARNED?

How much can be achieved by social skills and "problem solving" training? This depends on the circumstances and manner in which the training is conducted. Both approaches require several vital ingredients:

coaching and instruction, carefully graded to the skill of the learner;

demonstration and observation of the skills being taught, preferably with the opportunity to observe others learning, but with sufficient support to achieve good performance by the learner;

drawing the learner's attention to the aspects of behaviour to be observed;

practice, both in role play and in real life situations, which will provide rewarding experiences with a sense of achievement;

feedback which emphasises success, not mistakes; and which is able to reward appropriate behaviour in real life settings, both with positive comments and with rewarding experiences.

It should be remembered that many people with learning disabilities are not good at noticing the relevant features of a situation: they may have attention difficulties. If so, it is important to draw their attention to what they need to notice, so they can observe and learn from their own behaviour and that of others.

The most effective form of demonstration, guidance, and feedback in social situations is the behaviour and remarks of other people. A companion or facilitator in a social situation is often in a particularly good position to act as a model as well as to provide prompts in a natural way, for example, with remarks such as "Have you asked Mrs. Pearson about . . . ?", and to provide positive feedback immediately. One particularly useful medium of demonstration, which may easily be overlooked, is television. Some programmes, especially "soap operas" such as Brookside or East Enders, can prove helpful in illustrating both competent and less competent social skills models.

WHAT CAN BE ACHIEVED BY SOCIAL SKILLS AND PROBLEM SOLVING TRAINING?

Social skills training is a popular approach amongst professionals who are trying to help people with learning disabilities achieve an ordinary life in the community. Yet much of this training is quite limited in scope and in form (Robertson, Richardson, and Youngson, 1984), often due to lack of resources or because the people they are helping, or those in close contact with them, feel able to tackle only one problem at a time.

The following two examples (Firth and Firth, 1982) illustrate instances of "successful" social skills teaching:

Miss Masterson, a talkative lady in her forties, had a habit of continually interrupting people. In a social skills group she worked on identifying appropriate points to join a conversation. She began to recognise when she had interrupted inappropriately and to apologise for this.

Miss Lee, a shy and withdrawn lady who spoke very rarely in an almost inaudible whisper, had a tendency to look constantly at the floor. In a group with others living at a hostel she learned to hold up her head and look at people when speaking to them. She also became able to do this outside the group and away from the hostel.

A major problem with some social skills training is that there is little evidence that the skills learned in the "classroom" are actually used outside. Added to this, it often concentrates on the learning of specific behavioural routines or repertoires. Much less attention has been given to aspects such as motivation, or to the broader principles covered by interpersonal problem solving training.

Despite this, the value of specialist social skills training should not be underestimated. Moreover, it appears that teaching programmes which have concentrated on the thinking or "cognitive" aspects of behaviour may have led to the most enduring changes.

WHAT NEEDS TO BE DONE BY THOSE LIVING AND WORKING WITH PEOPLE WITH LEARNING DISABILITIES?

What is most significant is that in everyday life most "social skills training" occurs unconsciously and is provided by people who live and work with individuals with learning disabilities. The opportunity to

Identify their difficulties and their strengths

Enquire at a suitable opportunity whether they are aware of these

Let them know of their strengths and their difficulties, using your own social skills

Offer one or two helpful hints, if desired

Gently remind people of these points when the situation occurs (before, during, or afterwards, as appropriate) using:
    beforehand – gentle reminders
    at the time – discrete prompts or hints
    afterwards – helpful, positive feedback

Remember that it takes time to learn new skills

Try to ensure that the experience of trying out new skills is successful (as far as is possible)

Make sure that trying out new skills is noticed and rewarded, so that the learning experience encourages further attempts to succeed

**BOX 11. Helping people with learning disabilities
to improve their social skills**

practise skills in real life situations where those skills will be rewarded, is one of the most important elements in successful learning. Much of the learning of social skills does *not*, therefore, require teaching by specialist professionals.

There may be some advantages to be gained from "specialist" teaching where it is available. Complex and difficult skills, for example, can be taught intensively with much attention to detail and to successful practice in real settings. This can be especially useful if done in very small groups of, say, three people with a couple of leaders, who can work on a specific area of difficulty, such as how to start a conversation and how to keep it going, or how to ask someone out. Teaching in small groups may have the additional advantage of helping to focus attention on the importance of social skills.

The disadvantages of specialist teaching have been alluded to already. In particular, except where it is provided as part of an educational curriculum over a period of years, it cannot hope to cover half of the social skills that people need in order to form and keep relationships.

Parents naturally teach their children a wide variety of social skills in a more or less conscious way. People who live or work with adults with learning disabilities are also often in a position of consciously teaching the skills of social interaction. This kind of help may be particularly effective if friends, and other people closely involved in the lives of the people being taught, focus on one or two issues at a time, and do not expect their behaviour to change overnight.

Social skills learning is like most other learning which takes place in our lives: it takes place all the time, whether or not we receive formal teaching. We learn many of the important things in the course of everyday life from the people around us, be they friends, family, or workmates.

The most difficult individual habits to change, whether these are a tendency to drop the end of sentences or to come over as bossy, domineering, know-it-alls, will only respond to patient and persistent feedback from close friends and relatives over *long* periods of time. The most useful things which others can do to help people with learning disabilities (see Box 11) are to identify the individual problems, state them clearly, and offer one or two helpful hints. These may need to be repeated gently, without nagging, over a period of many, many months. It may also be important for them to accompany people into real situations, to remind them gently of the issues beforehand, to provide a competent model to imitate, and to make discreet suggestions during the experience. Lastly, they should try to ensure that the whole experience is not only successful but rewarding. Then, even if success is not achieved on every occasion, the learning experience itself will be well rewarded and will encourage further attempts to succeed.

Perhaps we can do no better than remind readers at this point of the chief individual abilities which are needed, in broad terms, to make and maintain relationships. These are:

an awareness and understanding of words describing feelings;

an understanding that others have differing feelings, thoughts, and wishes;

an ability to find out about others' feelings;

being able to think of alternative approaches, and their possible consequences, and to choose how to behave accordingly.

REFERENCES

ARGYLE, M. *The Psychology of Interpersonal Behaviour*. London: Penguin, 1983.

ARGYLE, M., HENDERSON, M. The rules of friendship. *Journal of Social and Personal Relationships*, 1984, 1, 211–237.

ATKINSON, D. How easy is it to form relationships after leaving long-stay hospitals? *Social Work Today*, 1987; 15 June, 18:41, 12–13.

ATKINSON, D. *Someone to Turn To: the social worker's role and the role of front line staff in relation to people with mental handicaps*. Kidderminster: BIMH Publications, 1989.

ATKINSON, D., WARD, L. Friends and neighbours: relationships and opportunities in the community for people with a mental handicap. *In* Malin, N. (Ed.). *Reassessing Community Care*. London: Croom Helm, 1987.

BASS, M. A. S., CAMP, B. W. *Think Aloud: Increasing Social and Cognitive Skills – a Problem-Solving Program for Children. 3. Classroom Program Grades 3-4.* Champaign, Ill.: Research Press, 1985a.

BASS, M. A. S., CAMP, B. W. *Think Aloud: Increasing Social and Cognitive Skills – A Problem-Solving Program for Children. 4. Classroom Program Grades 5-6.* Champaign, Ill.: Research Press, 1985b.

CAMP, B. W., BASS, M. A. *Think Aloud: Increasing Social and Cognitive Skills – A Problem Solving Program for Children. 1. Primary Level.* Champaign, Ill.: Research Press, 1981.

CAMP, B. W., BASS, M. A. *Think Aloud: Increasing Social and Cognitive Skills – A Problem Solving Program for Children. 2. Classroom Program Grades 1-2.* Champaign, Ill.: Research Press, 1985.

CARTLEDGE, G., MILBURN, J. F. *Teaching Social Skills to Children: innovative approaches.* Oxford: Pergamon Press, 1986.

CRAWLEY, B. *The Growing Voice.* London: Campaign for People with Mental Handicaps, 1988.

DINKMEYER, D. *Developing Understanding of Self and Others.* Circle Pines, Minn.: American Guidance Service, 1973.

DUPONT, H., GARDNER, O., BRODY, D. *Towards Affective Development.* Circle Pines, Minn.: American Guidance Service, 1974.

ELARDO, P. T., COOPER, M. *AWARE – Activities for Social Development.* Menlo Park: Addison Wesley Innovative Publishing Division, 1977.

FIRTH, M., FIRTH, H. Improving the interpersonal skills of mentally handicapped people. *Mental Handicap*, 1982; **10**:4, 138–140.

FLYNN, M. C. *A Place of My Own: independent living for adults with mental handicap.* London: Cassell, 1989.

GOFFMAN, E. *Stigma: notes on the management of spoiled identity.* Englewood Cliffs, NJ: Prentice Hall, 1963.

GOLDSTEIN, A. P. Social skills training. *In* Goldstein, A. P., Carr, E. G., Davidson, W. S., Wehr, P., (Eds.). *In Response to Aggression.* Oxford: Pergamon Press, 1981; 158–218.

MATTHEWS, S. H. *Friendships Through the Life Course: oral biographies in old age.* London: Sage Publications, 1986.

RICHARDSON, S. A., KOLLER, H., KATZ, M. Appearance and mental retardation: some first steps in the development and application of a measure. *American Journal of Mental Deficiency*, 1985; **89**, 475–484.

RICHARDSON, A., RITCHIE, J. *Friends, Special Friends and Partners: Working Paper No. 2.* London: Policy Studies Institute, 1988.

RICHARDSON, A., RITCHIE, J. *Developing Friendships: enabling people with learning difficulties to make and maintain friends.* London: Policy Studies Institute/Social and Community Planning Research, 1989.

ROBERTSON, I., RICHARDSON, A. M., YOUNGSON, S. C. Social skills training with mentally handicapped people: a review. *British Journal of Clinical Psychology*, 1984; **23**, 241–264.

RYAN, A., WALKER, R. *Making Life Story Books.* London: British Agencies for Adoption and Fostering, 1985.

SHURE, M. D., SPIVACK, G. *Problem Solving Techniques in Child Rearing.* San Francisco, Cal.: Jossey Bass, 1978.

TROWER, P., BRYANT, B., ARGYLE, M. *Social Skills and Mental Health*. London: Methuen, 1978.

WILKINSON, J., CANTER, S. *Social Skills Training Manual: assessment program design and management of training*. London: Wiley, 1982.

YOUNG, J. E. Loneliness, depression and cognitive therapy: theory and application. *In* Peplau, L. A., Perlman, D. (Eds.). *Loneliness: a current source book of theory, research and therapy*. New York: Wiley-Interscience, 1982.

. . . spending time together, doing something enjoyable is one of the best ways to get to know someone well . . .

CHAPTER EIGHT

Personal attributes in fostering close relationships

ATTITUDES AND SKILLS IN DEVELOPING AND MAINTAINING FRIENDSHIPS

What makes it easier, or more difficult, to find and build close relationships? In Chapter 6 we referred to some situations which might make it easier for people who like each other to get to know one another better; situations where communicating about feelings might be easier. Here, we mention some aspects of people's behaviour which might affect the development of close relationships.

Amongst the most essential attributes people need to form any close relationship are the ability to share something of themselves – to show their feelings – and the ability to respond to the feelings of other people. These abilities are not particularly linked to academic or intellectual proficiency. Indeed, people who can neither talk nor communicate by signs may have the ability both to show their own feelings clearly and to respond appropriately to the feelings of others.

Given these two abilities, close relationships may readily form, especially when individuals spend time in pleasurable activities together. Many of the close friendships which develop out of caring relationships, or between people with learning disabilities and volunteers or "befrienders", do so in this way. Spending time together, doing something enjoyable, over a number of occasions, is one of the best ways to get to know someone well, and for each person to find out if the relationship becomes closer over time. Many people with learning disabilities, however, do not know anyone who wants to spend time with them in this way. This may be because they are isolated, and meet few other people. Or it may be because they are reluctant to approach others, either because they do not know how, or because their approaches have in the past not been rewarding.

Attitudes make a considerable difference to whether people wish to spend time getting to know one another better. Hopson and Scally's

(1980) *Life Skills Teaching Programmes* put especial emphasis on learning the right attitudes, as well as the right skills, in order to make and maintain close relationships. They stress the importance of attitudes of respect, genuineness, and empathy. The attitudes and the skills they believe are important are set out in Boxes 12 and 13.

Hopson and Scally emphasise two particular attitudes which are important in developing close relationships. First, it is necessary to want to spend time getting to know other people well. Second, it is important to recognise that any relationship involves giving as well as getting, and has difficult or unhappy parts as well as fun and closeness.

Much emphasis in homes, schools, and workplaces is inevitably placed on politeness, and socially acceptable behaviour: how to get on with others and avoid antagonising or annoying them. Often, however, people with learning disabilities are not encouraged in the idea that it is really worthwhile to get to know other people well; to share disappointments, anger, and difficulties as well as excitement, hopes, and dreams with other people. People who do not readily learn for themselves from others' experiences, can easily grow up without being sufficiently conscious that close relationships have their downs as well as their ups, and that they involve giving as well as receiving. If people hope to maintain a close relationship with someone – be it a friend, lover, or housemate – they must learn to help, and to give support or attention, not only when they feel like giving it, but when the *other* person wants it.

One of the features of women's traditional role, which was identified in Chapter 3, was that of maintaining and nurturing relationships. It is often

---

Wanting to spend time with other people

Believing that every human being is worthy of respect

Believing that any relationship involves give and take – wanting to give as well as to receive

Being prepared to talk openly but appropriately about ourselves to others

Seeing the value of getting and giving feedback from and to others

Being willing both to give and to receive help – to avoid relationships becoming unequal

Believing people to have mixtures of qualities – both strengths and weaknesses

Believing that most people respond positively when approached positively

Recognising that other people will not always behave how we would like

Realising that we will not like everyone, and that not everyone will like us

---

**BOX 12. Important attitudes in making relationships,
adapted from Hopson and Scally (1980)**

Conveying respect: helping people feel important

Conveying genuineness: coming across as real, not as a phoney

Conveying empathy: communicating that we understand other people; seeing it their way

Continuing self-disclosure: sharing a variety of past and new experiences

Gaining increasing self-awareness

Being positive about ourselves

Managing conflicts effectively

Communicating effectively

Managing negative emotions: developing skills for managing excesses of anger, depression, jealousy, or fear that can threaten any relationship is essential

Giving, receiving, and asking for help

Giving, receiving, and asking for feedback

Being assertive: stating our preferences clearly but not aggressively, and with a willingness to compromise

Adjusting to each other's development, including changing needs

BOX 13. The skills of maintaining and deepening relationships, adapted from Hopson and Scally (1980)

particularly important that the close relationships of people with learning disabilities are nurtured, through maintaining contact and constructing opportunities that allow some intimacy. Both men *and* women with learning disabilities may need encouragement to attend to these habits or skills if their close relationships are not to falter and fail.

Another factor which people have to tolerate in any long-term, close relationship is that the other person will not always behave in the way they would like. Intolerance of other people's habits – their untidiness, their mannerisms, their jokes, their noise, their use of money – can easily be the cause of the end of a relationship if people have not been prepared for the fact that such difficulties occur. Difficulties need to be talked about. One or other of the parties in the relationship needs to agree to try and change or else to accept a situation, if niggling irritation or resentment is not to occur. Nagging is not a useful approach to changing others' habits because, although it may be effective in the short-term, it generally induces resentment and eventually emotional distance. Change by another person takes time. Often it is difficult to judge how much change it is reasonable to expect in someone else, and how quickly.

People may seek to make changes in themselves for a close friend, a lover, or a housemate. They may need support in deciding what changes are reasonable – in the other party and in themselves. Finally, people

. . . offering help when the other person needs it . . .

may need support in deciding whether to stay in a relationship, work at trying to save it, or pull out.

Various skills are likely to be necessary to maintain a close relationship. These include:

offering help when the other person needs it;

being tolerant of the other's weakness or faults;

demonstrating warmth even when disagreements occur;

avoidance of unnecessary jealousy when the other person spends time with other people;

choosing to make criticisms of the other person in private, not in front of others;

helping the other person to have fun and be happy with you;

refraining from "nagging" someone to do, or not do, particular things;

demonstrating interest in the other person and his or her life;

offering, as well as expecting, favours;

allowing the other person some (appropriate) privacy;

keeping confidences;

being rewarding and positive about the other person and what he or she has been doing;

showing trust in the other person;

judging how much of the other person's time it is fair to expect.

These issues are *not* easy for people with learning disabilities to find out about, because they are not usually in any "curriculum" – they are not part of sex education or "social skills training". They are often not part of the basic self-help skills which parents endeavour to make sure their sons and daughters possess. They are all issues, however, which could be talked about in the home, the school, or workplace. They are all topics of which parents and teachers, instructors and tutors, paid staff and volunteers should be aware and with which they should be prepared to help.

A useful view of the skills needed to help relationships develop and deepen is that given by Hopson and Scally (1980). Their list of "Dos and Don'ts" for making relationships work is reproduced in Box 14. It could provide a basis for talking about many situations, both friendships and "girlfriend/boyfriend" relationships, either informally or as part of a school or college curriculum. The material in Box 1 (Chapter 3) from Argyle and Henderson (1984) may also be helpful.

DOs
Listen to what people say
Offer to help
Ask for help
Spend time with them
Talk about what you think and feel
Do things together
Remember what they have told you
Try to compromise if you want to do different things
See things from their point of view sometimes
Be cheerful
Tell them what you like about them sometimes
Be considerate
Be honest
Be consistent
Give and take
Be loyal
DON'Ts
Fight
Tell lies
Moan all the time, be miserable
Talk about people behind their backs
Keep everything to yourself, be secretive
Always try to get your own way
Help them and never ask for help yourself
Always do what they want to do
Tell them everything
Be unreliable
Take and not give

BOX 14. Dos and don'ts for making relationships work,
adapted from Hopson and Scally (1980)

One of the difficulties which often faces young people with learning disabilities is what to say to other people they would like to get to know well, perhaps as a girlfriend or boyfriend. Partly this may be the same kind of difficulty that many of us experience when we are with people we do not yet know well, that is, finding "things to talk about". People, activities, events, shared topics, or public topics can all provide material for conversation (see Chapter 7). Talking about people may be a good way to start exploring feelings and values.

Some people have difficulty in avoiding over-intimate conversation with people they do not (yet) know well. Hopson and Scally (1980) and Taylor and Altman (1966) have given thought to this and offer a number of different kinds of topics, graded roughly according to the appropriate degree of intimacy. These items are reproduced in Box 15. While this list covers only a few possible topics, again it could provide a useful starting point for discussing what it is, and what it is not, appropriate to talk about with different kinds of people, or at different stages in a relationship.

FRIENDSHIPS AND SEXUAL RELATIONSHIPS

Sexual relationships are different from friendships. For many people the two will overlap. Indeed, it is probably true that most sexual relationships are between people who would call each other friends. A few people, involved in more casual sexual relationships, will not. Sometimes a friendship will develop into a sexual relationship between two people. At other times a relationship may initially be motivated primarily by sexual interest but gradually develop into a friendship as well. Sometimes a boyfriend-girlfriend relationship breaks up, only to allow friendship to develop in time.

In this book we have concerned ourselves with friendship. Others have written specifically about sexual and marital relationships (Craft and

---

What kind of place I would like to live in
How often my family get together
Laws that I would like to see put into effect
What animals make me nervous
How often I go out on dates
My feelings about lending money
How angry I get when people push me around
The number of children I want to have after I am married
Who my favourite relatives are and why
How I feel about getting old
How I really feel about other people at work, school, etc.
My feelings about discussing sex with my friends
How much I spend on my clothes
Whether I cry when I am sad
What I am most afraid of
What I do to attract a member of the opposite sex whom I like
Times that I have lied to my girlfriend or boyfriend
The parts of my body I am most ashamed for anyone to see
What really hurts me
How I might feel if I saw my father hit my mother
What birth-control methods I would use
The kinds of things that I do that I do not want people to watch

BOX 15. Things to talk about – according to the degree of intimacy, from Hopson and Scally (1980) and Taylor and Altman (1966)

Craft, 1979, 1983; Craft, 1986; Dixon, 1988). However, many of the points we have made apply equally to sexual relationships. For example, much of the discussion about opportunities to make acquaintances applies equally to the opportunities people have to meet potential boyfriends or girlfriends. Many of the same principles apply in their development: there is a period of acquaintance, which may be short or long, leading to the formation of a relationship. Boyfriends and girlfriends are not easily made by "chatting up" at a disco or bar. Often acquaintances only develop after some time into friendship, on the one hand, or into a "couple" relationship on the other.

There are some particular difficulties which face people with learning disabilities, that have to do with the boundary between sexual and non-sexual relationships. The first is knowing what behaviour is appropriate in testing out or exploring the possibilities of a boyfriend or girlfriend relationship. Many people without disabilities find knowing how far to go, how far is acceptable in "flirting", difficult. This question may present extra difficulties for people with learning disabilities who may need an explanation of what is or is not appropriate, or a chance to experiment and learn from experience and feedback. Much of the discussion about social skills at the end of the previous chapter is relevant for helping them cope with such difficulties.

Another difficulty which may present itself is when a relationship which was a non-sexual friendship takes a possibly sexual turn. Handling such a situation sensitively probably presents most people with great difficulty. They may be uncertain about their interpretation of the other person's behaviour ("Was it a 'pass' or not?"), or about how to react, or what the consequences might be. Sometimes they may not know themselves what they would prefer to happen. It is not easy to offer specific help, but it is important to encourage people to talk about experiences with someone they trust. Also, discussion groups and classes, perhaps making use of video recordings (Elfrida Rathbone Centre, 1988) provide a good opportunity for people to talk about how to handle such situations. This can be of great value, as many people with learning disabilities have lived in situations which have not previously encouraged them to express their true feelings.

Different problems face people who are considering whether to get engaged, or how to handle their marital difficulties. Atkinson (1989) comments on how the issues of engagement, marriage, and sex within marriage were areas frequently discussed between people and their social workers. She also describes how some rather special problems may arise from someone's jealousy of the developing engagement or sexual relationship of his or her friends or companions.

Difficulty in expressing feelings, especially negative feelings, acutely affects many relationships between couples or partners. The ability to express feelings is essential if warm and empathic relationships are to develop between two people. Even when positive feelings can be expressed, many people experience problems in expressing negative or "critical" feelings towards the one person whom they most admire and whose affection they most need. Individuals, especially women, may need the confidence to say "No" in a firm voice. They may, more subtly, need the confidence and self-assurance necessary to say what they like and what they do not like if their close relationships, especially sexual ones, are to survive without bitterness or hurt.

One recent publication (Dixon, 1988) covers some of these issues in a resource book designed for small group teaching, in an exceptionally coherent, straightforward, and practical way. This book comprises exercises which cover not only body awareness, relationships, sexual behaviour, sexual health, and parenting, but also explore self-esteem and ways of attending to individual sensual needs. It discusses specific problem areas, like sexual decision-making and saying no within a relationship, thus addressing precisely the issues at the boundary of sexual and friendly relationships which are not dealt with elsewhere.

REFERENCES

ATKINSON, D. *Someone to Turn To: the Social Worker's Role and the Role of Front Line Staff in Relation to People with Mental Handicaps*. Kidderminster: BIMH Publications, 1989.

CRAFT, A., CRAFT, M. *Handicapped Married Couples*. London: Routledge, 1979.

CRAFT, A., CRAFT, M. *Sex Education and Counselling for Mentally Handicapped People*. Tunbridge Wells: Costello, 1983.

CRAFT, A. *Mental Handicap and Sexuality*. Tunbridge Wells: Costello, 1986.

DIXON, H. *Sexuality and Mental Handicap: an educator's resource book*. Wisbech: Learning Development Aids, 1988.

ELFRIDA RATHBONE CENTRE. *Between Ourselves*. (video, 15 mins.) Hove: Twentieth Century Vixen, 1988.

HOPSON, B., SCALLY, M. *Life Skills Teaching Programmes No. 1*. Leeds: Life Skills Associates, 1980.

TAYLOR, D. A., ALTMAN, I. Intimacy – scaled stimuli for use in studies of interpersonal relations. *Psychological Reports*, 1966; **19**, 729–730.

*. . . opportunities to spend time with and learn from children
who are not disabled . . .*

CHAPTER NINE

What can be done and how can we help?

INTRODUCTION

This chapter is an attempt to bring together the practical things that people in different settings can do. It has been organised in sections, to help describe with differing emphasis what can be done by people with learning disabilities, their relatives and educators, other service workers, and planners and managers.

Like most of this book, this chapter offers options and possibilities for action by individuals. Yet there are some common themes for readers who wish to influence for the better the lives of people with learning disabilities. The starting point for any action might be to ask the question:

What do I (we) want to do about this issue?

Where a number of people are considering this question, be they teachers or relatives, service staff or service managers, a useful beginning may be to organise some training around the themes described in the next chapter. Some of the issues which are especially relevant to the lives of many people with learning disabilities are:

What kinds of choices might individuals have had in the past in their activities and their relationships?

What opportunities do staff, relatives, and others bring through their membership of organisations, particular social worlds, or knowledge of individuals?

What possibilities exist for individuals to learn about relationships from non-disabled people?

What resources might be available in the locality and the wider district?

What changes can be made to improve the range of individuals' choices, opportunities, and access to these resources?

People who wish to help individuals meet acquaintances and form friendships may find it helpful to focus on their own experiences as well:

How did I first meet the friends I now have?

How did I get to know them better?

What helps me in social situations where I do not know people well? (Other people to help the flow? Particular situations or social activities?)

What barriers and difficulties, and what strengths and advantages, do the people I know have in getting to know other people?

What have I learned from other people about relationships?

What specific action can I undertake myself? (Looking again at some of the Boxes in this book may help)

What can I encourage others to do?

Beginning to answer some of these questions may prompt readers to look back again into earlier chapters that seem to be relevant. In reading the rest of this chapter it is helpful to bear in mind three broad issues.

The first is the value to be gained by people with learning disabilities from opportunities to mix with people who do not have disabilities, and to learn from them. Observation and imitation are powerful ways of learning. The combination of the opportunity to accompany and observe significant other people who can act as role models, together with specific hints or teaching in certain areas of relationship skills, can be particularly helpful as a way of improving relationship skills. The need to be able to observe others in this way is as great for people with severe or profound learning disabilities as it is for those with mild degrees of disability.

Second, it is worth recalling the importance of self-confidence as a precondition for effective and rewarding relationships. The suggestions put forward in this chapter will be of little benefit to people whose self-esteem is not supported and nurtured. One of the myriad ways of supporting self-esteem is to help people to have some pride and pleasure in their past; the value of life accounts or the life story should not be underestimated (Ryan and Walker, 1985).

Third, people need places where they can get to know each other. A degree of privacy is essential if some relationships are to survive and grow. Sons and daughters may need a place where they can have some privacy at home. People living in hostels or in hospital may have nowhere they can easily be alone with a visitor or friend, other than a bedroom or dormitory. Bedrooms are not usually appropriate places to meet people, except intimate friends. Staff and others may need to negotiate or agitate to try and ensure that people are provided with an appropriate room in which to meet their friends and acquaintances.

There are several more specific approaches which can be used in differing situations. We now turn to some of these.

WHAT CAN BE DONE BY INVOLVING PEOPLE WITH LEARNING DISABILITIES?

Self-confidence is so important in helping people to make and develop social contacts of any kind, that involving people with learning disabilities in the provision of opportunities and support can itself be important in helping them develop their relationships.

A good example of how this can be done is provided by Skills for People*, which puts on a number of courses in North East England on a variety of themes, one of which is "Making friends". Skills for People involves individuals with learning disabilities in both the planning and running of the courses, all of which aim to help build confidence. Particular sessions offer ways of dealing with common events or problems, such as trying to make a date, saying no, or avoiding an argument.

One very useful idea used has been to make photostrips of the courses. These are picture strips with "bubbles" on what to say and do in different situations. They are made as the courses progress, so they can later act as a reminder of the material presented. This excellent idea is one which other groups and workshops might wish to employ.

Another example of a group which has enabled its members to develop self-confidence in the area of personal and sexual relationships is provided by the Elfrida Rathbone Centre in Islington (1988), which has produced a video tape to illustrate its work.

Self-advocacy can be of enormous help to some people, both as a way of building self-confidence in social situations and as a way of meeting and getting to know others. Self-advocacy is, essentially, "speaking up for oneself". The self-advocacy movement encourages people to make choices and decisions, and to argue and act for themselves.

Crawley (1988) defines self-advocacy as "the act of making choices and decisions and bringing about desired change for oneself". It can be carried out by individuals or by groups of people who wish to learn or practise self-advocacy on their own or each others' behalf. Crawley distinguishes four kinds of self-advocacy groups, as follows.

Autonomous groups that are independent of professional services or wider organisations. Such groups need independent sources of finance and have to take responsibility for organisational issues themselves.

* Skills for People, Haldane House, Tankerville Terrace, Newcastle-upon-Tyne NE2 3AH. Tel. 091-281-8737.

Groups which operate as a division or section of parent organisations which are independent of professional services or agencies. Parent organisations can provide money and administrative back-up for groups set up in this way.

Coalition groups which bring together individuals from a wide number of fields or organisations (for example, groups including people with different kinds of disability).

Groups that are integral to a particular agency or service, such as those formed in adult training centres, which can provide premises and support. There is, however, a potential conflict of interest with this kind of group, which may find its work difficult or may even find itself closed down if agency staff decide it is not effective or worthwhile (Shearer, 1986). Some groups become only an extension of the agencies' activities which greatly reduces their impact and effectiveness.

Until recently there were few self-advocacy groups in Great Britain. This has changed radically over the past few years and there are now many groups in existence here. The majority by far fall into the last of the types described: they are groups formed within adult training centres, sixty per cent of which reported having a self-advocacy group or student committee made up mainly of trainees (Crawley, 1988). By contrast, autonomous groups set up to help people leaving hospital have been more common in the USA.

The groups in adult training centres in this country have reported a variety of achievements, mostly practical arrangements in services provided. Many have apparently been effective in improving the skills of individual members, and in enhancing participants' self-esteem and self-awareness. Some of their difficulties have been a lack of skill on the part of staff running groups and group members' conflict with staff.

Crawley (1988) has provided some helpful discussion of some of the difficulties faced by self-advocacy groups, both outside and inside training centres and hospitals. The King's Fund Centre (1988) has published an account of two workshops on self-advocacy skills training, which contains many helpful ideas about how to set up and manage groups. Williams and Shoultz (1982) have described the various approaches to self-advocacy. Cooper and Hersov (1986) have also produced valuable resource material for education on this subject.

WHAT CAN BE DONE BY PARENTS AND RELATIVES?

Spending time with other young people

Learning how to get on with other people takes a long time. Our learning starts very early: while we are toddlers, if not before. Parents have a special role to play, therefore, through the opportunities they help to provide. We have made reference earlier (Richardson and Ritchie, 1986, 1989a, 1989b) to the particular issues faced by parents whose sons and daughters with learning disabilities are adolescents or young adults. Here, we wish rather to focus on the part families can play in helping young children.

One of the greatest contributions families can make whilst children with disabilities are young is to foster and support their opportunities to spend time with and learn from children who are not disabled. Children and young people learn from each other, generally much faster than from adults.

Other children can be very cruel to those whom they see as different in some way. Flynn (1989) has documented the extent to which physical appearance can be associated with victimisation, and Jahoda, Markova, and Cattermole (1988) have described the stigma which some people experience and its effects on their self-concept. Gottlieb and Leyser (1981) also found that "visibility" of children affected acceptance by their peers. Dress and appearance were important factors, but acceptability was greatly affected, they argued, by children's social behaviour. They commented that social integration:

> "will not produce positive attitude change (amongst non-disabled children) unless the retarded children can be taught to exhibit behaviour that conforms to the standards expected by their non-retarded peers . . .".

Integration alone will not provide the right attitudes to enable non-disabled children to accept children with disabilities. Gottlieb and Leyser (1981) argued that opportunities for integration needed to be supplemented with the necessary support: either to teach appropriate appearance, habits, and social behaviour; or to mediate in the relationships between children with and without disabilities.

If young people are to be able to make friends they need, above all, to be rewarding to other young people. Also, they must not be too lacking in initiative, or too aggressive, bossy, or quick-tempered. It may be worthwhile spending time on such things as learning to understand jokes, learning to tell them, and learning to be the butt of them: the kind of skills which are not generally taught in school.

As we have emphasised, helping children mix and learn from others requires both opportunities and support. The support might come from a parent supervising children playing at home, from a teacher working with children with learning disabilities in a larger class, from family members who gently teach age-appropriate social behaviour as part of day-to-day living, or from school in offering coaching for pupils with relationship difficulties. Parents have a role in providing these kinds of support, both directly at home and indirectly in encouraging schools to do so.

. . . Volunteers and others have something to offer . . . the
time and commitment to follow through an enabling role . . .

How to make an early start

This discussion highlights the need for early intervention to prevent, or reduce, any socially inappropriate behaviour at the earliest possible stage.

Parents will teach traffic sense or self-care habits to their children from when they are quite small. Why should they not teach basic relationship skills about how to make, and how to keep, friends? In other areas where skills are needed, such as in using an electric drill, or making Yorkshire puddings, most parents' preference is to teach by demonstration, as well as by instruction.

Surprisingly, however, when it comes to their children's behaviour, parents often prefer to rely solely on the spoken word. Advice or instruction alone, sometimes embellished with explanation, is the norm. Parents rarely demonstrate, prompt, or guide. Yet making and keeping friends involves a great deal of skill – in fact, many individual skills – with similarities to cooking a meal or riding a bicycle.

Often adults show a curious reluctance to become involved in helping children get along with others. The most appropriate method of teaching the skills required to do this will vary according to each child's age and ability. In the long term, teaching such skills may have a very important outcome.

The best approach for parents is probably to identify one, two, or three particular skills to work on over a period of time. Frequent positive suggestions and reminders about actions involving these skills over a period of time can often be the most effective way to get particular points across. It is important always to emphasise the successes, and not the failures.

A particular focus

There are several kinds of skill on which it may be worth focusing attention at different levels over many years. They are illustrated in some of the boxes in Chapter 7.

The first of these is *observation* of others and their reactions and responses. Young people who are better at making and maintaining friends have been found to be more accurate and more detailed in their observations of their peers. Teaching young people to observe others' behaviour carefully, and to interpret others' feelings and attitudes, appears to be vital in the process of helping them learn how to get on with others.

The second area concerns not observation, but *thinking*. Shure and Spivack (1975, 1978) have described the skills of thinking about how to behave in tricky situations. Young people who have little speech and communication may not know or understand the words that describe emotions. They may need to be taught the meanings of sad, angry, cross, hurt, upset, pleased, excited, glad, surprised, unhappy, bored, or worried.

They may also need to be reminded to think, consciously and carefully, about what others might be feeling and thinking. Young people, with or without learning disabilities, may not be able to get on easily with others because they lack the skills of thinking of alternative ways of behaving, and choosing the best approach.

It is helpful to be able to think of different ways of reacting to any particular situation. When somebody ignores you, do you walk away, ask them another question, speak louder, try later, get angry, or try a different approach? The ability simply to realise that there are different courses of action, and to think of at least two, is important in getting on well with other people.

It is useful to be able to guess how other people might react. If I get annoyed, will they reject me, will they get angry, will they not ask me to join them next time, or will they just answer back? It takes skill to be able to judge this. Reminders and discussion can at least help people to learn that others, too, may react in one of several different ways. It is helpful, too, to be able to put these skills together, make a decision about what is best, and try it out. All this requires much practice if decisions are to be made in time to respond appropriately to others.

There is a further major area in which parents and others should attempt to "teach" young people social skills. One of the most important of these skills is the ability to *distinguish* between aspects of different social situations: between family and work, between meetings with acquaintances and friends, between behaviour that is appropriate with the young and with the elderly. It is this kind of process, of distinguishing between the social rules that operate in different social situations, which is least often taught in social skills training programmes. Nevertheless, it is the kind of thing which parents, relatives, and friends can fairly easily talk about on a day-to-day basis.

Finally, there is a need to encourage and help young people to find the right way, the right time and place, and the right words to *express emotions*. Sharing feelings, joy as well as hurt, is vital to close relationships. Young people with learning disabilities may have to be encouraged to do so; otherwise the many disappointments, barriers, and rejections they experience in their lives may lead them to keep their feelings to themselves for fear of further hurt.

How might this work in practice?
Parents and relatives are well placed to support young people in learning from their encounters with others. It is possible for them to do much in the course of day-to-day interaction, both by discussion and by example. Some of the possibilities for learning through discussion are illustrated in Box 16.

Television provides many useful examples of good and poor social skill and problem solving. If using it for teaching such skills a video recorder is

Helping them to observe ("Did you see the expression on her face?")

Teach the meaning of words expressing emotions ("He looked down-in-the-mouth. Maybe he was cross. I wonder why. Perhaps . . .")

Encourage attention to others' likely feelings and reactions ("How do you think she felt?")

Encourage them to think of more than one way of reacting ("What else could you have done?")

Get them to think of what else might have happened ("Actually he turned away – but he might have done something else . . . What else might he have done? . . . well, might he have shouted at you?")

Help them choose the best course of action ("Let's go through that again . . . What do you think, now, would have been best?")

Help them learn from experience ("Why do you think she did that?")

Help them learn from suggested courses of action ("Why not ask her . . . ?")

Help them learn by suggested remedies for difficulties ("Next time, why don't you . . . ?")

Help them learn from demonstrations of particular behaviour ("Look, when John does something for me, I always thank him")

Encourage persistence ("Try again tomorrow")

Encourage motivation and commitment ("Don't wait for them – you go and ask")

Encourage reciprocity ("It is your turn to invite someone") and offers to help or do something *for* others

Emphasise the need to keep up and nurture friendships ("Have you seen Julie recently? Maybe you should go and see her tomorrow?")

Help distinguish the difference between various kinds of social situations ("Yes, but she was his girlfriend . . .")

Box 16. Areas where parents or educators can help young people learn

helpful, allowing particular sequences to be "frozen" or repeated. As we have already noted, some of the popular British soap operas, such as *Brookside, East Enders,* and *Coronation Street,* provide useful illustrations.

Activities
We have already pointed out the importance of doing things with people as a way of making relationships. We will not elaborate this further here, except to emphasise its importance and to stress how difficult it is to meet people if most spare time is only spent at home with the family, or on hobbies alone.

WHAT CAN BE DONE BY EDUCATORS – IN SCHOOLS, FURTHER EDUCATION, AND ADULT EDUCATION?

It may seem surprising that, although the nation spends vast sums teaching its young people skills, teaching does not include the personal skills which are so crucial to effective working and social relationships in later life. Given the influence that relationships have on the nature and quality of the lives of people with learning disabilities, it is increasingly important for teachers and those who plan education to address themselves to the whole area of interpersonal and relationship skills. Apart from the influence of family and upbringing, education has perhaps the greatest contribution to make *in the long term* to their ability to make and sustain rewarding relationships. This is so for several reasons.

First, the education system is the one place, above all others, where young people can learn the personal skills needed to make relationships, both through the formal teaching and learning process, and by the natural demonstration, imitation, and modelling of other young people.

Second, integrated schooling could provide, we think, far more opportunities for young people with learning disabilities to meet peers without disabilities, who could communicate with them, from whom they could learn, and who have open to them access to a wide range of activities and relationships. In the very long term the changes in attitude toward people with learning disabilities, which would be entailed by integrated education, accompany, and follow from it, would mean they would be able to experience a range of opportunities for making relationships that would be more like those other young people have.

Geographical proximity can be important to the friendships young people form. One effect of segregated education of those with moderate and severe learning disabilities, through the large catchment areas of special schools, is that it is much more difficult for them to meet their schoolfriends outside of the school situation. Cheseldine and Jeffree (1981) identified this problem in their survey of handicapped adolescents. They are disadvantaged in two ways: they attend a different school from their neighbours, and they may not be able to meet their schoolfriends outside of school. Only integrated and supported placements within existing junior and secondary schools will overcome this problem.

Third, a wide range of experiences and opportunities to learn about relationships would enhance the social skills and the social opportunities available to young people with learning disabilities after leaving school.

Available evidence, however, indicates that such benefits will not accrue without an active process, and efforts to support integration into mainstream classes (Gottlieb and Leyser, 1981). Contact and physical presence alone are not sufficient to ensure effective integration in relationships. The concept of a link person, an enabler, as part of this active process has been tried in some further education settings in ways which have been very successful in helping the social integration of students. For example, the "Gateway 2" scheme described by Shearer (1986) integrated students with learning disabilities in keep fit, cookery, music, yoga, and typing classes by a two-stage process. During an introductory course, which emphasised how to meet people, talk to them, and make relationships, they were able to learn and practise social skills. Following this, they were paired with existing members of the regular class.

Educators need to prepare young people for the roles they might take on in adulthood. One central issue, in preparing young people with learning disabilities for later relationships, is to encourage them to be or become interested in other people, in *their* experiences, views, and interests. Encouraging appropriate ways of expressing feelings and emotions is also important if they are to be helped to communicate, and subsequently to develop close relationships.

The teaching skills educators possess could be invaluable for the targeted teaching of personal skills and attitudes which could help their students later make successful relationships. Much of what has been explored in Chapters 2, 3, 7, and 8 provides material for this important educational task. It is sufficient here to state the task and refer to some examples of approaches which have been developed and tried out.

As we have already stated, video recordings of material from television can be especially useful, in conjunction with other approaches for demonstrating and discussing social skills and their consequences. Demonstration and discussion, however, need to be supported by other measures, some of which are worth mentioning here.

Shure and Spivack (1978) have put together an extensive programme for use by teachers, with many examples of how teachers and parents can help young people in their relationships. Their approach has been discussed and illustrated in Chapter 7. A useful summary of their rationale is presented by Shure (1981). It was devised for young people without learning disabilities, and, as such, is geared to the kinds of relationships they need to make with their peers in a local community. This thinking has been developed into an extensive set of classroom curricula (the *Think Aloud* programme) for children and young people of different ages and abilities (Bass and Camp, 1985a,b; Camp and Bass, 1981, 1985).

Hopson and Scally (1980) have also drawn on many different ideas and approaches to develop a major curriculum and set of exercises on *Lifeskills Teaching*. This includes a great deal of material on developing relationships which is particularly suitable for older children and young adults.

Oden and Asher (1977) have pioneered and developed (Oden, 1986) a "coaching" approach for young people with social skill difficulties, focusing on the following four areas:

participation;

cooperation;

communication;

being rewarding.

These are illustrated more fully in Box 17.

Oden (1986) has described how coaching techniques have developed which can be employed in activities such as creative arts experiences and small group games. Such coaching involves:

individual instruction in the behaviours which may help individuals;

encouragement to help individuals suggest specific actions they could take;

Target behaviours for individual instruction and practice

Participation:
get involved
get started
pay attention to the activity

Cooperation:
take part, but allow others to do so also
share materials
make a suggestion if you have a problem
give an alternative if you disagree

Communication:
talk with the other person
say things about the activity or about yourself
ask questions about the activity
ask questions about the other person
listen when the other person talks
look at the other person to see how he or she is doing

Being rewarding:
give some attention to the other person
say something nice (or positive) to the other person sometimes
smile sometimes
have fun with the other person
offer some help or suggestions
give some encouragement to the other person when appropriate

**Box 17. Social skills coaching, using cooperative
activities as a focus, from Oden (1986)**

opportunity for individuals to practise the skills they learn;

positive feedback on performance immediately afterwards;

encouragement and suggestions to enable the skills learned to be transferred and used outside the coaching sessions.

These programmes have been tried and tested for children who do not play or socialise with their peers, or who are not included in play because others regard them as "handicapped". Classmates have also been taught strategies for involving them in their activities in order to support such efforts. Furman (1984) describes some of these approaches. More recently, researchers have begun systematic comparisons of the effectiveness of such coaching strategies, often referred to as "peer-tutoring", with "befriending" strategies, as alternative ways of teaching skills to children with disabilities, and altering attitudes amongst their peers. Both strategies currently appear to be valuable (Haring *et al.*, 1987).

The most comprehensive overview of social skill teaching approaches with children to date is undoubtedly that by Cartledge and Milburn (1986). They describe a considerable number of assessment and teaching approaches in some detail, and refer to several educational curricula.

WHAT CAN VOLUNTEERS AND OTHER MEMBERS OF LOCAL COMMUNITIES DO?

One traditional role for volunteers working with people with learning disabilities has been that of companion. Befriending schemes have recently extended this role by encouraging volunteers to try to *be* a friend. Is this possible? We have argued that it may be, in individual circumstances, but not as a matter of course. This is because friendship primarily involves a free choice by each party.

We have tried to go beyond this and put forward a vital role; that of facilitating opportunities for people to make acquaintances and develop relationships. The role we would encourage is that of a "bridge" or "enabler" between individuals with learning disabilities and acquaintances and activities which might offer those individuals opportunities to get to know other people. Volunteers and others in the community have something to offer here which only they may be able to give: the time and commitment to follow through such an enabling role. What might this role look like in practice? Some possible ingredients are shown in Box 18.

Enablers may need to do more than provide or encourage activities, membership, or participation in clubs of one kind or another. They may need to provide support to ensure that individuals who have some appropriate skills are given necessary prompts or reminders to use them at the moment they are needed. Much "behind the scene" effort may be required to do this, by way of preparatory work with other people. Additionally, it may be necessary to accompany individuals in chosen activities, where it may often be quite appropriate, and very important, quite literally to "whisper in their ear" to prompt or remind them about what to do or how to behave.

One starting point for this kind of support may be to construct a "relationship map". This is simply a list or diagram of all of someone's relatives, acquaintances and friends, work relationships, and other contacts. Such "maps" can be used to begin to find people who can help in one way or another: people who can find out information, help with one or more of the roles listed in Box 17, act as a companion, or quite simply be "looked up".

It is probably helpful to involve other people wherever possible. The chairman of a local enthusiasts' club might be approached, for example, and might agree to provide an introduction to members of the club, ensuring that the person with a learning disability and the accompanying enabler are introduced to a few people on their first evening. The chairman might be able to give some thought as to which club members might be best at helping the new member fit in, might even mention to one or two people beforehand that they would probably be coming that evening, might give them their names and some information about them (such as whether they had moved into the area recently), just as they

---

Getting to know individuals and helping them to consider or express their interests and preferences

Acquiring information about what is available locally

Helping individuals to "sample" a variety of activities not previously experienced

Talking with other people about what they could offer – especially by way of information or people they could approach

Approaching organisations, such as colleges and voluntary services, for opportunities to contribute, help, or learn

Approaching specific people with a request to help facilitate an introduction

Accompanying individuals in activities and social encounters to provide support and advice

Talking about individuals' experiences afterwards to help with any difficulties, identify preferences, and consider ideas for the future

Getting in touch with people after events to thank them for their help and to discuss any problems

Box 18. Possible roles for volunteers, relatives, and service workers

Getting information on local organisations, groups, activities

Helping to arrange initial meetings

Introducing people

Speaking to the people involved beforehand, to give them some information about each other that will help make the encounter rewarding, for example, reminding them of people's names, jobs, where they come from, and what they are interested in

Presenting the person with a learning disability in as valued a manner as possible

Helping to cement the initial introduction with appropriate conversation or activity

Prompting the person with a learning disability beforehand or during the actual interaction, possibly by whispered hints or unobtrusive prompts, such as "You were telling me yesterday about what you did at the weekend . . ."

Staying and helping to support activity and conversation if the person with a disability is socially unskilled or uncertain what to say, or if the person without a disability is equally shy, embarrassed, or uncertain what to say to someone with a disability

Suggesting another meeting or reminding people to arrange to meet again

Talking about the event afterwards so that what was said and done is not forgotten

Giving feedback to the people involved, including specific advice, guidance, or comment for either party

Helping the person with a disability to learn from the experience, suggesting alternative courses of action in preparation for future encounters

Box 19. What "enabling" introductions might involve

would for any other new member who might be shy or ill at ease when joining the group. The enabler would be able to ease the flow of conversation, and possibly make some acquaintances which could be followed up on later occasions. Afterwards, the enabler can discuss with the person how the time went, and may be able to offer a couple of helpful comments or ideas for next time.

Enablers can also help by finding out information about what kinds of activities and organisations are available locally, not only from official sources, but by talking to people about what they know of their locality or possibilities nearby. Having found a suitable activity in which the person with a disability seems interested, some of the ideas given in Box 19 may be helpful. The book *Breaking Barriers*, by McConkey and McCormack

(1983), may also be useful in providing ideas about how to facilitate introductions to new people.

WHAT CAN BE DONE BY SERVICE WORKERS?

The role of service workers in helping people make and develop friendships is not to provide those friendships themselves. Their task is to help create opportunities and to help ensure support for people in using them.

Creating opportunities

Service workers have much to contribute in helping create opportunities for people to develop friendships and relationships. The issues have already been thoroughly explored in Chapter 6 and will not be repeated here. Very often service workers, both direct care staff and other professionals, are in a position to act as "enablers" in the ways we have described earlier in this chapter in relation to volunteers and others in the community. We will not reiterate all the points here but we do wish to emphasise the importance of the enabling role which staff can perform. Getting to know the neighbourhood and the resources within it is one important task; constructing a "relationship map", as already described, can prove another particularly useful first step in helping people meet new acquaintances.

Service agencies, however, need to be careful that their staff are pursuing the wishes of service users and are not imposing unwanted relationships upon them. A particular danger is that of "over activity", in other words, scheduling a whole variety of activities for people without allowing them time to relax, or to develop activities and relationships of their own choosing. People's need for privacy may also require careful attention. Their ability to spend time alone with friends of their own choice has already been stressed. Service workers may often be able to help make this possible.

On what, then, should service workers focus? First, they may need to consciously reappraise the priority which their agency gives to issues that affect the relationships of service users. This is *not* a plea for services to "make provision for friendships"; indeed, such provision may be quite inappropriate. Some vocational services, for example, might consider the acquisition of marketable work skills as a prime objective, and it might not be appropriate for them to allocate time and resources to the teaching of interpersonal skills. Even so, there are ways in which they could increase the opportunities of service users. They could, for instance, provide one canteen where service users, workers, and supervisors could mix and socialise. They could site their premises in a city commercial district rather than an out-of-town trading estate, which might make it easier for service users to attend social or leisure activities after work.

They could provide some guidance and training for workers and service users on their workplace attitudes and interpersonal behaviour.

It is certainly *not* appropriate for services to take it upon themselves to "provide friendships" (King's Fund Centre, 1988). Instead, they should aim to support people's ability to lead ordinary lives within a community of acquaintances and friends of their own choosing.

Service staff may need to go through some of the training stages suggested in the next chapter, to grasp the kinds of opportunities which may need to be sought. People meet new friends, and keep up existing relationships, in a variety of very individual ways which reflect their personalities, age, sex, and class. Staff need to be alert and sensitive to these issues if they are to be able to create the *right* opportunities for people to meet others, whether their choice is other young people at a disco, or one close friend in town for tea each week. Some people may want to meet others who share their interest in cars or embroidery; others may wish to get to know their neighbours. Staff might be able to help, by arranging events and introductions, involving others to act as "enablers", or simply finding out about local events, costs, and public transport. The information in Chapters 3 and 6, the issues in Chapter 5, and the ideas from Chapter 10 can, we believe, be put together by staff to meet a very wide variety of individual circumstances.

The single most important action staff can take is to find one person who can take on an enabling role for a service user. The enabler can simultaneously act as a "model" of appropriate behaviour, be someone with whom the service user can share experiences, and facilitate other social contacts (see Boxes 17 and 18).

Citizen advocacy (Sang and O'Brien, 1984) offers one effective way of involving other people to help individuals. The advocate's role covers two of the strands just mentioned. One is the "instruments" role of helping to solve practical problems: in this case, helping to facilitate social encounters. The other is the "expressive" role: listening to and sharing experiences. This is essential if the advocate is to be able, when necessary, to communicate or advocate for the individual. Richardson and Ritchie (1989a) have provided a helpful discussion of the ways in which citizen advocacy schemes can help people to develop friendships.

One point deserves special mention here. Very often, work connections and relationships may be very distinct from relationships outside of work, and professionals and care staff supporting people in their homes or residential settings may be unaware of relationships made at work and *vice versa*. A very deliberate effort may be needed to develop a relationship from acquaintance in one setting, for example, work, towards a closer friendship extending beyond that setting. People who know an individual well may be able to offer suggestions, encouragement, or prompts about how or when it is best to do this: but this does require familiarity with the individual's relationships both at work and outside work.

Staff also have an obligation to pay attention to the opportunities people have for keeping up existing relationships. People may need privacy or support to maintain contact with friends and acquaintances. When people move house, and particularly when they leave hospital, staff may need to suggest or provide opportunities for them to maintain contact with the people they leave behind.

Providing support

The second major role which service workers can fulfil, or help ensure that others fulfil, is to support people with learning disabilities in their relationships with others. This may involve a great deal of sensitive and time-consuming attention to personal attitudes and skills (discussed in Chapters 7 and 8), as well as more practical support appropriate to an enabling role (Box 18). They also have a particularly valuable, but easily neglected, role in supporting others, such as volunteers, who may need guidance and advice themselves as they act as "enablers".

One especially common form of *poor* support occurs when staff (or others) attach little importance to people's lack of previous opportunities and learning experiences, rationalising their present poor social skills and behaviour as being either their "fault", or their choice, or part of their personality.

Identifying specific, poorly developed social or interpersonal skills, which might present people with problems in making relationships, is a key task for staff. The important and sometimes subtle requirement here is to be able to identify whether people have any particular difficulties which can act as barriers in developing relationships and, if so, to pinpoint them accurately. Once this is done, there is much that can be achieved on a day-to-day basis, with or without formalised social skills training. Much has already been said about this in Chapters 7 and 8, and also in the earlier section in this chapter on what can be done by parents and relatives. We would like to emphasise here the importance of being able to recognise and communicate feelings, in order to maintain and develop closer relationships.

Another issue with implications for service workers is the importance of providing people with experiences of various kinds as a basis for conversational topics. Many people with learning disabilities will have had a very limited range of experience in comparison to other people. They may therefore not be able to converse on many topics. There may, thus, be enormous value in involving them in a wide variety of experiences and activities, outside of segregated provision, in order to give them something "ordinary" to talk about.

Helping people with learning disabilities to present themselves so that their appearance, as far as possible, does not distinguish them from others is also important if others are not to reject or victimise them. Occasionally, medical advice may need to be sought to correct or disguise physical deformities. More often, service workers may need to help people consider, not only their dress and hair styles, but also such features as posture and gait. As we discussed more fully in Chapter 7, particular attention may need to be paid to facial expression (Richardson, Koller and Katz, 1985; Flynn, 1989).

Facilitating good introductions, including preparation beforehand and follow-up afterwards, is a vital part of creating social opportunities. It is essential, however, that service workers do not think that they should always, or even often, perform these functions themselves. There are advantages in involving others wherever possible, provided they are clearly briefed.

People who are going to facilitate introductions need to know exactly what is expected of them. McConkey and McCormack (1983) list a number of issues for which some thought or preparation may be necessary, such as maintaining people's status and allowing people choices in any social encounter, such as whether, and when, to leave. They also offer useful "rules of thumb" for those who have not previously met anyone with a learning disability, such as: "Share your thoughts"; "Ask again if you don't understand"; "Be yourself". We have added to these ideas some further thoughts on what the enabling process might involve, which are set out in Box 18.

Staff who wish to pursue these approaches, must first find people who will be willing to act as enablers, if asked. They might include their own close and distant relatives, friends, work contacts, teachers, household members, and neighbours, or those of people they are seeking to help. Additionally, people who live in the neighbourhood or members of local organisations in influential positions, who may or not already be known, can be approached to take on enabling roles.

Service workers will not always be familiar with this role. They may be more used to providing support or arranging events themselves. If staff are to facilitate and support the relationships of the people with whom they work, they will need to undertake careful preparation, enquiry, and diplomatic approaches to seek out and involve *other* people who can provide additional help in involving people with learning disabilities in social activities.

WHAT CAN BE ACHIEVED BY SPECIALIST PROJECTS?

We have emphasised elsewhere in this book that there are limitations to project-based approaches to helping people develop relationships. It is therefore worth highlighting what kinds of needs can be met especially effectively by "specialist" projects.

Besides parental influences, probably the most significant long-term influence on the social relationship of people with learning disabilities will be the impact of education. Hence, projects which aim to develop educational curricula, add to existing curricula, or provide education in the area of personal relationships are of particular importance.

A different kind of project-based approach is the provision of advice, suggestions, information, or guidance – to individuals, relatives, staff in residential, day, or field services, community workers, and volunteers. An advice and information service can be a useful, cost-effective way of reaching many people who require support or ideas.

Projects can set out to develop the role of "enablers" in primary, secondary, or adult education settings, in vocational settings, and elsewhere. They can thus have a considerable impact on the lives of people who are served by those taking on an enabling role.

Citizen Advocacy type programmes can bring two major benefits. First, they are likely to involve advocates who will act for and link with a number of other people and may do so over a prolonged period of time, in contrast to many staff in the lives of people with learning disabilities who frequently come and go. Second, the one-to-one relationship between individuals and their advocates can be important in itself, as well as being a source of further relationships (Richardson and Ritchie, 1989a; Sang and O'Brien, 1984). Conversely, there is the potential disadvantage of Citizen Advocacy as an approach, which it shares with volunteer programmes: a possible dependence on one found "friend".

A further avenue which projects can usefully address is that of providing companionship which may fulfil a need that is very important to some people. Some projects of this kind describe themselves as "providing friends" or "befriending" people with learning disabilities (Lyons, 1986; Walsh, 1985a,b). One scheme which set out very specifically to provide "friends", or more accurately "companions", has been described by Walsh (1986). Its aims included:

> providing each of the people in the scheme with a companion;

> expanding their experiences through social events with their companions, or in recreational activities;

> encouraging acceptance and integration of people with disabilities into everyday life;

> giving families a break during which someone else would care for their son or daughter.

The scheme linked volunteers to the recipients, people with learning disabilities, most of whom lived with their parents. The volunteers invited them to their homes, or accompanied them in some activity. Most of the activities undertaken might be regarded as unremarkable, except that they occurred in settings where there were few, if any, other people with learning disabilities. This was in marked contrast to much of the activity of the recipients prior to joining the scheme. Whilst it is highly questionable whether such schemes provide friendship, they do fulfil an often much needed function in providing companionship. Some of these companion relationships may possibly develop into close friendships.

Richardson and Ritchie (1989a) have provided a particularly valuable discussion of the ways in which a number of different models of befriending schemes work in practice in this country, and the effects of these schemes on the relationships of their users. Although they comment very positively on the benefits of many of the schemes they visited, they note that, under some circumstances, the relationships can become very "closed", and people with learning disabilities can become increasingly dependent on their befrienders.

The ideas we have just put forward represent a few directions which specialist projects could take.

The benefits and possible shortcomings of social skills training projects have been discussed already (Chapter 7). Very different professional models and approaches have historically been involved in attempts to maximise the presence of people with learning disabilities in the community, and to overcome their difficulties or teach them appropriate skills in the course of step-by-step habilitation or rehabilitation programmes. These differences of approach are now beginning to be overcome. It would, therefore, be pleasing to see the establishment of projects which adopted a systematic approach to providing new opportunities for meeting people, and then offered further support by helping people to learn particular social skills to enable them to gain the greatest possible benefit from such opportunities.

WHAT CAN BE DONE BY SERVICE MANAGERS AND PLANNERS?

Probably the most important contribution which service managers and planners can make is to be aware of the importance of personal relationships – including friendship – to people's mental and physical health and to their quality of life. We have argued repeatedly that it is not possible to arrange for people to have friends, whether through friendship schemes or otherwise. It should certainly be possible to provide people with companions. It should also be possible to ensure that individual projects or services are aware that people with learning disabilities may wish to meet people and make friends, and to ensure that steps are taken which make this easier, rather than more difficult.

What kind of steps?
Primarily, services should not hinder people's ability to make and maintain their own relationships. Community services should not prescribe where people should live or when they should move in such a way as to unnecessarily disrupt their relationships. Provision of small segregated and isolated residential establishments can effectively prevent the people who live in them from making contact with others who are not

. . . If people choose to move . . . they should be helped to keep in touch with people they already know . . .

disabled in their local neighbourhood. Segregated services of any kind restrict people's ability to develop relationships of their choice. Staffing numbers, lack of flexible budgets, and staff attitudes can all hinder or dissuade service users from making social relationships outside of their residence or place of work.

One of the most basic needs of people with learning disabilities is privacy. Some people who have left hospital have expressed their prime reason for doing so as a desire for a room of their own. Richardson and Ritchie (1989a), in their interviews with people with learning disabilities, documented lack of privacy as a major barrier to their ability to make and maintain close friendships. A single lounge or sitting room in a house does not permit one member of the household any privacy for entertaining friends if others are using the room at the same time, to talk, listen to music, or watch television.

Careful thought is required to make sure that, when people move, their relationships are disrupted as little as possible. If people choose to move from hospital to live in the community, or to leave home, or to move from one locality to another, they should be helped to keep in touch with people they already know, if they so wish. This may mean making special provision in budgets for transport, over and beyond what would usually be needed by someone living in a particular locality. Visiting people regularly, whether they be a few miles away or thirty miles away, is expensive. Services which in the past have separated people from friends and relatives should at least contribute to minimising further disruption of their social contacts when the process is repeated as a result of changed policies some years later.

We have stressed repeatedly that acquaintances and friends are made and developed by doing things together with other people. We have pointed out also the frequent need for a third person, to enable and support many such activities.

Two requirements follow from this. Organisers of schemes, who wish to maximise people's chances of making acquaintances and friends, will need first to make sure it is easy for them to join in a variety of activities locally. Secondly, they will need to ensure that sufficient staff are available to support this process, either indirectly or directly. They may well need to provide an appropriate range of work or training schemes in order to achieve this.

The availability of transport dramatically alters people's chances of access to a great variety of activities. Where people live in relation to the vocational and social centres of local population, therefore, is most important. If discos, night-school, gardening, angling, or model building are the preferred activities of various individuals, then it is important that where they work and where they live are within reasonable access of social clubs, colleges of further education, allotments, rivers and ponds, or model building shops.

If staff or volunteers are to help people develop their interests, and spend time in company with others, they may need to devote time: either directly or by involving others. In the long run it can be more effective to involve others in the role of enablers. In the short-term this takes time and energy. Neither kind of work is possible in projects that are run on a shoe-string.

Recruitment and training

The importance given to recruitment and training will have an impact on the selection of staff, whether in residential, vocational, or other kinds of project. Particular qualities may be needed, either to introduce people with learning disabilities to new activities and new relationships, or to engage others in such a process. These qualities will vary enormously according to circumstance. The ability to think creatively, to involve others enthusiastically while tactfully suggesting to them the role they may need to play, to gently persist in making sure that opportunities are not lost, are all the kinds of qualities which may be needed.

Staff training, therefore, is an area to which project leaders, planners, and senior management will need to give attention. It may be needed to sensitise staff or volunteers to the issues involved. It may help to identify particular needs, help explore choices, or offer support to people facing difficulties in their relationships. The next chapter will outline some areas which may usefully be addressed in such training.

It may also be desirable for job descriptions, for example, in field social work and community nursing services, to refer explicitly to relationship issues if supporting people within their own social networks is seen as part of the core service priorities (see also Chapter 6). In services of this kind, as well as in residential services of all kinds, policies may need to be developed to draw staff attention to the need to support people's choices in this area, and to avoid hindering, damaging, or breaking their relationships through lack of proper attention and action. The current initiatives to reduce or close hospitals, place them at particular risk of disrupting people's lives. They will therefore have a particular need to develop explicit policies in this respect.

Safeguards

Managers will be conscious that fostering a wider range of relationships may bring risks to individuals: risks of emotional, financial, or even sexual exploitation. Risks suggest the need for safeguards. Appropriate safeguards in this area would seem to hinge on the interest and attention of others, and their intervention if the need should arise.

The kind of people who might monitor service users in these respects can be internal or external to their living situation. Families of children or adults living at home generally show a marked and continuing interest in any risks they may face through the company they keep. Staff, particularly those working in residential support services, may not see it as their duty to monitor the relationships of their clients. If necessary, such obligations might need to be made explicit. Alternatively, various other people may be willing to monitor such risks.

Citizen advocates (Carle, 1984; Sang and O'Brien, 1984) have a brief which is essential to their role: to speak up on behalf of the person for whom they advocate. Sang and O'Brien (1984) have provided a particularly helpful account of the benefits of Citizen Advocacy, what is involved, and how Citizen Advocacy schemes can be initiated. In the absence of such schemes, involving outsiders of any kind in a service – whether volunteers, professionals in training, or researchers – will usually help to ensure that people are less likely to be subject to these risks, or that such risks are detected at an early stage. The openness of any service or organisation to outside scrutiny, monitoring, or evaluation will improve the likelihood of any risks being drawn to staff attention and acted on expeditiously.

Regular formal service monitoring of all service users, whether in the form of individual programme plans or case reviews, can provide an important additional safeguard, provided that one person from outside the service, perhaps a social worker, relative, or citizen advocate, clearly takes the "advocate" role.

Hopefully, a proper concern throughout any service for each of the people it serves will ensure that all service users benefit from the increasing recognition of the importance of choice and opportunity in personal relationships: that their lives are improved, not put at risk.

REFERENCES

BASS, M. A. S., CAMP, B. W. *Think Aloud: Increasing Social and Cognitive Skills – A Problem-Solving Program for Children. 3. Classroom Program Grades 3-4*. Champaign, Ill.: Research Press, 1985a.

BASS, M. A. S., CAMP, B. W. *Think Aloud: Increasing Social and Cognitive Skills – A Problem-Solving Program for Children. 4. Classroom Program Grades 5-6*. Champaign, Ill.: Research Press, 1985b.

CAMP, B. W., BASS, M. A. *Think Aloud: Increasing Social and Cognitive Skills – A Problem Solving Program for Children. 1. Primary Level*. Champaign, Ill.: Research Press, 1981.

CAMP, B. W., BASS, M. A. *Think Aloud: Increasing Social and Cognitive Skills – A Problem Solving Program for Children. 2. Classroom Program Grades 1-2*. Champaign, Ill.: Research Press, 1985.

CARLE, N. *Key Concepts in Community Based Services*. London: Campaign for People with Mental Handicaps, 1984.

CARTLEDGE, G., MILBURN, J. F. *Teaching Social Skills to Children: innovative approaches*. Oxford: Pergamon, 1986.

CHESELDINE, S. E., JEFFREE, D. M. Mentally handicapped adolescents: their use of leisure. *Journal of Mental Deficiency Research*, 1981; **25**:1, 49–59.

COOPER, D., HERSOV, J. *"We Can Change the Future"*. *Self-advocacy for People with Learning Difficulties: a staff training resource*. London: National Bureau for Handicapped Students, 1986.

CRAWLEY, B. *The Growing Voice: a survey of self-advocacy groups in adult training centres and hospitals in Great Britain*. London: Campaign for People with Mental Handicaps, 1988.

ELFRIDA RATHBONE CENTRE. *Between Ourselves*. (video, 15 mins.) Hove: Twentieth Century Vixen, 1988.

FLYNN, M. C., *A Place of My Own: independent living for adults with mental handicap*. London: Cassell, 1989.

FURMAN, W. Enhancing children's peer relations and friendships. *In* Duck, S. W. (Ed.). *Personal Relationships 5: Repairing Personal Relationships*. London: Academic Press, 1984.

GOTTLIEB, J., LEYSER, Y. Friendship between mentally retarded and non-retarded children. *In* Asher, S. R., Gottmann, J. M. (Eds.). *The Development of Children's Friendships*. Cambridge: Cambridge University Press, 1981.

HARING, T. G., BREEN, C., PITTS-CONWAY, V., LEE, M., GAYLORD-ROSS, R. Adolescent peer tutoring and special friend experiences. *Journal of the Association for Persons with Severe Handicaps*, 1987; **12**, 280–286.

HOPSON, B., SCALLY, M. *Lifeskills Teaching Programmes No. 1*. Leeds: Lifeskills Associates, 1980.

JAHODA, A., MARKOVA, I., CATTERMOLE, M. Stigma and self-concept of people with a mild mental handicap. *Journal of Mental Deficiency Research*, 1988; **32**, 103–115.

KING'S FUND CENTRE. *Ties and Connections: an ordinary community life*. London: King's Fund Centre, 1988.

LYONS, M. Students as buddies: a proposal for smoothing the path towards a broader life experience through recreation. *Occupational Therapy*, 1986; April, 111-114.

McCONKEY, R., McCORMACK, B. *Breaking Barriers*. London: Souvenir Press, 1983.

ODEN, S. Developing social skills instruction for peer interaction and relationships. *In* Cartledge, G., Milburn, J. F. *Teaching Social Skills to Children: innovative approaches*. Oxford: Pergamon, 1986.

ODEN, S., ASHER, S. R. Coaching children in social skills for friendship making. *Child Development*, 1977; **48**, 495–506.

RICHARDSON, S. A., KOLLER, H., KATZ, M. Appearance and mental retardation: some first steps in the development and application of a measure. *American Journal of Mental Deficiency*, 1985; **89**, 475–484.

RICHARDSON, A., RITCHIE, J. *Making the Break*. London: King's Fund Centre, 1986.

RICHARDSON, A., RITCHIE, J. *Developing Friendships: enabling people with learning difficulties to make and maintain friends*. London: Policy Studies Institute/Social and Community Planning Research, 1989a.

RICHARDSON, A., RITCHIE, J. *Letting Go*. Milton Keynes: Open University Press, 1989b.

RYAN, A., WALKER, R. *Making Life Story Books*. London: British Agencies for Adoption and Fostering, 1985.

SANG, B., O'BRIEN, J. *Advocacy: the UK and American experiences*. London: King's Fund Centre, 1984.

SHEARER, A. *Building Community – People with Mental Handicaps, their Families and Friends*. London: Campaign for People with Mental Handicaps and King's Fund, 1986.

SHURE, M. B. Social competence as a problem solving skill. *In* Wine, J. D., Smye, M. D. (Eds.). *Social Competence*. London: Guildford Press, 1981.

SHURE, M. B., SPIVACK, G. *Problem Solving Techniques in Child Rearing*. San Francisco, Cal.: Jossey Bass, 1978.

SHURE, M. B., SPIVACK, G. *Problem Solving Techniques in Child Rearing: a training script for parents of young children*. Mimeographed handbook, available from: Hahnemann Community Mental Retardation Center, Philadelphia, USA, 1975.

WALSH, J. Setting up a friendship scheme: Part 1. *Mental Handicap*, 1985a; **13**: 2, 58–59.

WALSH, J. Setting up a friendship scheme: Part 2. *Mental Handicap*, 1985b; **13**: 3, 110–111.

WALSH, J. *Let's Make Friends*. London: Souvenir Press, 1986.

WILLIAMS, P., SHOULTZ, B. *We Can Speak for Ourselves*. London: Souvenir Press, 1982.

*. . . training . . . designed to involve people with learning
disabilities . . .*

CHAPTER 10

Using these ideas:
approaches to training and learning

DIFFERENT CONTEXTS – DIFFERING APPROACHES

Some of those who were asked to comment on drafts of this book hoped we could describe the results of our approach in practice. Does it work, they asked? We do not yet know. This is not because these ideas have not been tested in a careful piece of evaluative research. It is, rather, because we are not suggesting any one set of ideas or a prescription which can simply be implemented in a project and evaluated. Demonstration projects can be of enormous value in disseminating a vision of what is possible. Yet one of our central themes has been that sociable relationships, especially friendships, are not specific to any one sphere of life: work, leisure, extended family, or neighbourhood. The "ties and connections" that knit individuals into a community – their community – simply cannot be provided or served by any *one* project or service (King's Fund Centre, 1988). We have tried to detail the limitations which any isolated approach must suffer, and we have examined specifically the limitations of both "befriending" and social skills training schemes.

What, then, are we advocating? An awareness of the variety of issues, and a preparedness to help meet people's individual needs, in numerous small ways over time, is what we seek.

We have used a focus on both opportunities and skills simultaneously in our day-to-day work helping people with learning disabilities. It is certainly our experience that helping people with their attitudes and skills is of scant value if the opportunities to use those skills to develop relationships are not present. Our experience has also shown us that exposure to social situations which might provide good opportunities to make acquaintance is avoided by people to whom we have not given sufficient personal support. But combinations – a job and personal help, for example, or the local amateur dramatic production and individual social skills coaching – have led to real changes in people's lives and their relationships.

The view we have put forward is that there is no way to find someone a friend. Developing people's attitudes and skills, and providing them with opportunities may enable them to make acquaintances. Although the opportunities may be readily arrranged, however, helping people to develop their personal social skills and attitudes is a long-term affair. One social skills programme may help people in one or two skills areas. But consolidating those gains, building on them, and developing social skill in the broader sense, takes time. It takes time for anyone to assimilate, practise, consolidate, pay attention to new aspects, practise these, adjust in the light of experience, practise again, and learn to use skills in unplanned or unforeseen situations.

Perhaps, therefore, we should emphasise the one, so far unacknowledged, issue inherent in our thinking: changing people's lives takes time. Social and leisure opportunities for people to meet other people can often be arranged within days, or at most a few weeks. But helping people to change their own behaviour only becomes effective after one, or even two, years. Intensive approaches do not generally address this issue, because people readily revert to their previous habits under a little stress. It is our experience that people often need much time if they are thoroughly to assimilate not only the content, but the rationale for the help they are being offered, and to adjust their own attitudes and motivation for change. Take one example. The grimace that followed a felt slight or rejection was so automatic that it took one, quite able, person whom we helped over twelve months to learn to suppress it, even then with occasional lapses which led to yet further rejection.

In consequence we see our ideas leading different people in a number of differing directions. By highlighting broad issues about how people develop relationships we hope to raise awareness of issues which will influence action in many spheres – ranging from choosing property for people leaving hospital to designing curricula for skills for living courses in schools and colleges.

One of the most effective ways to highlight a range of issues in people's minds is through training events. We will, therefore, describe in this chapter three kinds of approaches to training. First, is the course model developed by the training organisation Skills for People (see page 145), designed to involve people with learning disabilities in appreciating the attributes and value of friendship, raise individual confidence, and practise social skills in a non-threatening situation. Second, is the comparison of "cognitive" and "behavioural" approaches to social skills training. These models of training are usually delivered by professionals to people with learning disabilities, either as individual students or in classroom or workshop settings.

Third, is a training format we have used with staff of residential and community services which is also suitable for volunteers, or for parents and relatives. This training has been given in one-day or half-day workshops, but it could usefully be extended if more time were available. When only one day or less is available, considerable selection is required from the topics suggested. We have not described exercises in detail on the assumption that there is a wealth of skill amongst staff providing training, and that individual exercises need to be tailored to match the experience of participants and the time available. The various issues raised in each section of Chapter 9 might merit inclusion as part of such a training process for particular audiences.

INVOLVING PEOPLE WITH LEARNING DISABILITIES IN TRAINING

Something has been said earlier in this book about the important contribution of self-advocacy in building the confidence of people and so helping them make the social relationships of their choice. Here we describe a much more specific initiative: a course run by tutors, some of whom themselves have learning disabilities, for people with and without such disabilities, on the value and skills involved in making friends.

This type of course has been pioneered by Skills for People on the topic "Making Friends". In this project people with all kinds of disability, including learning disabilities, work with relatives, professionals, and volunteers both to plan and operate the courses and workshops.

The objectives of these courses have included:

emphasising the importance of having friends;

giving an idea of what exactly is involved in a friendship;

introducing the first steps in making friends;

showing that it is easier to make friends in some environments than in others;

showing that a friendship has to be worked at, and is a two-way process;

giving people opportunities to practise friendship skills in a safe and non-threatening situation;

meeting some new people and making new contacts;

raising people's confidence, especially in a mixed sex group.

The expectations of people attending the courses have included:

meeting new people;

gaining confidence;

finding out more about friendship;

increasing awareness of how to make friends.

The courses have included a number of different methods to meet this variety of aims, including:

short talks on various aspects of friendship and personal social interaction;

role plays devised and acted by two presenters with a "director" seeking suggestions for action or dialogue from the whole group;

group discussion involving small groups in discussion of news items, for example, or of particular interest areas;

small group work using groups as a forum to amplify group members' thoughts about the short talks, and to explore their experiences and ideas;

photostrips to provide records of course activities. (For example, small groups choose a topic concerned with friendship and develop a small story. This is enacted and photographed to provide a record and reminder of what was discussed. Subjects might include: striking up acquaintance; avoiding a clash with the neighbours; or introducing oneself in different situations.)

These methods have the advantage that much of the learning is achieved by participants learning from one another. The photostrip, in particular, seems an excellent way of recording issues for future reference.

LEARNING SOCIAL SKILLS

Mastering social skills, we have argued, is a process which requires attention and support to one or two issues over a long period of time. Nevertheless, targeted social skills training initiatives is of value in certain situations, either for individuals on a one-to-one basis or for a small group of participants. Health or local authority professionals and community mental handicap teams should be able to put possible participants in touch with people who are able to offer help in planning and carrying out social skills teaching.

Chapter 7 offers readers much material which can be drawn on for use by individuals. Readers who wish to be referred to more structured approaches will be interested in the following description of two strands of approach to the teaching of social skills. These are not incompatible and can be beneficially interwoven. They comprise cognitive and behavioural approaches.

A variety of social skills and problem-solving training approaches has been described in books which are readily available (Bass and Camp, 1985a, b; Camp and Bass, 1981, 1985; Cartledge and Milburn, 1986; Priestley *et al.*, 1978; Pope, McHale, and Craighead, 1988; Shure and Spivack, 1978; Spence and Shepherd, 1983; Trower, Bryant, and Argyle,

1978; Wilkinson and Canter, 1982). Some of the issues and the difficulties involved have been discussed in Chapter 7. Training can be offered for individuals or for groups of people. In the latter case there is usually an attempt to cover some kind of "syllabus" over a number of sessions. Most writers stress the importance of an adequate assessment of each person's difficulties and needs if training is to be of value, typically covering three main areas:

past and current relationships, and future expectations;

social situations which do and which do not present difficulties;

specific behaviour and skills which may or may not have been mastered, or which may present difficulty.

Cognitive problem-solving approaches (Cartledge and Milburn, 1986; Shure and Spivack, 1978; Bass and Camp, 1985 a, b; Camp and Bass, 1981, 1985) set out to teach a set of skills in a logical sequence. The basic skills, like thinking of alternative solutions, are few in number. The aim is to teach individuals to learn a skill and be able to use it in a variety of situations.

The "curriculum" is, therefore, fairly clearly defined. People vary as to their current level of skills and the point at which they need to join a programme of teaching, although it may be useful for everyone to go through all the elements of the programme. For those who do not, the following areas will probably be included in their programme:

understanding and use of language, especially words for feelings;

appreciating others' points of view, feelings, and preferences;

thinking of alternative courses of action (alternative-solution-thinking);

foreseeing different possible consequences;

understanding connections between actions, responses, and eventual outcomes (means-end thinking);

evaluating alternative courses of action in the light of possible consequences.

Teaching styles and format vary widely according to the circumstances and the needs of the people being taught. Cognitive approaches are used most commonly in schools and further education settings.

Behavioural approaches to social skills training (Trower, Bryant, and Argyle, 1978; Wilkinson and Canter, 1982), on the other hand, begin with an assessment which usually leads to the formulation of a small number of specific goals of training. Group teaching, in regular weekly sessions, often covers several areas, including:

observational skills;

listening skills;

speaking skills;

skills in conversation;

the expression of attitudes, such as warmth or assertiveness;

everyday social routines, such as introduction and parting, giving and receiving compliments;

problem-solving of particular social situations;

other specific areas of difficulty, such as asking for or declining a "date", refusing requests, and so on.

Training sessions usually include some initial information on each topic. This is typically followed by some demonstration in a role play situation. People are then asked to practise a particular behaviour demonstrated by the tutors in role play themselves. They then receive feedback on their performance. Further guidance may be offered, and further practice provided. Feedback is usually largely positive and focuses on people's strengths. Video is sometimes used, and can help some people to recognise errors and improved performance by themselves and other group members.

Behavioural and cognitive problem-solving training can also be provided on an individual basis.

One of the advantages of training in groups is the fact that some people feel less intimidated as one of a group of people with similar difficulties. Other advantages are that more people can participate in group training, given that limited time is available from the tutor, and groups can provide opportunities for members to role play and practise the skills they learn. Whether group training is actually more efficient, however, remains an open question. The major disadvantage of training groups is a loss of flexibility, which is often needed in order to concentrate on one person's particular needs. A second disadvantage is that there is likely to be little time for individual members to practise skills in the areas where they most wish or need to learn.

It may be that the advantages of both individual tuition and of working in groups is gained by organising short courses for very small numbers (three or four) of people, which focus on particular social requirements which those people have in common, such as making and maintaining conversation in developing acquaintance. In either case it is essential that tuition is only one element in the learning model, which also needs to include:

opportunities for observation and imitation of role models in ordinary settings;

opportunities for practice;

constructive feedback on people's actual behaviour in the social situation.

RAISING AWARENESS OF THESE ISSUES

Awareness of issues can be raised in many ways, but chiefly by changing practices which impinge on other people. A first step in achieving such changes is often the organisation of training events to discuss the issues involved. Training events would appear to be a very appropriate way to raise the issues discussed in this book with staff, parents, people with learning disabilities, their relatives, and volunteers.

On the basis of our own experience in pilot workshops, we conclude this chapter by offering some topic areas for such audiences. Workshops might cover exercises on the following themes, together with information and presentations which readers are encouraged to develop from the material elsewhere in this book. The first few exercises can usefully be spent in asking questions of course members to heighten their awareness of the issues and make them consider their own attitudes towards them. Having done this, subsequent exercises can offer opportunities for them to undertake activities which will help them to think about how they can use their own experiences to help people with learning disabilities.

Workshop discussion topics and exercises

Our own relationships
Who do we know – as acquaintances – as friends? Do we distinguish close relationships or friendships? If so, how?

How did we get to know them?
Through whom did we first meet? What activities did we do together that helped us get to know each other?

Learning about relationships: our past experience
Can we recall significant learning experiences, initially as children, and later as adults? How did this learning take place? Who was important, as a model to imitate, a model from whose mistakes we learned, or as someone who gave us feedback?

Which skills?
Which of our own social skills do we consider to be our strengths, and our weaknesses, in different social situations? Those of us without learning disabilities may need to give this some thought individually, and then consult someone else who knows our behaviour quite well. Becoming aware of our own social skills and social skill weaknesses usually requires explicit feedback from others.

How do we learn now?
What ingredients help us to learn our own weaknesses and improve upon them? Can we do this alone? Is feedback sufficient? How important is self-confidence? Do we learn by observing others? Do we learn by our own mistakes? Do we need others to remind us of our failings? How should reminders be given if they are to be helpful?

Activities as a basis for conversation and interaction
List and discuss activities in which *we* engage which provide *us* with topics of conversation. List and discuss activities in which people with learning disabilities might participate as a way of providing them with topics of interest or conversation.

Social worlds
Exploration of the social worlds in which we ourselves are involved can highlight possibilities for areas in which people with learning disabilities may develop an interest. Some time might also be spent considering how links could be made between these interest areas and some more active involvement with people locally.

Activities for meeting people
A brainstorming session can be useful for making a long list of possible activities. "Brainstorming" is a technique where all the people present put forward ideas which come to them. All are written down without criticism, comment, or discussion until the list is complete. The list of activities that might be drawn up in this type of workshop can be divided into those which involve doing things with other people, and relatively solitary activities. It can then be further broken into activities that are good for meeting new people and those that are useful for developing relationships with people who are already known. Plenty of time should be allowed for discussion, for example: to point out that an activity that is suitable for people in middle-age who wish to meet new people may not be suitable for younger people and *vice versa*; or to consider the possibility of activities in which people can be introduced by an acquaintance to a number of other people, such as social clubs and ethnic clubs.

The strengths and needs of individuals
It is likely to be helpful for the group to focus on the specific strengths and needs of individual people with learning disabilities who are known to group members. It is probably most useful to do this exercise after some time has been spent thinking about how other people, without disabilities, meet people and make friends.

Social skills
At this point, it can be helpful to identify the particular social skills, strengths, and difficulties of people whom group members wish to

help. It will almost certainly be necessary to make these as specific as possible for each individual. It may then be helpful to identify particular skills worth focusing on in the immediate future.

Background skills needed
Spend some time considering background skills that people may need: skill in chosen leisure activities or sports; the ability to use public transport or other means of transport to get to places; the ability to cope with particular social situations.

Choices
Consider what kinds of choices individual people with learning disabilities may have had in the past, and in what ways these choices may have been limited. If possible, spend some time considering how group members might be able to extend these choices so that people can try activities that they have not previously thought available to them. The booklet by Carle (1986) may be useful here.

Strengths and needs of staff, relatives, or volunteers
It will be important at some stage to consider the particular strengths of the relatives, volunteers, or staff who are attending the workshop. Each of these people will be involved in certain activities, will know various people, or be part of a social circle. Each is likely to know of a different set of resources, clubs, and specialist organisations locally. Different people know of different facilities. Highlighting each of these and pooling them may provide a number of ideas on how to proceed to help individuals with learning disabilities to meet people in appropriate ways.

Close personal relationships
It may be valuable to spend some time discussing the issue of close personal and sexual relationships, if group members feel this is relevant to the people with disabilities whom they know. Very close, long-term, emotional relationships present particular issues: in how to maintain close relationships, and how to deal with upsets, difficulties, rows, and other ups and downs that occur within them.

Risks: avoiding and coping with difficulties
Some time should be spent discussing the possible risks and dangers people with learning disabilities may face. Alongside such a list it is necessary to generate ideas about how these risks may be minimised. Ways should be explored of coping with or reacting to dangers if these arise. Some topics which might need to be covered are suggested in Box 20 in the next chapter.

Resources and opportunities available locally
If this has not already been covered, it would be useful to spell out a list of resources and opportunities available. List all the clubs, sports

and leisure facilities, specialist shops, libraries, amateur dramatics and other special interest societies, and so forth, which are local or can be easily reached with public or private transport.

The introduction and enabling process

It is essential for group members to spend time considering what is needed by way of introduction and enabling if people with learning disabilities are to make the best of the opportunities presented to them. A first step in this task is to list people (other than the participants) who could play an enabling role. Point out that this can include both close and distant family members as well as other people known either to individuals with disabilities or to those present. A second step is to consider what help may be needed to introduce individuals to different activities or social relationships. Note that the enablers may also need advice, information, and support after the initial introduction process is complete. Emphasise the link with the topics covered in the first two exercises: who do those of us without disabilities know, and how do we get to know them? Also highlight the importance of shared activity.

Practical action

It is generally helpful to complete training of this kind by having group members make some agreements – after careful discussion – about what specific things they intend to do as a result of the training experience.

Evaluation

Some form of evaluation may be helpful at the end of such a course as a way of judging its likely effects. Such evaluation might take one of many forms, depending on whether the training was intended primarily to raise awareness of an issue, alter the behaviour of staff, aid the preparation of volunteers, or actually achieve a significant impact on the opportunities or skills available to a number of people with learning disabilities.

REFERENCES

BASS, M. A. S., CAMP, B. W. *Think Aloud: Increasing Social and Cognitive Skills – A Problem Solving Program for Children. 3. Classroom Program Grades 3-4*. Champaign, Ill.: Research Press, 1981.

BASS, M. A. S., CAMP, B. W. *Think Aloud: Increasing Social and Cognitive Skills – A Problem Solving Program for Children. 4. Classroom Program Grades 5-6*. Champaign, Ill.: Research Press, 1985.

CAMP, B. W., BASS, M. A. *Think Aloud: Increasing Social Cognitive Skills – A Problem Solving Program for Children. 1. Primary Level*. Champaign, Ill.: Research Press, 1981.

CAMP, B. W., BASS, M. A. *Think Aloud: Increasing Social and Cognitive Skills – A Problem Solving Program for Children. 2. Classroom Program Grades 1-2.* Champaign, Ill.: Research Press, 1985.

CARLE, N. *Helping People to Make Choices: opportunities and challenges.* London: Campaign for People with Mental Handicaps, 1986.

CARTLEDGE, G., MILBURN, J. F. *Teaching Social Skills to Children: innovative approaches.* Oxford: Pergamon Press, 1986.

KING'S FUND CENTRE. *Ties and Connections: an ordinary community life.* London: King's Fund Centre, 1988.

POPE, A. W., McHALE, S. M., CRAIGHEAD, W. E. *Self-esteem Enhancement with Chiildren and Adolescents.* Oxford: Pergamon Press, 1988.

PRIESTLEY, P., McGUIRE, J., FLEGG, D., HEMSLEY, V., WELHAM, D. *Social Skills and Personal Problem-Solving.* London: Tavistock, 1978.

SHURE, M. D., SPIVACK, G. *Problem Solving Techniques in Child Rearing.* San Francisco, Cal.: Jossey Bass, 1978.

SPENCE, S., SHEPHERD, G. (Eds.). *Developments in Social Skills Training.* London: Academic Press, 1983.

TROWER, P., BRYANT, B., ARGYLE, M. *Social Skills and Mental Health.* London: Methuen, 1978.

WILKINSON, J., CANTER, S. *Social Skills Training Manual: assessment program design and management of training.* Chichester: John Wiley, 1982.

. . . access to many activities and opportunities is dependent on money . . .

CHAPTER 11

In conclusion –
barriers, pitfalls, and priorities

BARRIERS

Our society gives precious little help or education to any of its citizens in connection with the establishment or maintenance of personal relationships. Often it blames individuals when things go wrong. This situation persists, despite the damage that failed relationships cause to the parties involved and to other people, and the cost society pays to patch up that damage. This lack of recognition and attention to relationships, and their consequences for individuals, represents one of the most pervasive barriers to be surmounted in helping people with learning disabilities to overcome the social or emotional isolation that their disability often entails.

Our society also is one in which access to many activities and opportunities is dependent on money. People with learning disabilities are, by and large, poor. As adults, few have jobs, and those jobs are rarely well paid. Their income is thus strictly limited, and money available for membership fees, admission prices, refreshments, and transport is scarce. This does not only preclude yachting club fees. It means that people must budget carefully for bus fares, the price of a cup of coffee, a museum entrance fee, an afternoon at the leisure centre, or a ticket to the cinema. Even visiting friends on foot entails some financial cost if their hospitality is reciprocated, in provision of tea and biscuits. In our more mobile society anyway, many acquaintances will not live within walking distance. One of the most significant expenditures restricting the activities of people on low incomes is the cost of travel. Poverty, therefore, remains a major barrier for many people with learning disabilities who seek to make or sustain friendships.

The attitudes of people without disabilities present an obstacle of a broader kind, not only directly but indirectly through their consequences for services. In some residential facilities, for instance, close friendships are feared and frowned upon because of their potential for possible sexual relationships. Commonly, the social ties and bonds of people with learning disabilities are not regarded as important enough to play a part in the decisions that other people, including professionals, make about them.

The most insidious and pervasive consequence of such attitudes is segregation of services. The values which have contributed to this segregation in the past are slowly being challenged. However, moving towards services which coordinate support for people with learning disabilities in more "ordinary" lives (King's Fund Centre, 1982, 1988b) at school, work, leisure, or home will involve very great changes in the way they are organised. Services still generally separate schooling, separate training or work opportunities, and separate residential provision for people with learning disabilities. This separation constructs a gigantic barrier to possibilities of social contact with people who do not have disabilities. It restricts and limits learning of the very abilities people need if they are to make successful relationships with others when opportunities do arise. This in turn denies them experiences and chances that might come about through social activity as a part of those relationships. Segregation of services, therefore, perpetuates social segregation.

People with learning disabilities also face barriers of a different kind, which are imposed by or result from their original handicap. Alongside intellectual impairment, many people have impaired vision, hearing, movement, or communication, each of which entails its own disability. These impose further barriers to social interaction, which we have not elaborated in this book because they are widely recognised and discussed elsewhere.

The very knowledge that individuals have a learning disability leads many people to expect less of them: not only in intellectual achievements, but in social skill and competence also. This vicious circle, whereby uncertain or low expectations lead to fewer opportunities and so perpetuate a lack of skills, was discussed early in this book (see Chapter 2). The effects of others' expectations and uncertainties will not change rapidly as expectations are the product of many factors, information and personal experience being only two contributors. The impact of social policies that result in integrated or segregrated services remains one of the most significant of these factors.

At a more personal level, having a learning disability implies that someone will learn skills, including social skills, more slowly than others might do. Some social skills may be learned relatively easily, but most people can only change their habitual verbal and non-verbal social idiosyncrasies very slowly. So, acquiring the skills and abilities described in earlier chapters is likely to take people with learning disabilities much time. This requires recognition, because rapid provision of social opportunities may not lead to rapid acquisition of social skills. Even where skills and opportunities are both present, it may take a year or more to build up a "circle" of acquaintances or friends, as people who have moved house often testify.

Likewise those features of behaviour which lead to the weakening or loss of friendship may be ones which are difficult to identify, which we are reluctant to admit, and which may not be easily taught in a classroom setting. This kind of learning takes time. If people are led into social "opportunities" unsupported, social abilities that are not yet perfected may lead them to a sense of failure. If others then blame them for failing, which is not unlikely, their rejection will become an extra restriction on their future.

These major barriers, and the kinds of action which will be needed in future to help overcome them, are illustrated in Box 20.

RISKS AND SAFEGUARDS

Encouraging people to develop relationships with others carries risks. They may develop relationships that they choose, but which are ultimately harmful to them. Parents are frequently concerned that their sons and daughters should not get into "bad company". Apparent friendships may, on occasion, be abused for financial or sexual reasons, or for personal power and security. People's own friends and acquaintances may not present them with any direct risk of exploitation, but the contacts of those friends and acquaintances may do so. In consequence, individuals may be exposed to the risk of theft, burglary,

Barriers	Ameliorative action
Unawareness of the importance of relationships	Raising profile of the issue in public education and service planning and management
Lack of skill and inexperience	Education and opportunities
Rejection	Information, preparation, and support
Poverty	Action at a political level
Segregation	Changes in attitudes and policy changes
Difficulty communicating, phoning, and writing	Support and education
Difficulty getting to activities and visiting people	Siting of residential provision and budgets for transport
Lack of confidence	Support, experience, and feedback

Box 20. Barriers to developing valued relationships

exploitation, sexual harassment, or even rape or murder. Such risks are greatest amongst people – particularly adolescents – who are in the process of experimenting with and defining their identities.

There are three kinds of safeguards against such risks. The first lies in careful preparation and discussion of dangers, of how to make choices, of how to stop or gracefully withdraw, and of how to say no to others. These skills, however, depend in general upon self-confidence: personal security deriving from secure and positive relationships. Many people with learning disabilities do not have this security and self-confidence, and for them the risks will remain present. Nevertheless, there can be great value in careful discussion, either with individuals or with small groups, of the possible risks and dangers people may face, and what action they may be able to take to reduce them.   Ideas about how to avoid or cope with risks are usually best generated amongst small groups of people who know each other fairly well. Some topics for discussion are illustrated in Box 21. Discussion groups could involve listing and talking about a variety of possible dangers – for example, being mugged, being "picked up", being insulted, ridiculed, or bullied – and ways of minimising these risks or coping with the situation. Dixon (1988) offers examples of discussion exercises to cope with difficulties in sexual relationships, some of which may be adaptable to other kinds of problem situations. Role play, in particular, can help demonstrate difficult situations and ways of avoiding or escaping from them.

In addition, individual discussion can be valuable as a way of drawing attention to particular difficulties an individual might be likely to face, such as a need for status and companionship which might, in some circumstances, lead to danger of involvement with peers who engage in criminal activity.

The second kind of safeguard lies in protection. In childhood parents generally protect their children, first physically, then through rules and guidelines, and later through expectations and social or emotional sanctions for unwise or improper behaviour. These protections will be provided longer for many people with learning disabilities, either by parents or by professionals and services. How far such protection is seen as appropriate and necessary is likely to vary according to the perspective and experiences of the person judging a situation. Some people choose to be more protective than others. Parents are tied emotionally: for them the risks are proportionately greater.

The difficulties faced by parents of young people with learning disabilities are not of their making. Most parents, whose children do not have a learning disability, find their developing independence thrust upon them. They must react, even though this may often be with ambivalence and not without argument, and loosen the ties of emotional dependence and protection. If they do not, societal expectations and norms will influence their sons and daughters, drawing them away from their

Some topics	How to reduce risks	How to cope
Insults or ridicule	Discuss: dress; behaviour; where and when to go with a confident companion	How to react – silence, humour or firmness
Being bullied	Discuss: likely situations or people; not going alone; acting with self-confidence	How not to show fear. Who to tell now
Physical threats, verbal threats, threats not to tell anyone else about	Discuss: likely situations	Who to tell and why. What to say at the time
Approaches by strangers (especially men); being "picked up"	Discuss: likely situations; possible types of approach	When and how to say no. How to get out of the situation
A demand for sexual intercourse or attempted rape	Discuss: possible situations or people; when to be alone with a man	How and when to be firm. When and how to get help
Being told you agreed to more than you did (financially, sexually)	Discuss: when to be careful; when to be very clear	How to be firm. When and how to seek help
People offering to do jobs for you, or trying to sell you things	Discuss: whose offers to accept and why	How to say yes or no
People who come to the door for help	Discuss: who to be wary of	When to say OK or goodbye. When and how to seek help
People who come to "read the meter" or "fix" something but	Discuss: how to check people's identification	How to stay in charge
Being "mugged" in the street	Discuss: where and when to walk alone, or not walk alone; what to wear	Alarms or defence – helpful or harmful. How to react, who to tell

BOX 21. Risks and dangers: topics for individual discussion, group discussion, or role play

protection into independence and, often, marriage. Not so for parents of children with learning disabilities. As Richardson and Ritchie (1986) point out, these parents may place less value on their children developing maturity and demonstrating independence; that independence may seem to them to express itself through choices that are inappropriate and risky. These factors may delay the time when parents will acknowledge a need to reduce protection. Frequently their adolescent offspring will not demonstrate the same initiative as other young people to break away from parental control, partly because society's expectations, which are communicated to them in various ways over the years, are lower than they are for other people of their age. The "dignity of risk" is not easily defined: and there are powerful factors which encourage parents especially to adopt protectiveness as a solution to risk. It is a solution which in many ways only bides time: for most parents there will come a time when, by choice or circumstance, their son or daughter does leave home.

A third kind of safeguard lies in the concern and interest of others. The greater the number of concerned people in touch with people with learning disabilities, the greater the amount of solicited and unsolicited advice and feedback available to them. Many people with learning disabilities do not have many friends who can offer this kind of support. It may, therefore, be helpful to encourage the involvement of advocates or other responsible outsiders as a way of protecting them from exploitation or manipulation. Here, we merely mention the principle, as particular approaches – such as citizen advocacy (Sang and O'Brien, 1984); self-advocacy (King's Fund Centre, 1988a; Williams and Shoultz, 1982); the involvement of identified social work staff; and individual programme planning frameworks – have already been discussed in Chapter 9.

PITFALLS

The financial and management pressures on human service organisations are now so great that new services are rarely initiated. Yet development of a new service has traditionally been one way for organisations to meet newly identified needs. We hope we have said enough in Chapter 5 to caution against this risky "solution" to people's needs for company and intimacy. Confusion may arise about the nature of "befriending" schemes. Services can provide company, and within the last two centuries the employment of a "companion" has been seen as a valued relationship. Services, however, cannot provide friendships: only offer opportunities or support which may make them possible.

A second risk we foresee is that some people's lives may become so filled with planned activity that they have no time to develop the relationships they begin to make with those with whom they would like to spend more time. This kind of situation can develop when people are given a great deal of help in organising how they are going to spend their time, and are encouraged to fill it all. Regular literacy night classes on Mondays, swimming on Tuesdays, having a friend round every Wednesday, bingo on Thursdays, the cinema on Fridays, and the local for a drink every Saturday may not leave much opportunity for people in work or training to spend time with new acquaintances they have met during the week. Sensitivity is required if activities and chances to meet others are not to be imposed on people against their own wishes and preferences. Staff and other concerned individuals must tread a careful middle course; between neglecting unmet and unrecognised social needs on the one hand, and imposing unwanted social pressure and intrusion into the lives of people who prefer otherwise.

A similar kind of pitfall is the "active search" for a friend or friends, which can fail because of its very intensity. Friendships do not usually develop suddenly. Over-enthusiastic starts, followed by disappointments if acquaintances do not develop into hoped-for close friends, can reinforce people's feelings of failure, and lack of worth and value to others (Weiss, 1975). These feelings may then make it more difficult for them to make acquaintances or friends, because motivation may be lost and skill in making relationships may be impaired, so that subsequent opportunities are passed by.

We have, at various points in this book, touched on the importance of relationships as a way of developing and expressing personal identity. There is therefore always a need, in supporting others in their relationships, to remember that we each have our own preferences in what we do and the people with whom we like to spend time. It is important to accept that others' wishes may be very different from our own. It is all too easy simply to suggest to others what we would do ourselves. There are times when this is very appropriate and helpful, and others when it is less so.

This comment about the importance of awareness of personal identity is reflected in the need to be aware of ethnic and cultural identities and assumptions. Patterns of acquaintance and relationships vary widely amongst the many different cultures in Britain. This book could not do justice to the variations in expectations, education, and situations which exist in people with learning disabilities in different parts of Britain – and we therefore have not attempted the task. We hope, nevertheless, that readers will be able to assimilate the ideas we have put forward into their own cultural expectations and those of their relatives, friends, and clients.

PRIORITIES

Some two decades ago the Government White Paper, *Better Services for the Mentally Handicapped*, focused on and highlighted the lack of provision then available to meet many of the needs of people with learning disabilities and their families (DHSS, 1971). The 1970s saw an emphasis on expansion of existing services and the provision of new services, particularly those which sought to support people with such disabilities and their carers. The subsequent decade has seen a growing concern for the *way* in which services are delivered, and their unintended effects on service users. This concern for the value, respect, and dignity that should be accorded to people with learning disabilities has begun to be translated into a better quality of service and will ultimately lead to a better quality of life for some people. Yet only recently has this concern been extended from the areas of living and working environments to concentrate on people's personal relationships. One priority, therefore, must be to ensure that such relationships, both actual and possible, are recognised for the important contribution they make to people's quality of life.

Until recently, the "invisibility" of friendships and acquaintances to those involved in policy-making, planning, and providing support services for people with learning disabilities has been striking. The Independent Development Council's *Next Steps* (1984), for example, a brief but otherwise excellent comprehensive review of national policy and action, devoted no space to discussing this issue directly.

Grasping the practical implications, now that the importance of the issue has been recognised, remains difficult. The Social Services Committee of the House of Commons (1985) recognised the contradiction in a community care policy supposedly motivated by concern for the quality of life of people with learning disabilities when it said:

"Discharge of patients to a 'parish of origin' . . . is crude enough. When it leads to the separation of lifelong friendships and the fracture of local attachments, it is really inhumane".

Avoiding the unwanted break-up of people's friendships remains one of the important issues yet to be faced by residential services in a period of hospital closure.

Heller's review (1982) suggests that the ill-effects of involuntary re-settlement are likely to be reduced if people move to an environment of higher quality than the one they previously inhabited. Many people have left large hospitals for community services in recent years. It is in these community services that much remains to be done to ensure a high quality living environment in which people can be helped to widen their opportunities to make and sustain relationships of various kinds.

Friendship implies a mutual choice between individuals. Helping people to have a greater choice and opportunity to develop acquaintance does not necessarily lead to friendship. Friendship cannot be achieved simply by the provision of a "service" to meet this need. The most useful point from which to start thinking about this issue is the consideration of how the friendships and relationships of most people without disabilities develop, how people come to choose their friends, and how people learn to make and preserve their friendships. This book reflects that.

Yet it is vital to avoid projecting onto others personal preferences and inclinations about forming relationships, and it is important to observe and listen carefully to the individual wishes of every person. Efforts such as self-advocacy, which help people to experience and express choice, may help them to express and exercise that choice in their social activities, friendships, and acquaintances.

The narrowness of social life for many people with learning disabilities was illustrated in Chapter 2. The scope of the challenge in helping them to choose their relationships is, therefore, great. This book has offered some suggestions for practical action. We hope that these suggestions, together with the resources that will be discussed in the following pages, will allow some of the growing awareness about the importance of personal relationships to be translated into richer, more varied, and more rewarding lives for some people. If the process is started in school and at home for those people with learning disabilities who are now just infants, perhaps by the time they reach adulthood they will have acquired many of the abilities and opportunities that will enable them to develop the company and friendships of their choice.

REFERENCES

DEPARTMENT OF HEALTH & SOCIAL SECURITY. *Better Services for the Mentally Handicapped.* Cmnd. 4683. London: HMSO, 1971.

DIXON, H. *Sexuality and Mental Handicap: an educator's resource book.* Wisbech: Learning Development Aids, 1988.

HELLER, T. The effects of involuntary residential relocation: a review. *American Journal of Community Psychology,* 1982; 10, 471-492.

INDEPENDENT DEVELOPMENT COUNCIL FOR PEOPLE WITH MENTAL HANDICAP. *Next Steps: an independent review of progress, problems and priorities in the development of services for people with mental handicap.* London: Independent Development Council, 1984.

KING'S FUND CENTRE. *An Ordinary Life: comprehensive locally based services for mentally handicapped people.* London: King's Fund Centre, 1982.

KING'S FUND CENTRE. *Self-advocacy Skills Training.* London: King's Fund Centre, 1988a.

KING'S FUND CENTRE. *Ties and Connections: an ordinary community life.* London: King's Fund Centre, 1988b.

RICHARDSON, A., RITCHIE, J. *Making the Break.* London: King's Fund Centre, 1986.

SANG, B., O'BRIEN, J. *Advocacy: the UK and American experiences.* London: King's Fund Centre, 1984.

SOCIAL SERVICES COMMITTEE OF THE HOUSE OF COMMONS. *Community Care with Special References to Adult Mentally Ill and Mentally Handicapped People.* London: HMSO, 1985.

WEISS, R. S. *Loneliness: the experiences of emotional and social isolation.* London, Mass.: Massachusetts Institute of Technology Press, 1975.

WILLIAMS, P., SHOULTZ, B. *We Can Speak for Ourselves.* London: Souvenir Press, 1982.

*. . . look at a combination of approaches on how to plan and
conduct social skills teaching . . .*

CHAPTER 12

Resources

This chapter is an attempt to gather together information that will be of value to those helping people with learning disabilities develop relationships of their choice. The list contains some references for background reading, but most items are included because they provide practical ideas for use in day-to-day situations, or in training or sharing ideas.

This list of resource materials is in no sense exhaustive or exclusive. It gives details of some of the materials which came to our notice through this study which we think are of potential use to readers. In some areas – for example, activities and opportunities – our choice has had, of necessity, to be highly selective.

All these resource materials have weaknesses as well as strengths. People planning to use them may therefore find it advantageous to use several of those listed. For example, people contemplating conducting social skills training are recommended to look at a combination of approaches, such as those described by Shure and Spivack (1978), Wilkinson and Canter (1982), and Trower, Bryant, and Argyle (1978), as well as the programmes of Hopson and Scally (1980). Together these would provide much detailed material on how to plan and conduct social skills teaching, with an emphasis both on the thinking processes involved and the behaviour itself.

We have tried, immediately following the reference for each entry, to indicate who is likely to find the materials of particular interest. We hope that the list will be of use but that it will not inhibit readers from searching for other useful materials.

ADDRESSES OF PUBLISHERS

The addresses of some publishers of the materials listed may not be widely known. Some selected addresses are given at the end of the chapter which may be useful to readers who require materials which they find difficult to trace.

RESOURCE MATERIALS

ALLAN, G. Informal networks of care: issues raised by Barclay.
British Journal of Social Work, 1983; **13**, 417-433.

Staff and professionals involved with: lay people and volunteers;
management and planning;
support for people with
learning disabilities.

This paper discusses issues surrounding informal social contacts with relatives,
friends, and neighbours. It explores the concept of informal local caring
networks, distinguishing between caring about someone (as in friendship) and
caring for someone. It concludes that informal caring networks are unlikely to be
successful as an alternative to other forms of care because of the differing nature
of these relationships.

ARGYLE, M. *The psychology of interpersonal behaviour.* Harmondsworth:
Penguin, 1983.

Staff and professionals involved in: education;
social skills training.

The book provides a useful basis of information about social behaviour and an
overview of the psychological issues. Although the coverage of the book is wide,
the discussion of friendship specifically is not detailed, and is focused particularly
on research on the "rules" of friendship behaviour.

ASHER, S. R., GOTTMAN, J. M. (Eds.). *The development of children's
friendships.* Cambridge: Cambridge University Press, 1981.

Staff and professionals, parents and   education;
families involved with: social skills;
management and planning;
support for people with
learning disabilities.

An edited collection of research to that date on the development of friendship
amongst children and on the perceptions and the descriptions which children are
able to give about their own relationships. The book includes a chapter by
Gottlieb and Leyser, which reviews evidence on factors which facilitate contact
and friendship between children with and without learning disabilities.

ATKINSON, D. How easy is it to form friendships after leaving long stay
hospitals? *Social Work Today,* 1987; June 15, **18**:41, 12-13.

Parents and families, staff and   lay people and volunteers;
professionals involved with: education;
management and planning;
activities and opportunities;

                                            support for people with
                                              learning disabilities.

This is an excellently simple but insightful article, which draws out themes from
the author's research with people leaving hospital. It explores the meaning of
friendship in this context, particularly in relationships with current and former
professionals. The conclusions stress the value of relationships seen by
individuals as friendship, and the importance of preserving existing friendships
through major moves in people's lives.

ATKINSON, D. Someone to Turn To: the social worker's role and the role
of front line staff in relation to people with mental handicaps.
Kidderminster: BIMH Publications, 1989.

Staff and professionals involved with: lay people and volunteers;
                                                 support for people with
                                                   learning disabilities;
                                                 staff training.

This is a book which sets out to capture something of the relationships between
staff and service users. It occupies an important position for staff working with
people with learning disabilities living in or moving to community settings. The
first half of the book discusses the results of research which followed up the
situation of fifty-five people of all ages who left hospital to live with minimum
support in Somerset over a ten-year period. The second half of the book discusses
the implications of the research for the role and tasks of social workers and others
supporting people with learning disabilities in the community. The book
concludes with a discussion of the needs of staff, both by way of training, and by
way of support.

Overall, this is a sensitive and informative coverage of an area in which
analysis has been largely neglected till now: the nature of the relationship
between professionals and people with learning disabilities. It therefore deserves
to be read by members of all the professions in the mental handicap field.

ATKINSON D., WARD, L. *A Part of the Community: social integration and
neighbourhood networks*. London: Campaign for People with Mental
Handicaps, 1986.

Parents and families, staff and   lay people and volunteers;
professionals involved with: management and planning;
                                                 activities and opportunities;
                                                 support for people with
                                                   learning disabilities.

This booklet gives a clear and easily read account of some issues which need
to be addressed in the social integration of people with learning disabilities. It
discusses the importance, not only of developing relationships but of
maintaining them. It indicates the need to "lubricate" and "repair" social
relationships if people are to become and remain socially integrated into a
locality.

BIEGEL, D. E., McCARDLE, E., MENDENSON, S. *Social Networks and Mental Health. An annotated bibliography.* London: Sage Publications, 1985.

Staff and professionals

A very extensive bibliography of research relating to social support and mental health. It includes a number of references to work on the effects of poor social support upon mental and physical health. It covers literature on: theories and conceptual issues; social support and physical and mental health; intervention programmes (including self-help); professional roles and policy. Each reference is accompanied by a brief abstract or summary. This book provides a major source point for researchers in the field, referencing 1340 items.

BISHOP, J., HOGGETT, E. P. *Organising Around Enthusiasms: mutual aid in leisure.* London: Comedia Publishing Group, 1986.

Parents and families, staff and professionals involved with:

lay people and volunteers; education; activities and opportunities.

This short book is the result of some research into recreational organisations and the ways in which they function. It provides valuable insights in an easily readable text. It may be of particular interest as a source of ideas for people concerned with provision of leisure activities.

BROWN, G., HARRIS, T. *Social Origins of Depression: a study of psychiatric disorder in women.* London: Tavistock, 1978.

Staff and professionals

A classic and very important study of the factors contributing to depression amongst women. It contains a valuable discussion of the importance of a close or confiding relationship as a means of alleviating women's vulnerability to depression.

BULMER, M. *Neighbours: the work of Philip Abrams'.* Cambridge: Cambridge University Press, 1986.

Staff and professionals

A posthumous collection of the work of Philip Abrams on neighbours, neighbouring, and neighbourhood care. It brings together the results of important research into informal neighbouring, altruism, and reciprocity in relationships between neighbours, and neighbour care schemes. The manner in which Abrams' own (unfinished) writings are integrated into a composite text, which places them in context, is exemplary.

CAMP, B. W., BASS, M. A. S. *Think Aloud: increasing social and cognitive skills – a problem solving program for children. 1. Primary Level.* Champaign, Ill.: Research Press, 1981.

CAMP, B. W., BASS, M. A. S. *Think Aloud: increasing social and cognitive skills – a problem solving program for children. 2. Grades 1-2.* Champaign, Ill.: Research Press, 1985.

BASS, M. A. S., CAMP, B. W. *Think Aloud: increasing social and cognitive skills – a problem solving program for children. 3. Grades 3-4.* Champaign, Ill.: Research Press, 1985.

BASS, M. A. S., CAMP, B. W. *Think Aloud: increasing social and cognitive skills – a problem solving program for children. 4. Grades 5-6.* Champaign, Ill.: Research Press, 1985.

Parents and families, staff and professionals involved in:	education; social skills training.

The *Think Aloud* programme represents a development based around the Shure and Spivack problem-solving approach. Its contribution is to teach children to use thinking – initially out loud and later covertly – as a way to guide their problem-solving. The programme is also concerned both with interpersonal and impersonal problems.

The "classroom programmes" are presented in great detail, laid out in a loose-leaf style designed for use by teachers in a classroom situation. This is particularly advantageous for teachers looking for a step-by-step curriculum. The material needs adaptation for a British audience.

A major asset of the programme is that it is available in four versions, for use with primary children, and those who are progressively older – Grades 1-2, 3-4, and 5-6. The version for Grades 5-6 contains much material which might be useful with adolescents with learning disabilities.

CARLE, N. (Ed.). *Helping People to Make Choices: opportunities and challenges.* London: Campaign for People with Mental Handicaps, 1986.

Parents and families, staff and professionals involved with:	lay people and volunteers; education; management and planning; support for people with learning disabilities; activities and opportunities.

A useful short booklet which aims to help people think about and promote choices which are available to individuals with learning disability. The print quality is poor, but the ideas may prove useful in provoking discussion and learning about choices.

CARTLEDGE, G., MILBURN, J. F. *Teaching Social Skills to Children: innovative approaches.* Oxford: Pergamon, 1986.

Staff and professionals involved in:	education; social skills training.

This book aims to present practical ideas to an audience of teachers in mainstream and special education classrooms, and clinicians working with children in various settings. It has several major strengths. It is not prescriptive.

The cognitive or "thinking" aspects of social skill are given prominent attention. The book contains clear and specific examples that will be useful to teachers and others. Although many of the ideas and resources are geared to children, those working with adults may well find many ideas which they can borrow from this approach. Much of the book is readable and rich with practical ideas, although parts may prove heavy reading for those unused to an academic style.

Part I of the book is a detailed, up-to-date review of what is involved in teaching social skills, and is intended as a training text. Part II consists of five chapters on special applications of social skills teaching. These are: the cognitive and affective approaches – particularly the *Think Aloud* programme (see Camp and Bass above); teaching children with severe disabilities social skills through leisure; coaching techniques; using activities to teach cooperation; and teaching adolescents.

An additional strength of this book is its twenty-page appendix of resource materials: on curricula, printed materials and books for pupils and teachers, audio-visual materials (film strips, cassettes, records, and films), dramatic play materials, and games. This represents a reasonably comprehensive list of American resource materials in this area, with current publishers' addresses.

COOPER, D., HERSOV, J. *"We can change the future". Self-advocacy for People with Learning Difficulties: a staff training resource.* London: National Bureau for Handicapped Students, 1986.

Parents and families, staff and   lay people and volunteers;
professionals involved with: education;
                                             management and planning;
                                             staff training.

This resource comprises a manual, and an accompanying video tape which illustrates many of the points made in the manual. It presents a highly positive view of the potential of self-advocacy, but also passes on practical ideas to help people learn more about the concept. The manual is broad in its coverage, looking at the concept of "handicap", what self-advocacy is, and the historical perspective. Modules cover *Definitions*, *Skills*, *Issues and Outcomes*, and *Passing on the Skills*. An interesting emphasis is placed on the effect of different kinds of relationships on self-advocacy and *vice versa*: for example, staff relationships may hinder or foster the development of advocacy, and are affected by self-advocacy. The impact of self-advocacy for families is also examined. All of the discussion is illustrated by direct quotes from people with learning disabilities. One of the most valuable sections is possibly that on staff training, which contains suggestions for the organisation of training and the use of self-advocates as trainers, as well as suggestions for the evaluation of training. The suggested activities at the end of each module may be especially useful.

CRAFT, A., CRAFT, M. *Handicapped Married Couples*. London: Routledge, 1979.

Parents and families, staff and professionals

This is the report of a Welsh research study of couples with lifelong intellectual, physical, or personality disabilities. It is of interest in the present context because of its description of the marriages of some people with learning disabilities, given both from the researchers' point of view, and in their own words.

CRAFT, A., CRAFT, M. *Sex Education and Counselling for Mentally Handicapped People*. Tunbridge Wells: Costello, 1983.

Parents and families, staff and professionals involved with:	lay people and volunteers; management and planning; education; social skills training.

This volume covers a variety of aspects of sex education and counselling through a number of chapters written by different authors. Most of the chapters are extremely readable, and some are highly recommended. Pauline Fairbrother writes clearly on the parents' viewpoint. Hilary Brown provides an excellent introduction to sex education for young adults with disabilities. A chapter by Ann Craft and her colleagues offers a well-thought-out curriculum for health and sex education, together with an extensive list of resources. The following chapter by Ann Craft on teaching programmes and training techniques is useful in conjunction with the previous one. Linda Andron's chapter on sexuality counselling with couples with developmental disabilities may be of particular interest. The chapters are well organised and between them cover the material well.

CRAFT, A. *Mental Handicap and Sexuality*. Tunbridge Wells: Costello, 1986.

Parents and families, staff and professionals involved in:	education; social skills training.

Although more recent than Craft and Craft (1983), this edited volume is disappointing. Individual issues are generally better covered by the former text. Moreover, this volume includes a number of chapters which are somewhat rigid in their approach to sex education, and the chapter on inappropriate sexual behaviour involves observational and behavioural approaches which many people might find unsuitable for this kind of difficulty.

CRAWLEY, B. *The Growing Voice: a survey of self-advocacy groups in adult training centres and hospitals in Great Britain*. London: Campaign for People with Mental Handicaps, 1988.

Parents and families, staff and professionals involved with:	lay people and volunteers; management and planning; health and social services; education.

This report is valuable for its concise explanation of different types of self-advocacy, and for its analysis of the factors which support or fail to support the many self-advocacy groups surveyed in this study. It is especially helpful in its discussion of the role of advisors to self-advocacy groups.

DIXON, H. *Sexuality and Mental Handicap: an educator's resource book*.
Wisbech: Learning Development Aids, 1988.

Parents and families, staff and   education;
professionals involved in: social skills teaching;
                                              staff training.

This recent publication is highly recommended for its exceptionally coherent and
practical approach to education and training about relationships – especially
sexual relationships. A great strength is the way in which it begins with simple
issues of communication and body awareness, before moving on to a substantial
section on self-esteem. This is possibly one of the most important sections in the
book, as it lays a foundation for subsequent sections on *Looking after me*,
Relationships, Being sexual, Pregnancy, birth and parenting, and *Sexual health*.
Each of these sections has a number of exercises on specific topics (such as,
Touching me, Stages in a relationship, Behaving sexually; Saying no sexually).
The material is well laid out, with illustrations, although users will need
additional diagrams or pictures for much of the specific material on body
awareness and contraception, for instance. The book also includes a list of
references of books, videos, slides and photographs, kits, packs and other
materials in the field. This is very much a resource book, to be drawn on for ideas
and exercises, not only about sexual relationships but for work on other aspects
of relationships also.

DUCK, S. W. *Human relationships*. London: Sage Publications, 1986.

Staff and professionals involved with: students;
                                               lay people and volunteers;
                                               education;
                                               social skills;
                                               activities and opportunities.

A very readable account of the social psychology of personal relationships,
providing many interesting insights gathered from recent research work. The
style is accessible and the referencing good. The book is designed for students of
social psychology; the style and much of the material reflects this focus upon a
youthful audience.

DUCK, S. W., GILMOUR, R. *Personal Relationships 1: studying personal
relationships*. London: Academic Press, 1981.

DUCK, S. W., GILMOUR, R. *Personal Relationships 2: developing
personal relationships*. London: Academic Press, 1981.

DUCK, S. W., GILMOUR, R. *Personal Relationships 3: personal
relationships in disorder*. London: Academic Press, 1981.

DUCK, S. W. *Personal Relationships 4: dissolving personal relationships*.
London: Academic Press, 1982.

DUCK, S. W. *Personal Relationships 5: repairing personal relationships*.
London: Academic Press, 1984.

Staff and professionals involved in: education;
social skills training.

These five edited volumes comprise a formidable collection of academic analyses of various aspects of personal relationships. The articles are mostly theoretical and are not intended for a general audience. For those who wish to explore the subject further, however, they represent a very valuable source of information derived from academic research, covering many aspects of personal relationships.

ELFRIDA RATHBONE CENTRE. *Between Ourselves*. Video (colour 15 mins). Hove: Twentieth Century Vixen, 1988.

Parents and families, staff and lay people and volunteers;
professionals involved with: education;
activities and opportunities;
social skills training;
self-advocacy.

Between Ourselves is a video tape made about a group of young women with mild and moderate learning disabilities who attended the Elfrida Rathbone Centre, Islington. In fifteen minutes it illustrates some of the group's work, including extensive interviews with group members, who explored problems in their relationships, especially those with members of the opposite sex. It will be of particular interest to some audiences because of its illustration of the Centre's approach to sex education including contraception. Group members' comment about how the group raised their confidence in respect of relationships with others are of interest. This resource is likely to be of particular value to people helping women develop self-advocacy because the video tape itself is largely presented by women with learning disabilities.

ELLIS, R., WHITTINGTON, D. *A Guide to Social Skill Training*. London: Croom Helm, 1981.

Staff and professionals involved in: education;
social skills training;
management and planning.

This book describes itself as a practical guide for those about to set up social skills training programmes and also as a critical review of theory and practice in social skills training. It is written for professionals and documents research in the area up until 1980 in some detail. An unusual feature is its concern, not only with social skills teaching for children, people with learning disabilities or mental health problems, but with the social skills needed and used by professionals themselves.

FELCE, D., TOOGOOD, S. *Close to Home: a local housing service and its impact on the lives of nine adults with severe and profound mental handicaps*. Kidderminster: BIMH Publications, 1988.

Parents and families, staff and professionals, managers and planners.

Whilst not a book specifically, or even particularly, concerned with friendships, this is a unique description of the day-to-day efforts and results in a service attempting to offer social as well as physical integration into a local community for people with severe learning disabilities.

FIRTH, H. *A Move to Community: social contacts and behaviour.* Morpeth: Northumberland Health Authority District Psychology Service, 1986.

Staff and professionals involved in: management and planning;
                                                  staff training;
                                                  support for people with
                                                  learning disabilities.

This is an evaluative report of the move of a small number of people with very severe disabilities from hospital to a community, and the changes in their social contact as a result. It highlights the importance of staff selection, training, and practice, and their effects on people's lives. It illustrates, as well as documents, the social relationships and activities of the individuals involved. It offers comment about different sources of relationships and draws a number of conclusions for managers and planners regarding issues such as accommodation and staff selection and training.

FIRTH, H., RAPLEY, M. *Making Acquaintance.* Morpeth: Northumberland Health Authority District Psychology Service, 1987.

Parents and families, staff and   lay people and volunteers;
professionals involved with: management and planning;
                                                 education;
                                                 social skills training;
                                                 activities and opportunities.

This booklet reviews the literature on the development of acquaintance and friendship, with somewhat fuller referencing than is given in the present text. There is a discussion of relevant social skills and how opportunities, teaching, and support can best be provided for people with learning disabilities in order for them to develop acquaintance. It does not deal with issues involved in close relationships.

FIRTH, M., FIRTH, H. Improving the interpersonal skills of mentally handicapped people. *Mental Handicap*, 1982; 10:4, 138-140.

Staff and professionals involved in: education;
                                                  social skills training.

A short, non-academic presentation of one social skills training group with people with learning disabilities. The article describes one approach to training, and highlights some practical issues about teaching, demonstration, and role playing.

FLYNN, M. C. *A Place of My Own: independent living for adults with mental handicap*. London: Cassell Educational, 1989.

Staff and professionals, parents and families involved with:	lay people and volunteers; education; social skills training; activities and opportunities.

This is an important, powerful, and clearsighted report of independent living. It represents a major, recent, comprehensive British study of the situation of eighty-eight people with learning disabilities living independently. The book commences with an exceptionally clear but brief summary of what has been learned about people moving into and living in independent accommodation, both in Britain and in North America. People's life styles, backgrounds, skills, activities, circumstances, and burdens are described, including the victimisation that many suffered, and the links between victimisation and appearance. A major strength of this book is its style, which manages to combine a directness and extensive use of people's own words with a scholarly discussion of the issues. Whilst the scope of this study did not allow exploration of people's social networks, the book provides a valuable overview of the situation of people living independently. The conclusions in the penultimate chapter are clear and helpful.

FOXX, R. M., MCMORROW, M. J. *Stacking the Deck: a social skills game for retarded adults*. Champaign, Ill.: Research Press, 1983.

Staff and professionals involved in:	education; social skills training; activities and opportunities.

Stacking the Deck consists of three different games, covering general social skills, social-vocational skills, and social-sexual skills. It is designed to be played as an "overlay" to existing board games, with certain rule changes which are explained in the accompanying manual. The games are designed to teach appropriate verbal responses to a variety of situations. This has limitations, as the games do not teach general problem-solving skills or indicate how to respond to unforeseen problems. Some of the items are not wholly age-appropriate. The social-sexual game is unusual in that it addresses a variety of situations which are not covered in other sex education packages. It may be useful in some situations to supplement other approaches to social skills. Two examples illustrate:

"Someone makes fun of your boy/girlfriend – say 'It isn't nice to make fun of people. Please don't do it again'."

"A man says he will give you money to have sex with him – Tell him 'No, leave me alone'."

FURTHER EDUCATION CURRICULUM REVIEW AND DEVELOPMENT UNIT. *Skills for Living: a curriculum framework for young people in further education with moderate learning difficulties*. London: Further Education Unit, 1982.

Staff and professionals involved in:	education.

This document is intended to assist teachers, college managers, advisers, and others interested in extending skills-for-living curriculum development for young people in further education who have moderate learning disabilities. It proposes a curriculum framework for this student group. The document lists a set of aims and objectives for a skills-for-living curriculum which might be the core of a vocational preparation course. One of these aims is to bring about an ability to develop satisfactory personal relationships with others.

The curriculum is set out in the form of a set of eight "webs" relating to each main aim. Each section briefly describes activities and a few resources for work in that area. The webs are useful in providing ideas as to the range of issues which will need to be covered, or which could be used to facilitate learning. However, the description of activities and resources is extremely cursory. The document is therefore likely to be useful chiefly for the ideas it presents on a curriculum, rather than for activities or resources.

GATHERCOLE, C. E. *Residential Alternatives for Adults who are Mentally Handicapped*. Composite edition, with *Leisure Volunteers' Guide*. Kidderminster: BIMH Publications, 1984.

Parents and families, staff and   lay people and volunteers;
professionals involved with: management and planning;
                                               activities and opportunities.

This composite edition is concerned with four issues: staffed and unstaffed accommodation; family placements; resettlement processes; and leisure and social integration. It includes a section on the use of volunteers to help people with learning disabilities develop leisure interests and skills, as well as a *Leisure Volunteers' Guide* for people who may act as volunteers in this way.

The short guide for volunteers does not aim to address itself to the challenges of making acquaintances and friends through leisure. However, it should prove very useful to volunteers who wish to help people to engage in leisure activities because of its practical suggestions about activities, interests, motivation, and choices.

HARRIS, J. Citizen advocacy. *Mental Handicap*, 1983; **11:4**, 145-146.

Parents and families, staff and   lay people and volunteers;
professionals involved with: management and planning.

A brief description of what citizen advocacy may involve, which highlights clearly the main elements in the processes and function of citizen advocacy.

HERON, A. MYERS, M. *Intellectual Impairment: the battle against handicap*. London: Academic Press, 1983.

Staff and professionals involved in: education;
                                               management and planning;
                                               staff training.

This book aims to provide an overview of approaches to services for people with intellectual impairments, addressing the resultant disabilities, and mitigating the social consequences in terms of handicap. The book is unusual in its examination of services throughout the world, contrasting and comparing differing service delivery models, as well as exploring in depth one service initiative, the Sheffield Development Project. Chapter 5 provides the authors' viewpoint on the most helpful ways available of meeting needs. Its comments were apposite when published and remain so.

HOPSON, B., SCALLY, M. *Life Skills Teaching*. London: McGraw-Hill, 1981.

Staff and professionals involved in: education;
                                                 social skills training;
                                                 staff training.

This is a book designed for teachers or other professionals who wish to work with students on "life skills" issues. A whole chapter is given over as a guide to resources for life skills teaching. A strength of this guide for a British audience is that most of the material is published in Great Britain. Addresses for publishers are given.

Relatively little of the material is of immediate relevance to the development of friendship, but much would be very helpful for the development of associated skills, such as the expression of emotion. The authors comment that they were unable to find much material that would help to develop the skills of giving and receiving feedback, or managing conflict. Their own "life skills teaching programmes" would probably be the most helpful.

The book includes an extensive and practical chapter on methods and issues in work with groups, which covers: micro teaching, lecturettes, and drama; group size and teacher role; and preparation and management of sessions.

HOPSON, B. SCALLY, M. *Life Skills Teaching Programmes No.1*. Leeds: Life Skills Associates, 1980. Available from: Life Skills Associates, Clarendon Chambers, 50 Clarendon Road, Leeds.

Staff and professionals involved in: education;
                                                 social skills training;
                                                 staff training.

This resource is unusual because it presents material for an educational audience (as distinct from the social skills training material from a clinical perspective) which explores the skills involved in making a relationship of any significant depth.

The material covers: how to make and gain from life transitions; how to be positive about oneself; how to communicate effectively; how to be assertive; how to make, keep, and end a relationship; how to manage negative emotions; how to find a job. One major strength of this package is that it attempts to be reasonably comprehensive within this range of issues, and is usefully cross referenced. Each section is prefaced by some discussion for the teacher. This is followed by a number of specific and carefully described exercises. A major advantage is that this material is not geared for any particular age group, and can be used for work with children and adults who have either mild or moderate degrees of learning disability. Much of it could provide a basis for ideas for work with people with more severe disabilities. The programmes place a strong emphasis both on the attitudes which are essential to making positive relationships and on the skills involved, including how to convey respect, genuineness, and empathy.

The section on how to manage negative emotions includes material on learning the meanings of words for feelings, a frequently neglected topic, and on recent cognitive approaches to emotion, emphasising the beliefs involved behind feelings of anger, dejection, or rejection for example. The material is detailed, and carefully put together.

INDEPENDENT DEVELOPMENT COUNCIL. *Next Steps: an independent review of progress, problems and priorities in the development of services for people with mental handicap*. London: Independent Development Council, 1984.

Parents and families, staff and   management and planning.
professionals involved in:

This is the Council's clear and simply worded view following the DHSS review, *Progress, Problems and Priorities in Mental Handicap*. It offers a readable and stimulating viewpoint on priorities in mental handicap service provision, especially in regard to community care.

INDEPENDENT DEVELOPMENT COUNCIL. *Pursuing Quality. How good are your local services for people with mental handicap?* London: Independent Development Council, 1986.

Staff and professionals involved in: education;
                                                  management and planning;
                                                  staff training.

A carefully thought through and well laid out booklet which is designed to help people tease out how to assess, and how to foster, high quality services for people with learning disabilities. Its focus is on community services. It should be of use to anyone planning, managing, monitoring, or evaluating services or projects, whether formal or informal.

JEFFREE, D., CHESELDINE, S. *Junior Interest Profile*. Winslow: Winslow Press, 1984.

Staff and professionals involved in: activities and opportunities;
                                                  education.

This is a picture-based assessment tool useful for introducing and exploring attitudes to a number of leisure activities which might be of interest to teenagers. A second section allows preferences between activities to be assessed. It is likely to be useful in aiding and assessing choices. The activities are very age-appropriate for adolescents. The only regret is that the number of activities illustrated is limited to sixteen: TV, piano, snooker, football, shopping, disco dancing, horse-riding, ping pong, fishing, table football, swimming, records, tennis, pet care, cycling, and model aeroplanes. A major strength is that the profile can be used with people with very severe learning difficulties and people without speech.

JEFFREE, D. M., CHESELDINE, S. *Let's Join In*. London: Souvenir Press, 1984.

Parents and families, lay people and volunteers, staff and professionals involved in:	education; activities and opportunities.

This book is aimed at parents, teachers, club leaders, and volunteers working with young people with special educational needs. It describes some of the ways in which the authors have successfully taught leisure time activities. The assumption is that leisure activities are a good way to overcome social isolation among adolescents with severe learning disabilities.

A major part of the book is geared towards the description of a variety of table games. Possible ways of developing outside activities such as gardening, bird watching, and train and car spotting are also described. A strength of this book is that it focuses attention on the need to encourage and teach participation in leisure activities which involve other people. A weakness is that the games are unlikely to be encountered naturally outside "specialist" settings. A further disadvantage is that the games are likely to be age-appropriate only for younger teenagers.

However, this book is one of the few resources specifically directed towards people with severe learning disabilities and it may prove valuable as a source of ideas beyond the immediate situations it describes.

KING'S FUND CENTRE. *An Ordinary Life*. London: King's Fund Centre, 1982.

Parents and families, staff and professionals involved in:	management and planning.

This document put forward a view of what comprehensive residential and supportive services for people with learning disabilities might be like. It does not concern itself specifically with relationships, but addresses itself to the issues of social integration as they relate to where and how people live. It is likely to be of particular relevance to service managers and planners.

KING'S FUND CENTRE. *An Ordinary Working Life*. London: King's Fund Centre, 1984.

Parents and families, staff and professionals involved in:	activities and opportunities; education; management and planning; staff training.

A project paper which sets out a view of what vocational services might be like for people with learning disabilities. The paper is relevant here because of the impact which integrated work and training could have on the social lives of people with learning disabilities.

KING'S FUND CENTRE. *Self-Advocacy Skills Training*. London: King's Fund Centre, **1988**.

Parents and families, staff and professionals involved with:	lay people and volunteers; social skills training.

This short report sets out the results of two workshops in addressing practical issues about running self-advocacy groups. It is easily readable and offers many ideas which will be useful to anyone advising or helping with such groups.

KING'S FUND CENTRE. *Ties and Connections – An Ordinary Community Life*. London: King's Fund Centre, **1988**.

Parents and families, staff and professionals involved in:	activities and opportunities; education; management and planning; staff training.

This book is an extremely valuable discussion of many of the issues involved in becoming a part of a local community. It explores the nature of neighbourhood, family, friendship, and membership of social worlds and organisations, first for people without learning disabilities, and then for people with learning disabilities. It provides a background to many of the issues explored in the present book, in a more general context.

The style of the book is particularly helpful in laying out the general issues and the particular issues for people with learning disabilities. A valuable feature is the "What Helps" pages at the end of each section. These give a number of simple, down-to-earth, practical ideas that may help people with learning disabilities to become a part of their community.

MALIN, N. (Ed.). *Reassessing Community Care*. London: Croom Helm, **1987**.

Staff and professionals involved in:	education; management and planning; staff training.

This book brings together a number of chapters on various issues in the provision of community care for people with intellectual or psychiatric disabilities. Some of these reassess the role of community care as part of current social policy. Others describe various recent developments in residential, day, and support services. A few chapters link the two levels. The chapter by Atkinson and Ward, on friendship and neighbourhood relationships, is one of these. It is based on material from interviews with people with learning disabilities living in the community, and goes on to draw out a number of issues about developing opportunities for relationships within household, family, and work settings, and with neighbours and friends. It includes a very useful discussion, with analysis and conclusions about ways to foster the development of individual relationships.

MANSELL, J., FELCE, D. JENKINS, J., DE KOCK, U., TOOGOOD, S. *Developing Staffed Housing for People with Mental Handicaps.* Tunbridge Wells: Costello, 1987.

Staff and professionals involved in: management and planning; staff training; activities and opportunities.

This book aims to provide practical help for staff involved in organising the transition from institutional to community-based services for people with learning disabilities. It addresses the needs in providing such a service for people with severe or profound learning disabilities. It includes some helpful discussion of the opportunities which need to be made available, and the ways in which they can be used, if people are to build a network of relationships. There is a particularly helpful emphasis on the role of staff as enablers in this process.

MATTHEWS, S. H. *Friendships Through the Life Course: oral biographies in old age.* London: Sage Publications, 1986.

Staff and professionals involved with: lay people and volunteers; staff training; activities and opportunities.

This is a study of friendship through "oral biographies": interviews exploring the nature of individuals' friendships throughout their lives. It offers some useful distinctions between different friendship "styles", as well as a discussion of the significance of age and gender to friendship.

The material is richly illustrated with extensive quotations and thus provides a highly readable account of the nature of friendship in the lives of a particular sample of older citizens.

MCCONKEY, R., MCCORMACK, R. *Breaking Barriers – Educating People about Disability.* London: Souvenir Press, 1983.

Parents and families, staff and professionals involved with: lay people and volunteers; education; activities and opportunities.

This is a book which was written primarily for professional staff in services for people with disabilities, but it was also hoped that the families and friends of people with learning disabilities would find it helpful. It aims to provide ideas, guidelines, sources of information, and sample materials to help people devise experiences and events which offer community education and participation. It was written as a practical handbook, in four sections, covering: the need for community education; formulating community education programmes (with detailed and practical suggestions); examples of community education programmes, for schools, adult education, and sales assistants; and resources, which presents samples of materials used and lists other published materials.

This book is valuable in that it provides ideas and guidelines to show how community education and participation can become more common. The resources at the end of the book are likely to be of particular use.

MCCONKEY, R., MCCORMACK, R. *Community Education Kit: schools programme on mental handicap, training programme for sales assistants.* Stillorgan: St. Michael's House, 1985.

Staff and professionals involved in: education;
                                                     staff training.

This kit is intended to supplement the book, *Breaking Barriers,* and to provide practical materials for use as part of the community education approach, with schools, as part of adult education courses on mental handicap, or in wider community education. It includes three short video programmes: *Interviews with people who are mentally handicapped; Parents talking;* and *The right choice.* The interviews with people attending a training centre present a positive picture of their lives. *Parents talking* deals with support, or absence of it, immediately after the birth of a child with Down's syndrome. *The right choice* illustrates situations encountered during shopping in stores. The kit also includes: tutors' notes, notes on resources, on meeting disabled people, on using video, and a schools programme folder. Some of the materials in this kit are reproduced in *Breaking Barriers.* The package may be useful for people organising schools teaching or other community education programmes.

OPEN UNIVERSITY. *Patterns for Living (Course P555)* and *Patterns for Living: Working Together (Course P555M).* Milton Keynes: The Open University, 1986, 1989.

People with learning disabilities, parents   activities and opportunities;
and families, lay people and volunteers,   education;
staff and professionals involved in: management and planning;
                                                      staff training.

The P555 course is designed for parents as well as professionals, volunteers as well as staff, and for "all those closely involved with people with a mental handicap". These readable, accessible, often humorous, and well-illustrated materials are designed to provoke thinking about a variety of issues in the lives of people with learning disabilities. They cover a wide variety of issues, such as living with one's family, living in hospital, having a home of one's own, and learning about leisure. Much attention is paid to how people cope with the changes they have to face in their lives. The materials also focus on sexual relationships, advocacy, and self-advocacy. The approach of the whole course is rooted in a concern with human relationships as the central issue in people's experiences in life. The course also views relationships as being central to other issues in living in the community. The materials indicate options and alternatives which may be valuable in promoting relationships. However, the course emphasises that, although friendship is invaluable, it cannot be prescribed, rushed, or created. The course makes extensive use of excellent case material, in a style which is clear, simple, and readable, and uses many good stories from real people. Video and audio tapes are also available. The course is written simply and extensive use of the ideas presented could be made in working with people with learning disabilities.

The P555M course covers the same issues, of family life, relationships, independence, and integration, in a format for use by people without reading or writing skills. It comprises: eight dramatised stories on four audiotapes; a videocassette; a student workbook which uses pictures instead of words; and study partner or group leader notes (for student or group study packs). The course represents a very significant achievement in translating the *Patterns for Living* materials into a form for people with learning disabilities who may subsequently act as study partners for others.

This Open University material can be ordered by people who are not registered students, from: Open University Educational Enterprises Limited.

OPEN UNIVERSITY. *The Handicapped Person in the Community (Course P251)*. Milton Keynes: The Open University, 1982.

Staff and professionals involved in: activities and opportunities;
education;
staff training.

This "post-experience" course relates to people with all kinds of disability. Hence the material varies widely in its degree of relevance to the issues discussed in this book. A unit on *Mental Handicap: aiding social integration* (Block 3, Part 1) is particularly pertinent. This unit examines the social and personal significance of human relationships, as well as important barriers to the formation of personal relationships by people with learning disabilities. For those who wish to study the place of personal relationships within the wider context of social integration and difficulty, this is excellent material. It can be ordered by people who are not registered students, from: Open University Educational Enterprises Limited.

PEALER, J., O'BRIEN, J. (Eds.). *Personal Relationships for Persons with Developmental Difficulties: proceedings of a conference on informal supports*. Columbus, Ohio: Ohio Society for Autistic Citizens, 1985.

Parents and families, staff and   lay people and volunteers;
professionals involved with: management and planning;
education and training;
activities and opportunities.

This report is a duplicated, easy to read description, in plain English, of some of the things which personal relationships mean for people with learning disabilities. It explores barriers and opportunities for personal relationships in a very down-to-earth and practical manner. It is well laid out, with much use of visual material and clear phrasing, for example: "relationships are sometimes *costly*. They take time and expenditure of one's self. Getting involved with another person is not easy".

PERLMAN, D., DUCK, S. *Intimate Relationships: development, dynamics and deterioration*. London: Sage Publications, 1987.

Staff and professionals involved in: education;
social skills training.

This recent collection of research material focuses specifically on intimate relationships. The volume may prove extremely useful for those concerned to pursue this particular area from a theoretical perspective. A chapter on jealousy in relationships by Buunk and Bringle may be of slightly wider interest.

POPE, A. W., McHALE, S. M., CRAIGHEAD, W. E. *Self-esteem Enhancement with Children and Adolescents*. Oxford: Pergamon Press, 1988.

Staff and professionals involved in: education;
                                                  social skills training.

This recent book may be of value to professionals, particularly teachers in secondary and further education, as a source of ideas. It discusses the development of problem-solving skills and different theoretical approaches, before moving on to discuss self-control, standard setting, communication skills, and issues of body image. There is a helpful chapter on assessment, including the identification of self-statements. Some individual tasks are described, but the breadth of coverage of the book means that it cannot attempt to provide exercises or detailed guidance for day-to-day educational or therapeutic work.

PRIESTLEY, P., McGUIRE, J., FLEGG, D., HEMSLEY, V., WELHAM, D. *Social Skills and Personal Problem-solving*. London: Tavistock, 1978.

Staff and professionals involved in: social skills training;
                                                  management and planning;
                                                  education and training.

The book is aimed at a wide spectrum of workers in the helping agencies, including schools, hospitals, social services, youth work, advisory bureaus, community work, and self-help organisations. It is described as a practical handbook of methods for working with people to help them solve their problems. It is not specifically addressed to people with learning disabilities. It may, however, present a variety of ideas for people who intend to teach social skills to others.

The book makes an explicit claim to plagiarism, and what its authors describe as the "jackdaw" approach of collecting ideas from many different sources is one of its strengths. Some may find this feature very stimulating. Although designed for educators, teachers, and other professionals, its style is refreshingly different from other books on social skills training, many of which are much more academic in tone. Moreover, the authors have a very sound grasp of social skills theory.

The book does not set out to develop acquaintance or friendships specifically. Moreover, as the material was designed for adults without learning disabilities, many of the ideas would require considerable modification for use with people with such disabilities.

RICHARDSON, A., RITCHIE, J. *Developing Friendships: enabling people with learning difficulties to make and maintain friends*. London: Policy Studies Institute/Social and Community Planning Research, 1989.

Parents and families, staff and   lay people and volunteers;
professionals involved with: management and planning;

education and training;
support for people with
learning disabilities.

This book occupies a key position in this field, presenting the results of the first major empirical study of the quality of relationships of people with learning disabilities living in this country. The material is in four sections. The first introduces the issues, discusses the meanings and functions of friendship, and considers some issues in the development of intimate friendships. The second discusses the context and the findings of the authors' research into the nature of the relationships of a sample of sixty people with learning disabilities who were interviewed in the course of the research. It includes a particularly helpful viewpoint on parents' perspectives. The third discusses the perspectives gained from the research into initiatives and projects which aimed to foster friendships. This is followed by some discussion of the contribution that skills training, confidence building, self-advocacy, and other avenues may make to the development of friendships by people with learning disabilities. The discussions of the roles of befriending schemes and citizen advocacy are particularly helpful. The final section draws some conclusions and implications for policy and practice.

Besides its importance as a piece of research, this book complements the present work by providing a discussion of how friendships may develop, drawing heavily on the perspectives of people with learning disability themselves.

RICHARDSON, A., RITCHIE, J. *Letting Go: dilemmas for parents*. Milton Keynes: Open University Press, 1989.

Parents and families, staff and   lay people and volunteers;
professionals involved with: education and training;
                                             support for people with
                                             learning disabilities.

This book is about parents living with their adult sons and daughters; and letting go. It is not directly about the relationships of their adult sons and daughters with learning disabilities, but it offers an invaluable insight into the situation from which many such adults leave, as their parents and they themselves grow older.

RICHARDSON, A., RITCHIE, J. *Making the Break: parent's views about adults with a mental handicap leaving the parental home*. London: King's Fund Centre, 1986.

Parents and families, staff and   lay people and volunteers;
professionals involved with: management and planning;
                                             education and training;
                                             support for people with
                                             learning disabilities.

This short and highly readable book is refreshing in that it addresses the issues involved in preparation for the future, and leaving the parental home, from the perspective of parents themselves. The book explores many practical issues in relation to this. It also explores at length the emotional disengagement which is normally a part of that process. As such it provides an invaluable background to many of the issues raised in this book.

ROBINSON, F., ROBINSON, S. *Neighbourhood care – an Exploratory Bibliography*. Berkhamsted: The Volunteer Centre, 1981.

Staff and professionals

A bibliography of literature on neighbourhoods, neighbouring, and neighbourhood care up to 1981. Each publication is described and summarised in an easily read, accessible style. The book represents a valuable resource for those wishing to explore the field.

ROGERS, C. *On Becoming a Person*. London: Constable, 1961.

Parents and families, staff and professionals involved with:	education and training; social skills training.

This book comprises a number of chapters on different issues within the single theme of personal (and interpersonal) development and growth. A key chapter of relevance to the qualities inherent in friendship is "The characteristics of a helping relationship", in which Rogers argues that *all* helpful relationships share common qualities, the most important being an attitude of wanting, and trying, to understand the other person.

RYAN, T., WALKER, R. *Making Life Story Books*. London: British Agencies for Adoption and Fostering, 1985.

Parents and families, staff and professionals involved with:	lay people and volunteers; education and training; activities and opportunities; support for people with learning disabilities.

This slim volume provides information and suggestions as to how to set about creating life story books, in an exceedingly accessible and direct style. The book is written for people working with children, particularly children in care. The approach advocated should be able to be translated without much difficulty by those working with adolescents or adults.

The central processes in making a life story book are identity building; and building bridges between the past, the present, and the future. These processes are likely to be of great value for many people with learning disabilities.

This book may be of particular use in assisting people in making acquaintance for two reasons: knowing about their past provides them with a ready-made topic of conversation; and positive self-concept is important for making acquaintances and friends. Although not aimed primarily at people with learning disabilities, the principles of the book apply equally to them as the author has made clear.

The book is both clearly written and down-to-earth. It should provide an excellent resource for anyone who wants ideas on how to help people develop a clear sense of their past and their present.

SANG, B., O'BRIEN, J. *Advocacy: the UK and American experiences*. London: King's Fund Centre, 1984.

Parents and families, staff and professionals involved with:	lay people and volunteers; management and planning; activities and opportunities; support for people with learning disabilities.

Sang was the first coordinator of the Advocacy Alliance in Great Britain from 1982. In America, O'Brien, through the Georgia Advocacy office, has extensive experience of citizen advocacy. This jointly produced Project Paper is thus able to provide an authoritative discussion of the issues surrounding citizen advocacy. Sang's description of the implementation of programmes in the UK will be of especial value to those considering or wishing to facilitate citizen advocacy schemes.

SEED, P. *Mental Handicap: who helps in rural and remote communities?* Tunbridge Wells: Costello Educational, 1980.

Parents and families, staff and professionals involved with:	lay people and volunteers; management and planning; education and training.

This book describes research into the lives of people with learning disabilities and their families in the Highlands of Scotland. The research focused on the social support that was available and used by the individuals and their families, relating families' needs to the services provided and the policies behind these. The study is of particular interest because of its description of the actual day-to-day contacts made by people with learning disabilities. A graphic picture is drawn of the activities and relationships of the individuals, in readable presentation.

SHEARER, A. *Building Community – People with Mental Handicaps, their Families and Friends*. London: Campaign for People with Mental Handicaps and King's Fund Centre, 1986.

Staff and professionals, parents and families, lay people and volunteers involved in:	management and planning; education and training; activities and opportunities.

This compelling and readable book addresses a variety of aspects of life in the community for people with learning disabilities: family support, self-advocacy, education, work, housing, and leisure. It describes a number of schemes or projects in these different fields, and in so doing builds a picture of possible developments which could help to provide quality community services.

There is no separate chapter on friendships or relationships, reflecting the fact that the projects described all have a significant impact on the relationships of the people who use them. Yet the book contains many and varied references to ways in which projects and services in different contexts can facilitate the growth and choice of relationships.

SHURE, M. B., SPIVACK, G. *Problem-Solving Techniques in Child Rearing*. San Francisco: Jossey Bass, 1978.

Parents and families, staff and   education;
professionals involved in: social skills training.

This book summarises much of the important work done by the authors in exploring the thinking and problem-solving processes in relating to others. It is concerned with children, but the ideas are readily adaptable to adolescents or adults. The book is particularly useful in that it includes a curriculum for problem-solving teaching, as well as a "script" for this curriculum. Two of the chapters include a large variety of dialogues illustrating the approach for children who have difficulty interacting with their peers or with adults.

A major strength of the approach is its constant emphasis on the principles behind it: encouraging young people to think for themselves, by guiding them to think through the problem rather than supplying the answer. The focus is on the skills involved in thinking out alternative ways of reacting to a situation, foreseeing possible consequences, and choosing how to react. The book does not cover the non-verbal social skill issues which are addressed in much behavioural social skills training.

Parents, as well as teachers, may find the very readable dialogues extremely useful. The first and last chapters provide heavier reading, but can be skipped by those less concerned with details of the theoretical approach.

SHURE, M. B., SPIVACK, G. *Problem-solving Techniques in Child Rearing: a training script for parents of young children*. Philadelphia: Hahnemann Community Mental Retardation Centre, 1975.

Staff and professionals involved in: education;
          social skills training.

This script, which was devised in 1975, covers the details of a programme that mothers and professionals working with young children can use to improve children's social skills and problem-solving abilities. Virtually all of this script is reproduced in the book *Problem-solving Techniques in Child Rearing* (Shure and Spivack, 1978), in a layout which is easier to read and follow. It is suggested that the book is preferable as a resource, both because of its easier availability and because it puts the training script in context.

SPENCE, S. *Social Skills Training with Children and Adolescents: counsellor's manual*. Windsor: NFER-Nelson, 1980.

Staff and professionals involved in: education;
          social skills training.

This manual, which is available to teachers, psychologists, and counsellors through NFER, aims to provide basic background information on the assessment and training of social skills for those professionals. The preface makes it clear that it is designed for use in addition to supervised experience and further reading and that it is not a handbook which can be appropriately used in isolation. The manual explains clearly the basic skills involved in interpersonal interaction from a behavioural viewpoint (non-verbal and verbal responses, basic and complex conversation skills, and a perception of emotion). It does not discuss the thinking or problem-solving skills in social interaction which are the focus of the various books by Shure and Spivack and their colleagues.

The book offers a variety of assessment techniques for use with children and adolescents, and useful suggestions for setting up social skills training programmes. A detailed example is given of a twelve-session social skills training programme for adolescents.

SPENCE, S., SHEPHERD, G. *Developments in Social Skills Training*. London: Academic Press, 1983.

Staff and professionals involved in: education;
                                                social skills training.

This book, aimed at practitioners who wish to teach social skills training, is a review of training as practised in a number of different areas. The style is somewhat academic, although the contributors to this edited volume were selected because of their experience as practitioners and were asked to concentrate on practical rather than research issues. There is no chapter specifically on work with people with learning disabilities. However, one chapter by Sue Spence, on work with adolescent offenders, may be of interest to those wishing to conduct social skills teaching with adolescent offenders who have learning disabilities.

SPIVACK, G., SHURE, M. B. *Social Adjustment of Young Children: a cognitive approach to solving real life problems*. San Francisco: Jossey Bass, 1974.

Staff and professionals involved in: education;
                                                social skills training.

This book was the initial report of the interpersonal problem-solving approach developed by these authors for use with children. The training programme script which is reproduced in full in this book was adapted and improved for the authors' 1978 publication *Problem Solving Techniques in Child Rearing*. The only material in this book which is not included in the later publication is a brief chapter on teacher and parent reports.

SPIVACK, G., PLATT, J. J., SHURE, M. B. *The Problem-solving Approach to Adjustment: a guide to research and intervention*. San Francisco: Jossey Bass, 1976.

Staff and professionals involved in: education;
                                                social skills training.

This book will be of most use for professionals who wish to use interpersonal problem-solving teaching in a systematic way, or to read in detail about the basis for this approach. The first part of the book discusses research evidence on elements of the interpersonal, cognitive problem-solving approach, namely: alternative solution thinking; means end thinking; perspective taking; consequential thinking; and causal thinking; with people of different ages – early childhood, middle childhood, adolescence, and adulthood. It also discusses the role of the family and child rearing practices in the development of interpersonal problem-solving. The second part discusses enhancement of these skills. Separate chapters cover: early intervention; a programme for mothers of young children; a programme for chronic psychiatric patients; and programmes for groups of young adults and patients in psychiatric hospitals.

TROWER, P., BRYANT, B., ARGYLE, M. *Social Skills and Mental Health*. London: Methuen, 1978.

Staff and professionals involved in: education;
                                               social skills training.

This book has acquired a position almost as a textbook on social skills training. Its analysis of traditional behavioural social skills training remains very good. It is written with adults who do not have learning disabilities in mind, but represents a very useful source book for professionals engaged in social skills training with people with learning disabilities. It does not cover the "thinking" skills of the problem-solving approach, and may therefore best be used in conjunction with other materials listed in this chapter.

WALSH, J. *Let's Make Friends*. London: Souvenir Press, 1985.

Parents and families, staff and   lay people and volunteers;
professionals involved with: activities and opportunities.

This book describes and documents one approach to trying to provide companionship for people with learning disabilities. The scheme described aimed to provide adults with a companion or "befriender". It also aimed to expand their experiences and their integration into community life.

The book provides a very readable description of an innovative scheme to try and meet some of the needs discussed in the present book. It may prove useful to people who wish to set up similar schemes, providing the distinction is borne in mind between companionship and friendship.

WALSH, J. Setting up a friendship scheme. Part 1 – *Mental Handicap*, 1985; **13**:2, 58-59. Part 2 – *Mental Handicap*, 1985; **13**:3, 110-111.

Parents and families, staff and   lay people and volunteers;
professionals involved with: management and planning;
                                           activities and opportunities.

These two articles document the scheme which is described more fully in the book *Let's Make Friends*. They may be useful as providing a briefer description, and may be more accessible to some readers. The book gives a more complete account.

WEISS, R. S. *Loneliness: the experience of emotional and social isolation*. London, Mass: Massachusetts Institute of Technology Press, 1975.

Parents and families, staff and   lay people and volunteers;
professionals involved with: activities and opportunities;
                                     education and training.

This book provides a detailed but coherent view of the nature and the effects of loneliness, through a number of different authors whose contributions are deftly welded together by the main author into an informative and perceptive whole. It is significant because it provides an important theoretical contribution to the understanding of loneliness. A particular strength is that it illuminates, in a highly readable style rich with illustration, the situation of people experiencing both social and emotional isolation.

The material does not relate specifically to people with learning disabilities: the issues remain equally salient nevertheless. It is of relevance because it provides understanding and insight into the situation of people without either friends and acquaintance, or close supportive relationships.

WILKINSON, J., CANTER, S. *Social Skills Training Manual: assessment, programme design and management of training*. Chichester: Wiley, 1982.

Staff and professionals involved in: education;
                                           social skills training.

This book is a practical guide to social skills training with a very accessible style. It is aimed at professionals such as nurses, teachers, psychologists, psychiatrists, occupational therapists, social workers, and probation officers. It is not primarily concerned with people with learning disabilities. The direct reference to this client group (an introductory training programme on pages 98 to 108) is unfortunately very limited, and at times positively unhelpful. However, the early chapters are clear. They draw attention to advantages and disadvantages of individual and group teaching and discuss practical issues such as the length, number, and frequency of sessions.

The chapter on assessment and goal setting is very clear about the purpose and importance of assessment. Although less comprehensive than other descriptions of assessment, its clarity and readability give it a strong recommendation for anyone contemplating social skills teaching.

A disadvantage of this book is its restricted view of social skills development, from a narrowly behavioural viewpoint. The examples given are very limited and carry the risk of being used in a "cookbook" fashion.

WILLIAMS, P., SHOULTZ, B. *We Can Speak for Ourselves: self-advocacy by mentally handicapped people*. London: Souvenir Press, 1982.

Parents and families, staff and professionals involved with:

lay people and volunteers; management and planning; education and training; activities and opportunities.

This book describes what self-advocacy is, and documents how it can be developed. The book provides good stories and factual information on developing and supporting a self-advocacy group. There is a chapter on self-advocacy in the United Kingdom.

WILLMOTT, P. *Social Networks, Informal Care and Public Policy*. London: Policy Studies Institute, 1986.

Staff and professionals

An excellent discussion of some of the issues behind community care. The changing nature and function of kinship, friendship, and neighbourliness is extremely valuable and readable, and provides an up-to-date perspective on recent work in these areas. Some of the issues in this book are taken up in more detail in Willmott's more recent publication *Friendship Networks and Social Support* (1987).

WILLMOTT, P. *Friendship Networks and Social Support*. London: Policy Studies Institute, 1987.

Staff and professionals

This recent book is a description of the results of a study of over a hundred people with children in the London area. It provides an opportunity for the author to comment and draw together many results and interpretations from his own and others' research, besides a wealth of factual data. It is mainly concerned with informal social relationships, with friends, with neighbours, and with relatives. The focus is on the role they play in social support, and on the meaning of friends as a source of help, company, confidante, and trust. The book includes a brief section on possible strategies for countering social isolation and lack of social support.

This book will be of particular interest to people wishing to gain a more thorough understanding of the role friendship plays among adults who do not have learning disabilities.

ADDRESSES OF PUBLISHERS

American Association on Mental Retardation
1719 Kalorama Road NW, Washington, DC 20009, USA.
Tel. 800/424-3688.

American Guidance Service
Publisher's Building, Circle Pines, Minnesota 55014 – 1796, USA.

British Agencies for Adoption and Fostering
11 Southwark Street, London SE1 1RQ.
Tel. 071-407 8800.

CMH
12a Maddox Street, London W1R 9PL.
Tel. 071-491 0727.

Comedia Publications
9 Poland Street, London W1V 3D9.
Tel. 071-439 2059.

Further Education Unit
Grove House, 2-6 Orange Street, London WC2H 7WE.
Tel. 071-321 0433.

Hahnemann Community Mental Retardation Center
Department of Mental Health Sciences, Hahnemann Medical College and
Hospital, Philadelphia 19102, USA.

Independent Development Council for People with Mental Handicap
126 Albert Street, London NW1 7NF.
Tel. 071-491 0727.

King's Fund Centre
126 Albert Street, London NW1 7NF.
Tel. 071-267 6111.

Learning Development Aids
Duke Street, Wisbech, Cambridge PE13 2AE.
Tel. (0945) 63441.

Life Skills Associates
Clarendon Chambers, 50 Clarendon Road, Leeds LS2 9NZ.
Tel. (0532) 467128.

NFER/Nelson
2 Oxford Road East, Windsor, Berkshire SL4 1DF.
Tel. (0753) 858961.

(Northumberland Health Authority) District Psychology Service
St. George's Hospital, East Cottingwood, Morpeth, Northumberland NE61 2NU.
Tel. (0670) 512121.

Ohio Society for Autistic Citizens
751 NW Boulevard, Columbus, Ohio 43212, USA.
Tel. 614-294 5784.

Open University Press
12 Cofferidge Close, Stony Stratford, Milton Keynes MK11 1BY.
Tel. (0908) 566744.

Policy Studies Institute
100 Park Village East, London NW1 3SR.
Tel. 071-387 2171.

Research Press
2612 North Mattis Avenue, Champaign, Illinois 61826, USA.

SKILL – National Bureau for Students with Disabilities
336 Brixton Road, London SW9 7AA.
Tel. 071-274 0565.

St. Michael's House Research
Upper Kilmacud Road, Stillorgan, Co. Dublin, Ireland.
Tel. (0001) 88 58 05.

Twentieth Century Vixen
28 Southampton Street, Brighton, Sussex BN2 2UT.
Tel. (0273) 692336.

Volunteer Centre
29 Lower King's Road, Berkhampstead, Herts., HP4 2BA.

Winslow Press
Telford Road, Bicester, Oxon OX6 0TS.
Tel. (0869) 244644.